KENNEDYS

STORIES OF LIFE AND DEATH FROM AN AMERICAN FAMILY

KENNEDYS

STORIES OF LIFE AND DEATH FROM AN AMERICAN FAMILY

EDITED BY CLINT WILLIS

Thunder's Mouth Press
New York

KENNEDYS: STORIES OF LIFE AND DEATH FROM AN AMERICAN FAMILY

Compilation copyright © 2001 by Clint Willis
Introductions copyright © 2001 by Clint Willis

Adrenaline ® and the Adrenaline® logo are trademarks of
Avalon Publishing Group Incorporated, New York, NY.

An Adrenaline Book®

Published by
Thunder's Mouth Press
An Imprint of Avalon Publishing Group Incorporated
161 William Street, 16th floor
New York, NY 10038

A Balliett & Fitzgerald book

Book design: Sue Canavan

frontispiece photo: The Kennedy children with Mother Rose, 1923,
© Associated Press

Library of Congress Cataloging-in-Publication Data
Kennedy: stories of life and death from an American family / edited
by Clint Willis.
    p. cm
    "Adrenaline."
    ISBN 1-56025-333-9
    1. Kennedy, John F. (John Fitzgerald), 1917-1963—Anecdotes. 2.
Kennedy family—Anecdotes. 3. Presidents—United States—
Biography—Anecdotes. 4. Legislators—United States—Biography—
Anecdotes. 5. Politicians—United States—Biography—Anecdotes. I.
Willis, Clint.

E842.1.K46 2001
973.92'092'2—dc21   2001048041
[B]

9 8 7 6 5 4 3 2 1

Printed in the United States of America
Distributed by Publishers Group West

For Jay Schwamm
with love and thanks

contents

p h o t o g r a p h s

introduction

My best friend when I was ten years old was named Hampton. He had five or six brothers and sisters, and they all lived in a huge brick house—it struck me as a mansion—in the fanciest subdivision in Lafayette, Louisiana. They owned a motorboat and went fishing and water-skiing on weekends; they spent vacations at their grandmother's even bigger house on Mississippi's Gulf Coast; and everywhere they had cousins and friends and aunts and uncles.

I remember them as a beautiful family. The children dressed up for Mass seemed immaculate—the girls with hair ribbons and pretty, well-cut dresses; the toddlers and babies in white or sky-blue outfits from the right stores; Hampton and the other big boys in blue blazers and oxford shirts and ties. I liked being around all that beauty, which I associated with money and generosity and excitement.

The family adopted me for a time—I was quasi-family—and that status was important to me. They took me skeet shooting and craw-fishing, and fed me dinners at a long, shiny table in their enormous dining room. I baited crab nets and caught a huge garfish off the grandmother's pier. My friend's father, a big, cigar-smoking surgeon with a huge voice, taught me to water ski and took us to see the

Harlem Globetrotters. Since I spent many weekends at their house, the family often took me to Mass on Sundays; the parents were very religious and I think they hoped to make a Catholic of me.

All of this was important to me, but painful. I wanted to be like my friend and his family—I wanted their glamour and energy and style—but I knew that I was different in various ways, darker and less formed. They might or might not be better than I was, but they seemed so certain and so rewarded by life that I sometimes felt second-class around them; like a hanger-on. So while I loved them, I was mad at them.

I thought of Hampton's family as a version of the Kennedys. That's how I put it to myself at the time, which is remarkable since I knew only a little about the Kennedy family. I remembered the day of JFK's assassination—my mother cried and my first-grade teacher asked us to say a prayer for him. But the news in 1968 that Robert Kennedy was shot barely made it to my neighborhood, and didn't mean much when it got there.

Now I realize that I wanted Hampton's family to elevate and identify me in the way JFK's or RFK's friendship seemed to distinguish a person from the crowd. The Kennedys in their prime had that kind of power; they could change the way a person—even a stranger—saw himself and was seen in the world. We admired the family for their energy and style and looks and achievements—their sheer purposefulness; they were always doing something. We also envied those and other qualities, and we envied the Kennedys each other; their clannishness seemed like something anyone would want. And it sometimes felt like we were invited to join them: We could vote for them, campaign for them, love them—if we couldn't be Kennedys, we could be in their lives.

Actual contact with the family seemed to elevate a person. A friend of mine played with John F. Kennedy, Jr. when they were both toddlers. Another friend went to the opera with Robert and Jackie Kennedy in 1964. Still another had his tooth chipped by a Kennedy in a hockey game in the early '70s. It's interesting to realize that talking about this feels like showing off, and it almost certainly is: Even now, after decades of gossip and malice, the most remote connection to the Kennedy clan confers some kind of status. Still, none of us is a Kennedy: We're by definition outsiders. That still makes some people mad, even if they don't like to admit or even notice that they're angry.

All of this makes it hard to simply see the family or the individuals who belong to it. When we try to do so, setting aside our wishes and judgments and politics, we catch glimpses of a story. The facts and century-long chronology of that story are in hundreds of books. But those things matter less than the characters and their development—for the major actors did, to various degrees, grow and change, much like characters in a good novel. That's one reason their premature deaths—Joe, Jr. at 29, Kathleen at 28, JFK at 46, RFK at 42, JFK, Jr. at 38—sometimes torment us: We want to know how the story might have ended; we want to know who each of them would have become; we want them to show us how to live.

We can't know what would have been, and so we're left to judge them—or to wonder who they really were. This anthology is not meant to praise the Kennedys or to attack them. Instead, the book as a whole shows various members of the family—in particular, the brothers John, Robert and Edward—through the eyes of observers who have tried to understand them over the years. The writers succeed only partly, in part for a reason that their work illuminates and that many of us forget: The Kennedys are real people, and as such they belong not to us nor to history nor even to the stories we like to tell, but to themselves.

—Clint Willis

from **Superman Comes to the Supermarket**

by **Norman Mailer**

Norman Mailer (born 1923) has written 30 books and countless essays, short stories, poems and articles. This excerpt from his 1960 Esquire piece brilliantly foreshadows John F. Kennedy's emerging role as a man apart—a new and powerful and mysterious force in American culture.

P anic was the largest single sentiment in the breast of the collective delegates as they came to convene in Los Angeles. Delegates are not the noblest sons and daughters of the republic; a man of taste, arriving from Mars, would take one long look at a convention floor and leave forever, convinced he had seen one of the drearier squats of Hell. If one still smells the faint living echo of a carnival, it is regurgitated by the senses into the fouler cud of a death gas one must rid oneself of—a cigar smoking, stale-aired, slack-jawed, butt-littered, foul, bleak, hard-working, bureaucratic death gas of language and faces ("yes, those *faces*," says the man from Mars: lawyers, judges, ward heelers, *mafiosos*, Southern goons and grandees, grand old ladies, trade unionists, and finks), of pompous words and long pauses that lay like a leaden pain over fever, the fever that one is in, over, or is it just behind history? A legitimate panic for a delegate. A delegate is a man who picks a candidate for the largest office in the land, a President who must live with problems whose borders are in ethics, metaphysics, and now ontology. The delegate is prepared for his office of selection by emptying wastebaskets, toting garbage, and saying yes at the right time for twenty years in a small political machine of some small or large town; his reward, one of them anyway, is that he arrives at an invitation to the convention. An expert on local catch-as-catch-can, a small-time, often mediocre practitioner of small-town political judo, he comes to the big city with nine-tenths of his mind made up, he will follow the orders of the boss who brought him. Yet of course it is not altogether so mean as that: His opinion is listened to—the boss will consider what he has to say as one interesting factor among five hundred, and what is most important to the delegate, he has the illusion of partial freedom. He can, unless he is severely honest with himself— and if he is, why sweat out the low levels of a political machine?—he can have the illusion that he has helped to choose the candidate, he can even worry most sincerely about his choice, flirt with defection from the boss, work out his own small political gains by the road of loyalty or the way of hard bargain. But, even if he is there for no more than the ride, his vote a certainty in the mind of the political boss, able to be thrown here or switched there as the boss decides, still in some peculiar sense he is reality to the boss; the delegate is the great American public, the bar he owns or the law practice, the piece of the union he represents, or the real-estate office, is a part of the political landscape that the boss uses as his own image of how the votes will go and if the people will like the candidate. And if the boss is depressed by what he sees, if the candidate does not feel right to him, if he has a dull intimation that the candidate is not his sort (as, let us say, Harry Truman was his sort, or Symington might be his sort, or Lyndon Johnson), then vote for the candidate the boss will if he must—he cannot be caught on the wrong side, but he does not feel the pleasure of a personal choice. Which is the center of the panic. Because if the boss is depressed, the delegate is doubly depressed, and the emotional fact is that Kennedy is not in focus, not in the old political focus, he is not comfortable; in fact it is a mystery to the boss how Kennedy got to where he is, not a mystery in its structures—Kennedy is rolling in money, Kennedy got the votes in primaries, and, most of all, Kennedy has a jewel of a political machine. It is as good as a crack Notre Dame team, all discipline and savvy and go-go-go, sound, drilled, never dull, quick as a knife, full of the salt of hipper-dipper, a beautiful machine; the boss could adore it if only a sensible candidate were driving it, a Truman, even a Stevenson, please God a Northern Lyndon Johnson, but it is run by a man who looks young enough to be coach of the Freshman team, and that is not comfortable at all. The boss knows political machines, he knows issues, farm parity, Forand health bill, Landrum-Griffin, but this is not all so adequate after all to revolutionaries in Cuba who look like beatniks, competitions in missiles, Negroes looting whites in the Congo, intricacies of nuclear fallout, and NAACP men one does well to call Sir. It is all out of hand, everything important is off the center, foreign affairs is now the lick of the heat, and senators are candidates instead of governors, a disaster to the old family style of political measure, where a political boss knows his governor and knows who his governor knows. So the boss is depressed, profoundly depressed. He comes to this convention resigned to nominating a man he does not understand, or let us say that, so far as he understands the candidate who is to be nominated, he is not happy about the secrets of his appeal, not so far as he divines these secrets; they seem to have too little to do with politics and all too much to do with the private madnesses of the nation. Yes, this candidate for all his record, his good, sound, conventional liberal record, has a patina of that other life, the second American life, the long electric night with the fires of neon leading down the highway to the murmur of jazz.

Not all the roots of American life are uprooted, but almost all, and the spirit of the supermarket, that homogenous extension of stainless surfaces and psychoanalyzed people, packaged commodities, and ranch homes, interchangeable, geographically unrecognizable, that essence of the new postwar SuperAmerica is found nowhere so perfectly as in Los Angeles' ubiquitous acres. One gets the impression that people come to Los Angeles in order to divorce themselves from the past, here to live or try to live in the rootless pleasure world of an adult child. As one travels through the endless repetitions of that city which is the capital of suburbia with its milky pinks, its washed-out oranges, its tainted lime-yellows of pastel on one pretty little architectural monstrosity after another, the colors not intense enough, the styles never pure, and never sufficiently impure to collide on the eye, one conceives the people who live here—they have come out to express themselves, Los Angeles is the home of self-expression, but the artists are middle-class and middling-minded. No passions will calcify here for years in the gloom to be revealed a decade later as the tessellations of a hard and fertile work, no, it is all open, promiscuous, borrowed, half bought, a city without iron, eschewing wood, a kingdom of stucco, the playground for mass men—one has the feeling it was built by television sets giving orders to men. And in this land of the pretty-pretty, the virility is in the barbarisms, the huge billboards, the screamers of the neon lighting, the shouting farm-utensil colors of the gas stations and the monster drugstores, it is in the swing of the sports cars, hot rods, convertibles, Los Angeles is a city to drive in, the boulevards are wide, the traffic is nervous and fast, the radio stations play bouncing, blooping, rippling tunes, one digs the pop in a pop tune, no one of character would make love by it, but the sound is good for swinging a car, electronic guitars, and Hawaiian harps.

So this is the town the Democrats came to, and with their unerring instinct (after being with them a week, one thinks of this party as a crazy, half-rich family, loaded with poor cousins, traveling always in caravans with Cadillacs and Okie Fords, Lincolns and quarter-horse mules, putting up every night in tents to hear the chamber quartet of Great Cousin Eleanor invaded by the Texas-twanging steel-stringing geetarists of Bubber Lyndon, carrying its own mean high-school principal, Doc Symington, chided for its manners by good Uncle Adlai, told the route of march by Navigator Jack, cut off every six months from the rich will of Uncle Jim Farley, never listening to the mechanic of the caravan, Bald Sam Rayburn, who assures them they'll all break down unless Cousin Bubber gets the concession on the garage; it's the

Snopes family married to Henry James, with the labor unions thrown in like a Yankee dollar, and yet it's true, in tranquility one recollects them with affection, their instinct is good, crazy family good) and this instinct now led the caravan to pick the Biltmore Hotel in downtown Los Angeles for their family get-together and reunion.

The Biltmore is one of the ugliest hotels in the world. Patterned after the flat roofs of an Italian Renaissance palace, it is eighty-eight times as large, and one-millionth as valuable to the continuation of man, and it would be intolerable if it were not for the presence of Pershing Square, that square block of park with cactus and palm trees, the three-hundred-and-sixty-five-day-a-year convention of every junkie, pot-head, pusher, and queen. For years Pershing Square has been one of the three or four places in America famous to homosexuals, one of the avatars of the good old masturbatory sex, dirty with the crusted sugars of smut, dirty rooming houses around the corner where the score is made, dirty book and photograph stores down the street, old-fashioned out-of-the-Thirties burlesque houses, cruising bars, jukeboxes, movie houses; Pershing Square is the town plaza for all those lonely, respectable, small-town homosexuals who lead a family life, make children, and have the Philbrick psychology (How I Joined the Communist Party and Led Three Lives). Yes, it is the open air convention hall for the small-town inverts who live like spies, and it sits in the center of Los Angeles, facing the Biltmore, that hotel which is a mausoleum, that Pentagon of traveling salesmen the Party chose to house the headquarters of the Convention.

So here came that family, the delegates dispersed over a run of thirty miles and twenty-seven hotels: the Olympian Motor Hotel, the Ambassador, the Beverly Wilshire, the Santa Ynez Inn, the Mayan, the Commodore, the Mayfair, the Sheraton-West, the Huntington Sheraton, the Green, the Hayward, the Gates, the Figueroa, the Statler Hilton, the Hollywood Knickerbocker—does one have to be a collector to list such names?—beauties all, with that up-from-the-farm Los Angeles decor, plate-glass windows, patio and terrace, foam-rubber mattress, pastel paints, all of them pretty as an ad in full-page color, all but the Biltmore where everybody gathered every day—the newsmen, the TV, radio, magazine, and foreign newspapermen, the delegates, the politicos, the tourists, the campaign managers, the runners, the flunkies, the cousins and aunts, the wives, the grandfathers, the eight-year-old girls, and the twenty-eight-year-old girls in the Kennedy costumes, red and white and blue, the Symingteeners, the Johnson Ladies, the Stevenson Ladies, everybody—and for three days before the convention and four days into it, everybody collected at the Biltmore, in the lobby, in the grill, in the Biltmore Bowl, in the elevators, along the corridors, three hundred deep always outside the Kennedy suite, milling everywhere, every dark-carpeted gray-brown hall of the hotel, but it was in the Gallery of the Biltmore where one first felt the mood which pervaded all proceedings until the convention was almost over, that heavy, thick, witless depression which was to dominate every move as the delegates wandered and gawked and paraded and set for a spell, there in the Gallery of the Biltmore, that huge depressing alley with its inimitable hotel color, that faded depth of chiaroscuro which unhappily has no depth, that brown which is not a brown, that gray which has no pearl in it, that color which can be described only as hotel-color because the beiges, the tans, the walnuts, the grays, and all those dumb browns merge into that lack of color which is an over-large hotel at convention time, with all the small-towners wearing their set, starched faces, that look they get at carnival, all fever and suspicion, and proud to be there, eddying slowly back and forth in that high block-long tunnel of a room with its arched ceiling and square recesses filling every rib of the arch with art work, escutcheons, and blazons and other art, pictures I think, I cannot even remember, there was such a hill of cigar smoke the eye had to travel on its way to the ceiling, and at one end there was galvanized pipe scaffolding and workmen repairing some part of the ceiling, one of them touching up one of the endless squares of painted plaster in the arch, and another worker, passing by, yelled up to the one who was working on the ceiling: "Hey, Michelangelo!"

Later, of course, it began to emerge and there were portraits one could keep. There was Lyndon Johnson, who had compromised too many contradictions and now the contradictions were in his face: When he smiled, the corners of his mouth squeezed gloom; when he was pious, his eyes twinkled irony; when he spoke in a righteous tone, he looked corrupt; when he jested, the ham in his jowls looked to quiver. He was not convincing.

Stevenson had the patina. He came into the room and the room was different, not stronger perhaps (which is why ultimately he did not win), but warmer. One knew why some adored him—he did not look like other people, not with press lights on his flesh; he looked like a lover, the simple truth, he had the sweet happiness of an adolescent who has just been given his first major kiss. And so he glowed, and one was reminded of Chaplin, not because they were the least alike in features but because Charlie Chaplin was luminous when one met him and Stevenson had something of that light.

There was Eleanor Roosevelt, fine, precise, hand-worked like ivory. Her voice was almost attractive as she explained in the firm, sad tones of the first lady in this small town why she could not admit Mr. Kennedy, who was no doubt a gentleman, into her political house. One had the impression of a lady who was finally becoming a woman, which is to say that she was just a little bitchy about it all—nice bitchy, charming, it had a touch of art to it, but it made one wonder if she were not now satisfying the last passion of them all, which was to become physically attractive, for she was better-looking than she had ever been as she now spurned the possibilities of a young suitor.

Bobby Kennedy, that archetype Bobby Kennedy, looked like a West Point cadet, or, better, one of those unreconstructed Irishmen from Kirkland House one always used to have to face in the line in Harvard house football games. "Hello," you would say to the ones who looked like him as you lined up for the scrimmage after the kickoff, and his type would nod and look away, one rock glint of recognition your due for living across the hall from one another all through Freshman year, and then bang, as the ball was passed back, you'd get a bony king-hell knee in the crotch. He was the kind of man never to put on the gloves with if you wanted to do some social boxing, because after two minutes it would be a war, and ego-bastards last long in a war. And then there was Kennedy, the edge of the mystery. But a sketch will no longer suffice.

The afternoon he arrived at the convention from the airport, there was of course a large crowd on the street outside the Biltmore, and the best way to get a view was to get up on an outdoor balcony of the Biltmore, two flights above the street, and look down on the event. One waited thirty minutes, and then a honking of horns as wild as the getaway after an Italian wedding sounded around the corner, and the Kennedy cortege came into sight, circled Pershing Square, the men in the open and leading convertibles sitting backwards to look at their leader, and finally came to a halt in a space cleared for them by the police in the crowd. The television cameras were out, and a Kennedy band was playing some circus music. One saw him immediately. He had the deep orange-brown suntan of a ski instructor, and when he smiled at the crowd his teeth were amazingly white and clearly visible at a distance of fifty yards. For one moment he saluted Pershing Square, and Pershing Square saluted him back, the prince and the beggars of glamour staring at one another across a city street, and then with a quick move he was out of the car and by choice headed into the crowd instead of the lane cleared for him into the hotel by the police, so that he made his way inside surrounded by a mob, and one expected at any moment to see him lifted to its shoulders like a matador being carried back to the city after a triumph in the plaza. All the while the band kept playing the campaign tunes, sashaying circus music, and one had a moment of clarity, intense as a *déjà vu*, for the scene that had taken place had been glimpsed before in a dozen musical comedies—it was the scene where the hero, the matinee idol, the movie star comes to the palace to claim the princess, or what is the same, and more to our soil, the football hero, the campus king, arrives at the dean's home surrounded by a court of open-singing students to plead with the dean for his daughter's kiss and permission to put on the big musical that night.

And suddenly I saw the convention, it came into focus for me, and I understood the mood of depression that had lain over the convention, because finally it was simple: The Democrats were going to nominate a man who, no matter how serious his political dedication might be, was indisputably and willy-nilly going to be seen as a great box-office actor, and the consequences of that were staggering and not at all easy to calculate.

Since the First World War Americans have been leading a double life, and our history has moved on two rivers, one visible, the other underground: There has been the history of politics, which is concrete, factual, practical, and unbelievably dull if not for the consequences of the actions of some of these men; and there is a subterranean river of untapped, ferocious, lonely, and romantic desires, that concentration of ecstasy and violence which is the dream life of the nation.

The twentieth century may yet be seen as that era when civilized man and underprivileged man were melted together into mass man, the iron and steel of the nineteenth century giving way to electronic circuits which communicated their messages into men, the unmistakable tendency of the new century seeming to be the creation of men as interchangeable as commodities, their extremes of personality singed out of existence by the psychic fields of force the communicators would impose.

Nowhere as in America, however, was this fall from individual man to mass man felt so acutely, for America was at once the first and most prolific creator of mass communications, and the most rootless of countries, since almost no American could lay claim to the line of a family that had not once at least severed its roots by migrating here. But, if rootless, it was then the most vulnerable of countries to its own homogenization. Yet America was also the country in which the dynamic myth of the Renaissance—that every man was potentially extraordinary—knew its most passionate persistence. Simply, America was the land where people still believed in heroes: George Washington; Billy the Kid; Lincoln, Jefferson; Mark Twain, Jack London, Hemingway; Joe Louis, Dempsey, Gentleman Jim; America believed in athletes, rum-runners, aviators; even lovers, by the time Valentino died. It was a country that had grown by the leap of one hero past another—is there a county in all of our ground that does not have its legendary figure? And when the West was filled, the expansion turned inward, became part of an agitated, overexcited, superheated dream life. The film studios threw up their searchlights as the frontier was finally sealed, and the romantic possibilities of the old conquest of land turned into a vertical myth, trapped within the skull, of a new kind of heroic life, each choosing his own archetype of a neo-renaissance man, be it Barrymore, Cagney, Flynn, Bogart, Brando, or Sinatra, but it was almost as if there were no peace unless one could fight well, kill well (if always with honor), love well and love many, be cool, be daring, be dashing, be wild, be wily, be resourceful, be a brave gun. And this myth, that each of us was born to be free, to wander, to have adventure, and to grow on the waves of the violent, the perfumed, and the unexpected, had a force that could not be tamed no matter how the nation's regulators—politicians, medicos, policemen, professors, priests, rabbis, ministers, *idéologues*, psychoanalysts, builders, executives, and endless communicators—would brick-in the modern life with hygiene upon sanity, and middle-brow homily over platitude; the myth would not die. Indeed a quarter of the nation's business must have depended upon its existence. But it stayed alive for more than that—it was as if the message in the labyrinth of the genes would insist that violence was locked with creativity, and adventure was the secret of love.

Once, in the Second World War and in the year or two that followed, the underground river returned to earth, and the life of the nation was intense, of the present, electric—as a lady said, "That was the time when we gave parties which changed people's lives." The Forties was a decade when the speed with which one's own events occurred seemed as rapid as the history of the battlefields, and for the mass of people in America a forced march into a new jungle of emotion was the result. The surprises, the failures, and the dangers of that life must have terrified some nerve of awareness in the power and the mass, for, as if stricken by the orgiastic vistas the myth had carried up from underground, the retreat to a more conservative existence was disorderly, the fear of communism spread like an irrational hail of boils. To anyone who could see, the excessive hysteria of the Red wave was no preparation to face an enemy but rather a terror of the national self: free-loving, lust-looting, atheistic, implacable—absurdity beyond absurdity to label communism so, for the moral products of Stalinism had been Victorian sex and a ponderous machine of ideology. Yes, the life of politics and the life of the myth had diverged too far. There was nothing to return them to one another, no common danger, no cause, no desire, and, most essentially, no hero. It was a hero America needed, a hero central to his time, a man whose personality might suggest contradictions and mysteries that could reach into the alienated circuits of the underground, because only a hero can capture the secret imagination of a people, and so be good for the vitality of his nation—a hero embodies the fantasy and so allows each private mind the liberty to consider its fantasy and find a way to grow. Each mind can become more conscious of its desire and waste less strength in hiding from itself. Roosevelt was such a hero, and Churchill, Lenin, and De Gaulle; even Hitler, to take the most odious example of this thesis, was a hero, the hero-as-monster, embodying what had become the monstrous fantasy of a people, but the horror upon which the radical mind and liberal temperament foundered was that he gave outlet to the energies of the Germans and so presented the twentieth century with an index of how horrible had become the secret heart of its desire. Roosevelt is of course a happier example of the hero; from his paralytic leg to the royal elegance of his geniality he seemed to contain the country within himself—everyone from the meanest starving cripple to an ambitious young man could expand into the optimism of an improving future because the man offered an unspoken promise of a future that would be rich. The sexual and the sex-starved, the poor, the hard-working, and the imaginative well-to-do could see themselves in the President, could believe him to be like themselves. So a large part of the country was able to discover its energies because not as much was wasted in feeling that the country was a poisonous nutrient which stifled the day.

Too simple? No doubt. One tries to construct a simple model. The thesis is after all not so mysterious; it would merely nudge the notion that a hero embodies his time and is not so very much better than his time, but he is larger than life and so is capable of giving direction to the time, able to encourage a nation to discover the deepest colors of its character. At bottom the concept of the hero is antagonistic to impersonal social progress, to the belief that social ills can be solved by social legislating, for it sees a country as all-but-trapped in its character until it has a hero who reveals the character of the country to itself. The implication is that without such a hero the nation turns sluggish. Truman for example was not such a hero, he was not sufficiently larger than life, he inspired familiarity without excitement, he was a character but his proportions came from soap opera: Uncle Harry, full of salty common-sense and small-minded certainty, a storekeeping uncle.

Whereas Eisenhower has been the anti-Hero, the regulator. Nations do not necessarily and inevitably seek for heroes. In periods of dull anxiety, one is more likely to look for security than a dramatic confrontation, and Eisenhower could stand as a hero only for that large number of Americans who were most proud of their lack of imagination. In American life, the unspoken war of the century has taken place between the city and the small town: the city, which is dynamic, orgiastic, unsettling, explosive, and accelerating to the psyche; the small town, which is rooted, narrow, cautious, and planted in the life-logic of the family. The need of the city is to accelerate growth; the pride of the small town is to retard it. But since America has been passing through a period of enormous expansion since the war, the double-four years of Dwight Eisenhower could not retard the expansion, it could only denude it of color, character, and the development of novelty. The small-town mind is rooted—it is rooted in the small town—and when it attempts to direct history the results are disastrously colorless because the instrument of world power which is used by the small-town mind is the committee. Committees do not create, they merely proliferate, and the incredible dullness wreaked upon the American landscape in Eisenhower's eight years has been the triumph of the corporation. A tasteless, sexless, odorless sanctity in architecture, manners, modes, styles has been the result. Eisenhower embodied half the needs of the nation, the needs of the timid, the petrified, the sancti-monious, and the sluggish. What was even worse, he did not divide the nation as a hero might (with a dramatic dialogue as the result); he merely excluded one part of the nation from the other.

Some part of these thoughts must have been in one's mind at the moment there was that first glimpse of Kennedy entering the Biltmore Hotel; and in the days that followed, the first mystery—the profound air of depression that hung over the convention—gave way to a second mystery, which can be answered only by history. The depression of the delegates was understandable: No one had too much doubt that Kennedy would be nominated, but if elected he would be not only the youngest President ever to be chosen by voters, he would be the most conventionally attractive young man ever to sit in the White House, and his wife—some would claim it—might be the most beautiful first lady in our history. Of necessity the myth would emerge once more, because America's politics would now be also America's favorite movie, America's first soap opera, America's best-seller. "Well, there's your first hipster," says a writer one knows at the convention, "Sergius O'Shaug-nessy born rich," and the temptation is to nod, for it could be true, a war hero, and the heroism is bona-fide, even exceptional, a man who has lived with death, who, crippled in the back, took on an operation that would kill him or restore him to power, who chose to marry a lady whose face might be too imaginative for the taste of a democracy that likes its first ladies to be executives of home-management, a man who courts political suicide by choosing to go all out for a nomination four, eight, or twelve years before his political elders think he is ready, a man who announces a week prior to the convention that the young are better fitted to direct history than the old. Yes, it captures the attention. This is no routine candidate calling every shot by safety's routine book ("Yes," Nixon said, naturally but terribly tired an hour after his nomi-nation, the TV cameras and lights and microphones bringing out a sweat of fatigue on his face, the words coming very slowly from the tired brain, somber, modest, sober, slow, slow enough so that one could touch emphatically the cautions behind each word, "Yes, I want to say," said Nixon, "that whatever abilities I have, I got from my mother." A tired pause . . . dull moment of warning, ". . . and my father." The connection now made, the rest comes easy, ". . . and my school and my church." Such men are capable of anything.)

One had the opportunity to study Kennedy a bit in the days that followed. His style in the press conferences was interesting. Not terribly popular with the reporters (too much a contemporary, and yet too difficult to understand, he received nothing like the rounds of applause given to Eleanor Roosevelt, Stevenson, Humphrey, or even Johnson), he carried himself nonetheless with a cool grace that seemed indifferent to applause, his manner somehow similar to the poise of a fine boxer, quick with his hands, neat in his timing, and two feet away from his corner when the bell ended the round. There was a good lithe wit to his responses, a dry Harvard wit, a keen sense of proportion in disposing of difficult questions—invariably he gave enough of an answer to be formally satisfactory without ever opening himself to a new question that might go further than the first. Asked by a reporter, "Are you for Adlai as vice-president?" the grin came forth and the voice turned very dry, "No, I cannot say we have considered *Adlai* as a vice-president." Yet there was an elusive detachment to everything he did. One did not have the feeling of a man present in the room with all his weight and all his mind. Johnson gave you all of himself, he was a political animal, he breathed like an animal, sweated like one, you knew his mind was entirely absorbed with the compendium of political fact and maneuver; Kennedy seemed at times like a young professor whose manner was adequate for the classroom but whose mind was off in some intricacy of the Ph.D. thesis he was writing. Perhaps one can give a sense of the discrepancy by saying that he was like an actor who had been cast as the candidate, a good actor, but not a great one—you were aware all the time that the role was one thing and the man another—they did not coincide, the actor seemed a touch too aloof (as, let us say, Gregory Peck is usually too aloof) to become the part. Yet one had little sense of whether to value this elusiveness or to beware of it. One could be witnessing the fortitude of a superior sensitivity or the detachment of a man who was not quite real to himself.

from Of Kennedys and Kings:
Making Sense of the Sixties
by Harris Wofford

Activist and author Harris Wofford (born 1926) was a member of the Civil Rights Section of JFK's 1960 presidential campaign. Wofford's account of a crucial episode in that campaign offers an early glimpse of John and his campaign manager Bobby's dealings with Martin Luther King and his followers. Those dealings combined calculation, passion and the characteristic haste of two young men in a hurry.

It was a gray day in March 1965, and we were about six miles outside Selma on Highway 80. Coretta Scott King was walking with her chin high and looking straight ahead as she had learned to do during a long decade of civil rights marches. I had not seen her since John Kennedy was killed. At the front, leading the march to Montgomery, Andy Young signaled that we could rest on the roadside. Coretta saw me a few ranks behind and in her slow, measured way welcomed me back to Alabama—"There is plenty to be done here." Then with her usual steady calm, she turned to the subject we had never discussed after the 1960 election: "They say that his call to me made the difference, that it elected him President. I like to think so. He was beginning to do so much, he and his brother."

Much has been made of Kennedy's action and Nixon's inaction while Martin King was in a Georgia jail in October 1960. The impact on black voters and on electoral votes has been analyzed and reported. But the full story of the reactions of John and Robert Kennedy and of

Coretta, Martin, and Daddy King has not been told. The complexity and spontaneity and the irony of accident that surrounded and caused the call have nowhere been accurately conveyed.

The facts have sometimes been turned upside down. In his *Report of the County Chairman,* James Michener wrote that "when John Kennedy leaves the White House in 1968 he ought to erect a statue to the man who suggested that he make his urgent phone call . . ." but Michener had the call being made to Martin instead of Coretta King, which misses the point. In a television dramatization of King's life on NBC in 1978, Kennedy's motivation was assumed to have been cynical and merely political. In other versions the episode is treated as an example of an all-efficient, ever-calculating, well-coordinated Kennedy machine. The reverse is closer to the truth. Motivation was mixed, but at the time no one could predict whether the political consequences for Kennedy would be good or bad.

Kennedy's call was, in fact, precipitated by Coretta's call to me the day her husband was sentenced by a Georgia judge to four months of hard labor for driving with an out-of-state license. "They are going to kill him, I know they are going to kill him," she told me. The thought of the Georgia chain gang stirred old memories and fears. She wanted to do something and was turning anywhere for help. Having heard that Senator John Kennedy was concerned, she called me, an old friend, now the Senator's civil rights coordinator.

It was the second time I had heard her predict her husband's death. Late one evening in 1957, I was driving Martin and Coretta King from a meeting in Baltimore to their Washington hotel, and suddenly in the back seat she started telling my wife about a terrible, recurring dream in which Martin was killed. As a girl growing up in Marion, Alabama, near Selma, she had come to fear the violence of white people; her home had burned down under suspicious circumstances, and then her father's sawmill was burned by a white logger. "They will do any-thing," she said.

In October 1960, King had hoped there would be no new racial controversy during the presidential election. As the head of the nonpartisan Southern Christian Leadership Conference, he did not intend to endorse Kennedy, but he was "neutral against Nixon." He was impressed and encouraged by the far-reaching Democratic civil rights platform, and preferred to use the campaign period to negotiate civil rights commitments from both candidates, but particularly from Kennedy. When the Student Nonviolent Coordinating Committee, including Julian Bond and Marion Barry, proposed a sit-in against segregation in restaurants and lunch counters in downtown Atlanta stores, King urged a delay until after the election. When the young militants decided to go ahead anyway, King tried to arrange to be out of town on the day scheduled. He confided this to me when I had to cancel a meeting he had set with Kennedy for that day in Miami; with his one good reason for not being in Atlanta gone, he did not think he could avoid participating in the sit-in.

Negotiations for the meeting with Kennedy had been going on for weeks, with one complication after another. King had a larger personal following than any other Negro leader and could reach the mass of Negro voters as no one else then could. ("Black" was not yet the acceptable term.) We in the Civil Rights Section of the campaign wanted somehow to demonstrate Kennedy's support for King and King's respect for Kennedy, and thought a well-publicized meeting of the two would help. They had met privately earlier in the summer, after the Democratic convention, and King had urged Kennedy to "do something dramatic" to assure Negroes of his commitment to civil rights. In later discussions I had with King, he suggested a meeting in the South as one way to do this. That would symbolize Kennedy's concern and courage. Afterwards King would be willing to tell a news conference that he appreciated the Democratic Party's strong platform on civil rights and had confidence in the Senator's determination and ability to carry it out as President. Not quite an endorsement, but a near equivalent. We thought it would add important momentum to the campaign, and help counteract the anti-Catholic mood of many deeply Protestant Negro clergymen. King's own father, a Baptist minister, had signed a newspaper advertisement for Nixon, solely on religious grounds.

The difficulty was Martin's condition that the meeting take place in the South. Kennedy suggested Nashville, but King didn't think that was Southern enough to make the point. Deeper South, he urged. Kennedy would not agree to Atlanta because his chief supporters there—Griffin Bell, Governor Ernest Vandiver, Robert Troutman (an old friend from Choate)—thought it would lose a state he otherwise had a good chance to win. Finally Miami was agreed to, although it was not what King had meant by the Deep South.

Perhaps because of that venue and because both Kennedy and Nixon were to be in Miami to address the American Legion convention, King told us he would have to offer to meet Nixon, too. Since Nixon was more and more following a Southern strategy, he probably would have refused such a meeting, but Kennedy did not want to fall into a trap: Nixon might meet King and thus convey a sense of King's neutrality, diluting any pro-Kennedy effect among Negroes, while the Kennedy meeting, with its emphasis on the Democratic civil rights platform, would intensify the Southern white resentment. Reluctantly, I had to call off the Miami meeting. King stayed in Atlanta, joined the sit-in, and went to jail.

On Wednesday, October 19, 1960, cheered on by hundreds of supporters and jeered at by surprised white customers, some seventy-five Negroes sought luncheon service at ten downtown Atlanta stores. It was a dramatic break with tradition and prevailing law. "There was hardly a place outside our own neighborhoods," Coretta King wrote of the event, "where a Negro could even get a soda except by going to the side door of a drugstore and having it handed out." Martin King was in the forefront of those asking to be served in the Magnolia Room restaurant in Rich's, one of the largest department stores in the South. He and fifty-one others were arrested and charged with violating the anti-trespass law. Refusing to put up bail, King said, "I'll stay in jail a year, or ten years, if it takes that long to desegregate Rich's."

Thursday, several hundred Negroes sat in at or picketed some fifteen establishments, forcing the closing of many eating places; twenty-five protesters were arrested. Friday, few stores attempted to offer food service; one that did, Woolworth's, was closed when Negroes sat in and whites gathered threateningly. Two Negroes were arrested.

Saturday morning, October 22, I was home in Alexandria, Virginia, playing with our children and enjoying a brief break from night-and-day campaigning. The radio reported that the Ku Klux Klan was parading on downtown Atlanta streets. King's Southern Christian Leadership Conference had telegraphed both presidential candidates asking for help. At Kennedy headquarters we were daily becoming more concerned that even without the Republicans pressing the point, a Negro backlash against all Democrats might result from Atlanta's reminder of the segregation-forever stand of white Southern Democrats. But what brought me to telephone Atlanta was a simpler thought: King had been in jail four days and I, a friend and Kennedy's civil rights man, had done nothing.

In Atlanta, Morris Abram, a leading lawyer and civil libertarian, listened while I joshed him, seriously: "Atlanta's supposed to be the enlightened leader of a New South, Hartsfield's the best mayor in the country, and you're a lawyer who can do anything. So why is Martin still in jail?" Morris said that it was fortuitous I had called; he was leaving for a meeting at City Hall with Mayor Hartsfield and a group of Negro leaders. He would tell Hartsfield of my call and they would see what they could do. Senator Kennedy did not know of my call, I emphasized, but I knew he would appreciate a satisfactory resolution, with King's release from jail as soon as possible.

Two or three hours later the phone rang. "Sit down and hold on to your seat," Morris began. "The mayor has just told press and television people outside City Hall that in response to Senator Kennedy's personal intervention he has reached an agreement with Negro leaders for the release of King and the other sit-in prisoners."

"But Kennedy knows nothing about my call—I told you I was acting on my own," I said, holding on to my seat.

"The mayor knows that, but it is a good agreement and he wants to talk to you."

"This is Bill Hartsfield," a familiar voice said. "Now I know that I ran with the ball farther than you expected, Harris, my boy, but I needed a peg to swing on and you gave it to me, and I've swung on it. You tell your Senator that he and I are out on the limb together, so don't saw it off. I'm giving him the election on a silver platter, so don't pull the rug out from under me."

While Hartsfield was talking, in his warm Southern drawl, I began to think how I would explain the situation to Kennedy. Hartsfield was one of the best mayors, a Southern Fiorello La Guardia, and the agreement he had reached with Negro leaders for a thirty-day halt in demonstrations while he worked with business and civic leaders to desegregate downtown Atlanta exemplified why Atlanta was the most progressive city in the South: when the Civil Rights Commission held hearings on housing in Chicago, New York, and Atlanta in 1958 and 1959, Hartsfield was one of the star witnesses in the sessions I had organized in Atlanta; and his story was more promising than anything we heard in the Northern cities. But Kennedy's Georgia and Southern campaign managers were not going to be persuaded; they would consider the unauthorized intervention intolerable. Later Bobby Troutman told me that he was taking his kids to a ball game when he heard the mayor's announcement on the radio; he stopped the car and hurried into a phone booth to call Bob Kennedy and be assured that nothing like that had happened.

Racing against time to prevent the kind of denial that would damage both Kennedy and Hartsfield, I finally got through by radiophone to Kennedy's car in a motorcade in Kansas City. Pierre Salinger or Kenneth O'Donnell took the call. "Hartsfield said *what?* You did *what?*" I don't recall who spoke or the exact curses that came next. After a short argument and consultation with Kennedy, it was agreed, grumpily, that Salinger would issue a low-key explanation that did not saw the limb from under all of us. When I read it on the wire service, I did not like its inaccuracy but it did not pull the rug out from under the mayor or the sixty Negro leaders who had joined in the agreement:

• • •

As a result of having many calls from all over the country regarding the incident in Atlanta, Senator Kennedy directed that an inquiry be made to give him all the facts on that situation and a report on what properly should be done. The Senator is hopeful that a satisfactory outcome can be worked out.

Georgia campaign chief Griffin Bell, then a leading Atlanta attorney, did not sound so hopeful. On behalf of Governor Vandiver, Congressman George Smith III, his campaign co-chairman, and himself, he declared, "We know that Senator Kennedy would never interfere in the affairs of a sovereign state." Bell added that "Martin Luther King has violated a state law. He is charged with trespassing on private premises, has been offered bail, and refused it because he wants to be a martyr. He must stand trial and he will get equal treatment just as any other common law violator."

While consternation spread among white Southern Democratic leaders, Negroes were momentarily jubilant. Coretta King went to the victory celebration to greet the prisoners released from jail; to her dismay, Martin was not there. The previous spring he had been charged with driving without a Georgia license (he had his Alabama license). He had been stopped by a policeman who saw him driving with a white woman—the novelist Lillian Smith—whom he and Coretta were taking to a hospital in De Kalb County, a stronghold of the Ku Klux Klan. He had been fined twenty-five dollars and placed on twelve months' probation. just as Mayor Hartsfield was arranging the release of prisoners, a De Kalb County judge declared that King's arrest for the sit-in violated his probation and reinstated the earlier conviction.

King was taken to the county jail outside Atlanta and ordered to serve six months in a state prison at hard labor. On the traffic charge—which did not involve a law that King considered unconstitutional, as he did segregation laws—he was ready to post bail and appeal while on bail, but the judge refused to let him out.

At the sentencing, Coretta King cried in public, "for the first time," she said later, "since the Movement began in 1955." She feared that "such a long sentence meant that our baby would arrive while he was in jail." She was five months pregnant and the judge had announced a six-month sentence (later reduced to four). Daddy King scolded her for crying, but was shocked and upset himself. When they saw him in his cell, Martin said, "We must prepare ourselves for the fact that I am going to have to serve this time."

What should Kennedy do now? The incredible sentence to hard labor was causing worldwide comment and was a red-hot issue among millions of American Negroes. Mayor Hartsfield announced: "We wish the world to know that the City of Atlanta had no part in the trial and sentencing of Dr. King for a minor traffic offense." But the state of Georgia and its Democratic governor were parties to King's imprisonment, and Kennedy's earlier expression of concern seemed to have been ineffective. I argued that at least we should issue a strong public statement. That would increase the pressure for King's release and improve Kennedy's standing among Negro voters. I prepared a draft to which he at first agreed, but the telephone lines between Washington and Georgia were soon buzzing with protests from Governor Vandiver, Griffin Bell, and others around the South. Kennedy was told he would lose Georgia and several other states if he issued such a statement. Bell, however, was a fair man and was shocked by the four-month sentence; he thought King should be freed on bail and prepared a more moderate draft to that effect. Finally, the governor was said to have promised to get "the son of a bitch" released if Kennedy would refrain from any further public statement. "I agreed," Kennedy told me. "What we want most is to get King out, isn't it?"

It was certainly what we wanted. Yet three days after all the other prisoners had been released, King was still in the county jail. The judge was delaying a hearing on bail. It was at this point that I received the phone call from Coretta King, her voice breaking. Frustrated because I could not tell her about the governor's promise and Kennedy could not make any public comment on the case, I could only say we were doing everything possible. This was not very reassuring to a wife who felt her husband's life was in danger every minute he remained in jail.

Stirred by the desperation in her voice, I asked Louis Martin to commiserate with me over some beer. Aside from Sargent Shriver, who had overall responsibility for our Civil Rights Section, Louis was my closest colleague in the campaign.

"Who cares about public statements?" I said to Louis. "What Kennedy ought to do is something direct and personal, like picking up the telephone and calling Coretta. Just giving his sympathy, but doing it himself."

"That's it, that's it!" said Louis. "That would be perfect."

We pondered the proposal for a while and then decided to try to get it to Kennedy right away. This time, however, I could not get through to him or to any of his key associates, and Shriver's number didn't answer. The Kennedy aides didn't return my phone calls, probably fearing more pressure for public action.

Concerned about Coretta, I thought it would be good to have someone she respected reach her to express support that night, so I called Chester Bowles.* When I explained the situation, he said he would dial her immediately and tell her that every effort was being made to assure Martin's safety and achieve his early release. Moreover, he said, Adlai Stevenson was there for dinner, and he would get him to talk to her, too.

The next morning she called me to say that she had tremendously appreciated the warm talk with Chester Bowles; she didn't mention Stevenson. Later Bowles explained that he had tried to persuade Stevenson to come on the telephone but Adlai said he couldn't do it because he had never been introduced to her. Whether he really held back out of such scruples or because the call had an emotional quality he found distasteful, or because he didn't want to offend white Southern leaders who might support him for Secretary of State, or for

---

*As Ambassador to India from 1950 to 1952 and in his *Ambassador's Report* and other writings, Bowles had championed the idea of Ghandian action. The Kings particularly liked his article, "What Negroes Can Learn from Gandhi," in *The Saturday Evening Post* (August 20, 1957), on which I had collaborated.

some other reason, Stevenson's response reflected the reticence that appealed to some as a guarantee against demagoguery but so often frustrated those who sought decisive action.

Most urgently on Coretta's mind, however, was a fear that her nightmare was coming true. In the middle of the night Martin had been awakened roughly in his cell, put in handcuffs and leg chains, hurried out into a car, and driven two hundred miles into rural Georgia. He wondered whether he was being taken out to be lynched. When dawn came the car finally deposited him at the Reidsville state prison and he was able to telephone his wife. For Coretta, Martin's transfer that far out into "cracker country" was a terrible turn for the worse.

In fact, Morris Abram assured me a few minutes later, the move itself was a wise one, though the way it had been done was inexcusable. King indeed had been in great danger in a small county jail; he was much safer in a state prison where a reasonable warden was in charge. The last thing the governor of Georgia or the Georgia white establishment wanted was King's blood on their hands. Encouraged, but still concerned about both Martin and Coretta and about Kennedy's role, I talked with Sargent Shriver in Chicago and brought him up to date. He had been given the civil rights assignment in the campaign because of his long-standing involvement as head of the Catholic Interracial Council of Chicago. During the Montgomery bus boycott he had introduced Martin King to his first public audience in Chicago; I knew he would be responsive.

"The trouble with your beautiful, passionate Kennedys is that they never show their passion," I said. "They don't understand symbolic action. Last night Louis and I suddenly knew what Kennedy should do, but we couldn't get through to him and you weren't home, so Chester Bowles did it." I had hardly stated the idea when he said, "It's not too late, Jack doesn't leave O'Hare for another forty minutes, I'm going to get it to him. Give me her number and get me out of jail if I'm arrested for speeding."

When Shriver reached Kennedy's room at the O'Hare International Inn, he saw the usual set of top associates and knew that if he broached it in their presence, someone would shoot the idea down. He waited until Ted Sorensen had gone off to finish a speech, Salinger left to see the press, and O'Donnell went to the bathroom. Then he mentioned King's middle-of-the-night ride to the state prison and said, "Why don't you telephone Mrs. King and give her your sympathy?" Shriver recalls giving him a simple case for the call: "Negroes don't expect everything will change tomorrow, no matter who's elected. But they do want to know whether you care. If you telephone Mrs. King, they will know you understand and will help. You will reach their hearts and give support to a pregnant woman who is afraid her husband will be killed."

Kennedy listened intently and, after a thoughtful pause, said, "That's a good idea. Why not? Do you have her number? Get her on the phone." In another minute, while everyone else was out of the room, he was talking with her warmly, seriously, reassuringly.

Even before any word from Shriver, I heard from Mrs. King. She was very moved, and grateful. I asked her what Kennedy had said, and she quoted him as saying: "I want to express to you my concern about your husband. I know this must be very hard for you. I understand you are expecting a baby, and I just wanted you to know that I was thinking about you and Dr. King. If there is anything I can do to help, please feel free to call on me."

Soon afterwards Morris Abram called. "It's happened!" he said. "Kennedy's done it, he's touched the heartstrings." Martin's father and Coretta had just come to his law office and told him about the Kennedy call. "Daddy King says if Kennedy has the courage to wipe the tears from Coretta's eyes, he will vote for him whatever his religion." We agreed that Morris would urge the senior Dr. King to make his conversion public.

About this time, Anthony Lewis of *The New York Times* called to query me, and perhaps to goad me, about the King affair and Kennedy's apparent silence and inaction. I said that if there was any action it wouldn't be in Washington but in Atlanta, and that he should keep in touch with Mrs. King, not me. He called back shortly to say the

Times correspondent in Atlanta reported the odd response that Mrs. King would not talk to him unless Harris Wofford approved. I called her and asked if Senator Kennedy had requested her not to make any comment. When she said he had made no such request, I said I was sure Kennedy wouldn't be issuing any statement but she should feel free to say anything she considered appropriate. Louis Martin and I sat back and waited.

We didn't have to wait long. John Seigenthaler, Bob Kennedy's close aide, called with a summons: "Bob wants to see you bomb throwers right away." A fine and compassionate Pulitzer Prize-winning newspaperman from Nashville, John sounded worried.

In his Washington headquarters, Bob was pacing back and forth, angrily. On the plane to Detroit the candidate had rather nonchalantly told Salinger, "And by the way, I telephoned Mrs. Martin Luther King this morning." Salinger, sensing danger, had radioed the word to Bob, who had exploded. With fists tight, his blue eyes cold, he turned on us. "Do you know that three Southern governors told us that if Jack supported Jimmy Hoffa, Nikita Khrushchev, or Martin Luther King, they would throw their states to Nixon? Do you know that this election may be razor close and you have probably lost it for us?"

He gave us no chance to state our case. When he ordered that there be no publicity, I said that nothing could keep the story from spreading in Atlanta and was about to tell him that the *Times* was already on the track. Louis also knew that the New York *Post* was pursuing the story. But Bob declared that the Civil Rights Section was not to do anything more that was controversial—no new press release, no new editorializing literature, no nothing—and dismissed us.

Now it was our morale that was low. Late that night when the Senator landed in New York, a newsman asked him if it was true he had called Mrs. King. He is said to have muttered something under his breath about a traitor in his camp, but publicly he confirmed the call. "She is a friend of mine and I was concerned about the situation." The next morning the *Times* attached a very small item about the call at the end of a long story on King's transfer to the Reidsville prison. (Anthony

Lewis says the Washington bureau had submitted a substantial article on the call, but the editors did not see the event's significance.) The *Times* quoted Mrs. King briefly and then noted that some Republicans had urged a statement on the King case from Nixon but that "an aide said the Vice President would have no comment."

In the Atlanta press Coretta King was quoted at greater length:

> It certainly made me feel good that he called me personally and let me know how he felt. I had the feeling that if he was that much concerned he would do what he could that Dr. King was let out of jail. I have heard nothing from the Vice President or anyone on his staff. Mr. Nixon has been very quiet.

Unknown to any of us at the time, Nixon and Eisenhower were in fact considering issuing a statement. In his book *Six Crises*, Nixon says that upon learning of the King case he immediately talked with Attorney General William Rogers, who recommended strong White House action. The Department of Justice prepared a draft for President Eisenhower to read on television:

> It seems to me fundamentally unjust that a man who has peacefully attempted to establish his right to equal treatment, free from racial discrimination, should be imprisoned on an unrelated charge, in itself insignificant. Accordingly, I have asked the Attorney General to take all proper steps to join with Dr. Martin Luther King in an appropriate application for his release.

Who decided against it, and why, we do not know. It would have matched the Kennedy initiative, with less risk to Nixon since the action would have been Eisenhower's, still a magic name, North and South. From my experience with Eisenhower's White House in the late 1950s (when I was with the Commission on Civil Rights), I suspect that the President merely maintained his consistent resistance to any action in the area of civil rights. This was one of the many times when Eisenhower could have given Nixon crucial assistance and didn't. But in this case Nixon himself also had the option to do or say something, and didn't.

Also unknown to me, sometime during this period Lyndon Johnson is said to have told Senator Kennedy, "Well, we'll sweat it out—but you'll have the privilege of knowing that you did the right thing."

While we were sweating it out late in the afternoon of October 27, the day after the call, David Brinkley of NBC called to say that a bulletin had just come over the wires reporting that a brother of Senator Kennedy had called the De Kalb County judge to ask for King's release. "Did someone really call the judge?" he asked. Knowing how Bob felt and certain that Ted, in California, would not have intervened, I assured him no brother could have done it, and no brother-in-law either, I felt sure. Brinkley said he wouldn't use the story on the evening news.

Not long afterwards, John Seigenthaler got me on the phone. Bob was on the line from New York, asking us to draft a statement explaining why he called the county judge. John had already denied the story and could not believe Bob had done it; nor did he think it a good move, politically or legally.

"Can't you just say I was inquiring about Dr. King's constitutional right to bail?" Bob asked, sounding uncharacteristically sheepish.

"What did you say to him? Why did you call him?" we asked.

"I said that if he was a decent American, he would let King out of jail by sundown. I called him because it made me so damned angry to think of that bastard sentencing a citizen to four months of hard labor for a minor traffic offense and screwing up my brother's campaign and making our country look ridiculous before the world."

That is how I remember it, although his language was no doubt more colorful. But oral history is inexact, and John Seigenthaler recalls that Bob said, "It just burned me all the way up here on the plane. It grilled me. The more I thought about the injustice of it, the more I thought what a son of a bitch that judge was. I made it clear to him that it was not a political call; that I am a lawyer, one who believes in the right of all defendants to make bond . . . . I felt it was disgraceful." The conversation, Kennedy said, had been restrained, and the judge had not sounded hostile.** Bob had not told his brother about it.

Very late that night—he thinks around 3 a.m.—Louis Martin was awakened-by the telephone. "This is Bob Kennedy," the caller said. "Louis, I wanted you especially to know that I called that judge in Georgia today, to try to get Dr. King out." Louis shook himself awake, not believing his ears, and made Kennedy repeat himself; there seemed to be quiet pride in Bob's voice as he recounted his action.

"You are now an honorary Brother!" Louis Martin said. Ever afterwards, Bob claimed that title in dealing with Martin ("Tell him his honorary Brother needs his help," he would say to Martin's secretary), and in turn Martin would always be able to get through directly to Kennedy with those magic words.

On balance I, too, was as pleased by Bob's passion as I was surprised by his procedure. The impropriety of the call was obvious. The Canons of Professional Ethics of the American Bar Association provide that "a lawyer should not communicate or argue privately with the Judge as to the merits of a pending cause, and he deserves rebuke and denunciation for any device or attempt to gain from a Judge special personal consideration or favor." Yet that canon notwithstanding, if the call in fact influenced the judge to let King free on bail, Kennedy's political instincts—if not his legal tactics—were right. If King had remained in jail, the Senator's call to Mrs. King might have seemed a symbol without substance—the worst fate for any symbolic act. Not long after Bob's call, the judge, noting pressure "from both sides," released King on $2,000 bond.

** In his 1964 oral history interview with Anthony Lewis, Robert Kennedy recalled that the suggestion to call the judge came from Governor Vandiver himself, probably via Griffin Bell. Kennedy said he called the judge from a pay booth and told him that King's release would be very helpful. According to Kennedy, the judge had responded, "Bob, it's nice to talk to you." After the election Kennedy said that the judge called on him at the Department of Justice and they had a friendly visit.

Outside the prison, King said, "I am deeply indebted to Senator Kennedy, who served as a great force in making my release possible. For him to be that courageous shows that he is really acting upon principle and not expediency." He added, "There are moments when the politically expedient can be morally wise." To a reporter he said, "I hold Senator Kennedy in very high esteem. I am convinced he will seek to exercise the power of his office to fully implement the civil rights plank of his party's platform." He noted he had not heard from Nixon and did not know of any effort in his behalf by anyone in the GOP.

That Friday evening, October 28, some eight hundred people filled the Ebenezer Baptist Church in Atlanta to welcome Martin home. "We must master the art of creative suffering," he said. "We must continue to have the courage to challenge the system of segregation whether it is in schools, public parks, Christian churches, lunch counters or public libraries. We must be prepared to suffer, sacrifice and even die." While he did not endorse Kennedy outright, the Atlanta *Journal* reported that "he did just about everything short of it." To the congregation he said, "I never intend to be a religious bigot. I never intend to reject a man running for President of the United States just because he is a Catholic. Religious bigotry is as immoral, undemocratic, un-American and un-Christian as racial bigotry."

Dr. King, Sr., chose that evening to make his public announcement:

> I had expected to vote against Senator Kennedy because of his religion. But now he can be my President, Catholic or whatever he is. It took courage to call my daughter-in-law at a time like this. He has the moral courage to stand up for what he knows is right. I've got all my votes and I've got a suitcase and I'm going to take them up there and dump them in his lap.

There were just ten days left before the election. The press had carried the Kennedy-King story far and wide, but most of its readership was white. White bigots, North and South, were likely to know what one or both of the Kennedy brothers had done. At Democratic headquarters dire predictions were being made about how many votes—and states—the King affair had cost. Louis Martin and I wanted to do everything in our power to see that the prophesied losses were made up by a surge of black votes.

Negro-owned newspapers, mostly weekly publications with modest circulation, could not reach the mass of black voters in time. Yet we knew that the story, if well told, would convince many to switch from Nixon, and even more importantly, would inspire many registered but apathetic Democrats to vote who might otherwise stay at home. We thought we could arrange mass distribution of a good pamphlet, but with Bob Kennedy having directed us to publish no new statements or editorializing literature, we were stymied.

Putting the problem to Shriver, still in Illinois, we asked him to help persuade Bob to let us print and distribute a little pamphlet on the King case. "What do you want to put in it?" he asked. We said that all we wanted to do was reproduce the statements made by leading Negroes in the public press. "So you don't need to editorialize or make any new statement?" he said. "Then you don't need to ask Bobby's permission. He might say no, but what you're planning is not within his ban. Let's do it. If it works, he'll like it. If we don't do it, and we don't get enough Negro votes, he and Jack wouldn't like that, and we would all be kicking ourselves for a long time."

In six hours we went to press with *The Case of Martin Luther King.* To avoid embarrassing the Democratic National Committee we arranged for it to be published and sponsored by "The Freedom Crusade Committee" headed by two Philadelphia ministers (one of them the father of Congressman-to-be William Gray, Jr.). We stretched the non-editorializing rule to—or beyond—the limit with one bold caption: *"No Comment" Nixon versus a Candidate with a Heart, Senator Kennedy.* Otherwise, it simply contained, in very readable type, the statements by Coretta, Martin, and Dr. King, Sr., along with the following comments by Ralph Abernathy of the Southern Christian Leadership Conference, Gardner Taylor, president of the Protestant Council of New York, and the New York *Post.*

"I earnestly and sincerely feel that it is time for all of us to take off our Nixon buttons," Abernathy was quoted as saying. "Senator Kennedy did something great and wonderful when he personally called Mrs. Coretta King and helped free Dr. Martin Luther King. This was the kind of act I was waiting for. It was not just Dr. King on trial— America was on trial. . . .I learned a long time ago that one kindness deserves another. Since Mr. Nixon has been silent through all this, I am going to return his silence when I go into the voting booth."

The Reverend Gardner Taylor said, "This is the kind of moral leadership and direct personal concern which this problem has lacked in these last critical years." The New York *Post* editorial said that Senator Kennedy responded "with full awareness that his words and deeds would inflame the Southern racists and multiply his difficulties in Dixie. . . .In this dramatic human episode Senator Kennedy has looked a lot larger and warmer—and bolder—than his opponent."

During the weekend of October 29-30, the first 50,000 copies of the pamphlet, printed on light blue paper and dubbed "the blue bomb," rolled off a Washington press and were mailed in bundles all over the country. By Tuesday, November 1, Shriver had called and said they were reprinting 250,000 (later 500,000) copies in Illinois for distribution before every Negro church in Chicago and other cities in Illinois and Wisconsin on the following Sunday, two days before the election. As orders for hundreds of thousands of new copies came from Civil Rights Section campaign workers in many states, we telephoned around the country to organize a massive Sunday distribution at Negro churches. In a number of cities, extra copies were printed on local presses. Near dawn on Sunday, November 6, we loaded the last large shipments on Greyhound buses headed for Virginia and North and South Carolina. They were met at the terminals and the pamphlets taken straight to the churches. In all, nearly two million copies were distributed.

The printed word and churches were not our only recourse. Streetwise Louis Martin called Harlem leader Raymond Jones and other Northern Negro Democrats, suggesting they send runners into the bars with the word that Kennedy called Coretta and got Martin out of jail. When "Ray the Fox" reported back that the bars of Harlem were all going our way, and when we got widespread reports of whole congregations of Negro Baptists and Methodists standing up and pledging to vote for Kennedy, we sensed that a tide was running for the Senator in practically every Negro community, North and South.

When the votes were counted that Tuesday, it became clear that more than two-thirds of the Negroes voting were for Kennedy. (Gallup and Harris polls found 68 to 78 percent for the Senator.) Moreover, a higher proportion had voted—and had voted Democratic—then in 1956. In Illinois alone, which Kennedy carried by 9,000 votes, some 250,000 Negroes are estimated to have voted for him. Theodore White, in *The Making of the President 1960*, concluded that "it is difficult to see how Illinois, New Jersey, Michigan, South Carolina or Delaware (with 74 electoral votes) could have been won had the Republican-Democratic split of the Negro wards and precincts remained as it was, unchanged from the Eisenhower charm of 1956." If two or three of those states had gone Republican, Kennedy would have lost. He won by 84 electoral votes, with a popular margin of only 120,000 votes.

Afterwards, President Eisenhower in irritation blamed "a couple of phone calls"—by John and Robert Kennedy—for the decisive shift of Negro votes. Nixon, in turn, wrote in *Six Crises* that had the White House issued the statement that the Justice Department had recommended, "the whole incident might have resulted in a plus rather than a minus." Instead, Nixon wrote, despite what he considered a strong personal record in support of civil rights legislation, and earlier friendly association with Martin King himself (when they met in Ghana), "this one unfortunate incident in the heat of the campaign served to dissipate much of the support I had among Negro voters." He added that if he had "called the judge or done something similarly 'grandstand,' " it might have been a sure road to victory—one of sixteen such possible roads he listed.

Curiously, Nixon blamed it all on Bob Kennedy and made no reference to the Senator's call to Mrs. King. He explained the "no comment" attributed to him as a reaction to Bob's call to the judge. He said that on learning of Bob's call he told his press secretary, Herb Klein, "I think Dr. King is getting a bum rap. But despite my strong feelings in this respect, it would be completely improper for me or any other lawyer to call the judge. And Robert Kennedy should have known better than to do so." Klein, according to Nixon, concluded it would be better simply to say "no comment." Whatever he may have said later to Klein about Bob Kennedy, the "no comment" to *The New York Times* was given after the Senator's call to Mrs. King—the day before Bob's call to the judge.

Two days after the election, Nixon's chauffeur said, "Mr. Vice-President, I can't tell you how sick I am about the way my people voted in the election. You know I had been talking to all my friends. They were all for you. But when Mr. Robert Kennedy called the judge to get Dr. King out of jail—well, they just all turned to him." Nixon replied, "If there was any fault involved it was not with your people: it was mine, in failing to get my point of view across to them."

In such a narrow victory, credit goes to every successful part of the campaign, back to the very beginning, and to all the actions and inactions of the candidate (and in this case, the candidate's brothers, sisters, brothers-in-law, wife, mother, and father). Accidental and elusive factors play their part, too. Bernard Segal of Philadelphia, former president of the American Bar Association, tells how his and Bob Kennedy's mutual love of chocolate led by a circuitous route to Bob's close association with Congressman William Green, Sr., James P. Clark, and other key Philadelphia Democratic leaders, without whose support the crucial Pennsylvania delegation might not have cast their decisive convention votes to nominate John Kennedy. But if the election had been lost no one would have known about Bernard Segal's chocolates; the call to Mrs. King could easily have been singled out for a large share of the blame.

In his *Report of the County Chairman,* James Michener calls the King affair "the single event which came closest to being the one vital accident of the campaign." When King was jailed, Michener assumed it "was a situation that must work to the Democrats' disadvantage, for if Senator Kennedy did nothing, he would lose Negro support in the vital northern cities, and if he did something, he would alienate the South, where he had to pick up electoral votes." Michener concluded:

> What happened is history. . . . John Kennedy took the risk and did the gallant thing. . . . In doing this he did not lose Georgia or South Carolina or Texas. Instead he won the Negro vote in New York and Chicago and Philadelphia, and thus the Presidency.

In the original draft of *The Making of the President*, White had it that a single "command decision" was made for the candidate to call Mrs. King and for brother Bob to call the judge. After I gave him a very different version, he modified the account of the Senator's call but still wrote that "Bobby Kennedy, informed in the course of the day of the command decision . . . the next morning telephoned . . . the Georgian judge." And again, on the plan for the pamphlet, he wrote that since the "command decision had been made, the Kennedy organization could by now follow through." His view of a centralized super-efficient Kennedy operation would not let him write otherwise, but that is not how it happened.***

Bob Kennedy never discussed the calls to Mrs. King or the judge with me, except for that morning when he gave Louis Martin and me hell for suggesting his brother's action and the night he confessed to calling the judge. The New York *Post* writer Murray Kempton reported that he had asked Bob, after the election, whether he was glad he had called the judge. "Sure I'm glad," Kennedy said, "but I would hope I'm not glad for the reason you think I'm glad."

***Attributing more generous motives to Kennedy, White retold the story of the call to Mrs. King in his 1978 book, *In Search of History*. But the call was not an entirely humanitarian act either. Nor was the account in Sorensen's *Kennedy* correct. Kennedy phoned, according to Sorensen, against the advice of "almost all his advisers" who "initially opposed [it] as a futile 'grandstand' gesture which would cost more votes among Southerners than it would gain among Negroes." There was prior advice against issuing a public statement about King, but no advice about the call, except Shriver's, since none of the other "advisers" knew of it in advance.

John Kennedy never, to my knowledge, made any public comment on his call to Mrs. King, except the brief confirmation that he had done it, but in a conversation about it with John Kenneth Galbraith he said, "The finest strategies are usually the result of accidents."

On Sunday, October 30, while the blue pamphlets were being printed, I went to meet Senator Kennedy at Washington National Airport. It was the last time I was to call him "Senator" or "Jack," for he was about to fly off for his final campaign in Pennsylvania, New York, and California (where he would propose the Peace Corps). Our Civil Rights Section had one piece of unfinished business: the release of the report of the Conference on Constitutional Rights that Kennedy had convened in New York in mid-October. It was a document that had been cleared and then, for one reason or another, delayed. Kennedy had agreed to sign the covering letter at the airport.

He read it carefully, no doubt noting the far-reaching specific recommendations covering practically every area of civil rights. Then in his quizzical, sympathetic but humorous way, he looked me in the eye and asked, "Tell me honestly whether you think I need to sign and release this today in order to get elected a week from Tuesday. Or do you mainly want me to do it to go on record?" I had to agree that the release would have little effect on voters; it involved commitments for his presidency.

By now he had shot his bolt for civil rights in the campaign and done it well.

"Then we can wait, and release it when I'm elected," he said. "You can consider me on record—with you."

I walked with him out on the runway to his plane, the *Caroline*. He was carrying his three-year-old daughter on his back, and my five-year-old son, Daniel, was on mine. The sun was shining and his gaiety that day had the air of victory about it.

Then, in the only reference I ever heard him make to the King affair, he asked, "Did you see what Martin's father said? He was going to vote against me because I was a Catholic, but since I called his daughter-in-law, he will vote for me. That was a hell of a bigoted state-ment, wasn't it? Imagine Martin Luther King having a bigot for a father!"

He said it lightly, and as we parted, he grinned and added, "Well, we all have fathers, don't we?"

First Lady in Waiting

by Norman Mailer

Norman Mailer's 1960 take on the young Jackie Kennedy and her President-elect hus- band showcases Mailer as an almost super- naturally keen observer. He is alert to the central aspects of the young couple's respective personalities—including Jackie's "touch of that artful madness which suggests future drama" and JFK's sense of "death within him."

The weather was hectic. It was the Summer of 1960, a few weeks after the Democratic Convention yet before the presidential campaign had formally begun and one was out at Hyannisport, site of the Summer White House. Those of you who know Hyannis ("High-anus," as the natives say,) will know how funny is the title—all those motels and a Summer White House too, the Kennedy compound: An enclosure of three summer homes belonging to Joe Kennedy, Sr., RFK, and JFK, with a modest amount of lawn and beach to share among them. In those historic days the lawn was overrun with journalists, cameramen, magazine writers, politicians, delegations, friends and neighboring gentry, government intellectuals, family, a prince, some Massachusetts state troopers, and red-necked hard-nosed tourists patrolling outside the fence for a glimpse of the boy. He was much in evidence, a bit of everywhere that morning, including the lawn, and particularly handsome at times, looking like a good version of Charles Lindbergh at noon on a hot August day. Well, Jackie

Kennedy was inside in her living room sitting around talking with a few of us, Arthur Schlesinger, Jr., Prince Radziwill, Peter Maas, and Pierre Salinger. We were a curious assortment indeed, as oddly assembled in our way as some of the do-gooders and real baddies on the lawn outside. It would have taken a hostess of broad and perhaps dubious gifts, Perle Mesta, no doubt, or Ethel Merman, or Elsa Maxwell, to have woven some mood into this occasion, because pop! were going the flashbulbs out in the crazy August sun on the sun-drenched terrace just beyond the bay window at our back, a politician—a stocky machine type sweating in a dark suit with a white shirt and white silk tie—was having his son, seventeen perhaps, short, chunky, dressed the same way, take a picture of him and his wife, a Mediterranean dish around sixty with a bright, happy, flowered dress. The boy took a picture of father and mother, father took a picture of mother and son—another heeler came along to take a picture of all three—it was a little like a rite surrounding *droit du seigneur,* as if afterward the family could press a locket in your hand and say, "Here, here are contained three hairs from the youth of the Count, discovered by me on my wife next morning." There was something low and greedy about this picture-taking, perhaps the popping of the flashbulbs in the sunlight, as if everything monstrous and overreaching in our insane public land were tamped together in the foolproof act of taking a sun-drenched picture at noon with no shadows and a flashbulb—do we sell insurance to protect our cadavers against the corrosion of the grave?

And I had the impression that Jackie Kennedy was almost suffering in the flesh from their invasion of her house, her terrace, her share of the lands, that if the popping of the flashbulbs went on until midnight on the terrace outside she would have a tic forever in the corner of her eye. Because that was the second impression of her, of a lady with delicate and exacerbated nerves. She was no broad hostess, not at all; broad hostesses are monumental animals turned mellow: hippopotami, rhinoceri, plump lion, sweet gorilla, warm bear. Jackie Kennedy was a cat, narrow and wild, and her fur was being rubbed every which way. This was the second impression. The first had been simpler. It had been merely of a college girl who was nice. Nice and clean and very merry. I had entered her house perspiring—talk of the politician, I was wearing a black suit myself, a washable, the only one in my closet not completely unpressed that morning, and I had been forced to pick a white shirt with button-down collar: All the white summer shirts were in the laundry. What a set-to I had had with Adele Mailer at breakfast. Food half-digested in anger, sweating like a goat, tense at the pit of my stomach for I would be interviewing Kennedy in a half hour, I was feeling not a little jangled when we were introduced, and we stumbled mutually over a few polite remarks, which was my fault I'm sure more than hers for I must have had a look in my eyes— I remember I felt like a drunk marine who knows in all clarity that if he doesn't have a fight soon it'll be good for his character but terrible for his constitution.

She offered me a cool drink—iced verbena tea with sprig of mint no doubt—but the expression in my face must have been rich because she added, still standing by the screen in the doorway, "We do have something harder of course," and something droll and hard came into her eyes as if she were a very naughty eight-year-old indeed. More than one photograph of Jackie Kennedy had put forward just this saucy regard— it was obviously the life of her charm. But I had not been prepared for another quality, of shyness conceivably. There was something quite remote in her. Not willed, not chilly, not directed at anyone in particular, but distant, detached as the psychologists say, moody and abstracted the novelists used to say. As we sat around the coffee table on summer couches, summer chairs, a pleasant living room in light colors, lemon, white, and gold seeming to predominate, the sort of living room one might expect to find in Cleveland, may it be, at the home of a fairly important young executive whose wife had taste, sitting there, watching people go by, the group I mentioned earlier kept a kind of conversation going. Its center, if it had one, was obviously Jackie Kennedy. There was a natural tendency to look at her and see if she were amused. She did not sit there like a movie star with a ripe olive in each eye for the brain, but in fact gave conversation back, made some of it, laughed often. We had one short conversation about Provincetown, which was pleasant. She remarked that she had been staying no more than fifty miles away for all these summers but had never seen it. She must, I assured her. It was one of the few fishing villages in America that still had beauty. Besides, it was the Wild West of the East. The local police were the Indians and the beatniks were the poor hard-working settlers. Her eyes turned merry. "Oh, I'd love to see it," she said. But how did one go? In three black limousines and fifty police for escort, or in a sports car at 4 a.m. with dark glasses? "I suppose now I'll never get to see it," she said wistfully.

She had a keen sense of laughter, but it revolved around the absurdities of the world. She was probably not altogether unlike a soldier who has been up at the front for two weeks. There was a hint of gone laughter. Soldiers who have had it bad enough can laugh at the fact some trooper got killed crossing an open area because he wanted to change his socks from khaki to green. The front lawn of this house must have been, I suppose, a kind of no-man's-land for a lady. The story I remember her telling was about Stash, Prince Radziwill, her brother-in-law, who had gone into the second-story bathroom that morning to take a shave and discovered, to his lack of complete pleasure, that a crush of tourists was watching him from across the road. Yes, the house had been besieged, and one knew she thought of the sightseers as a mob, a motley of gargoyles, like the horde who riot through the last pages in *The Day of the Locust*.

Since there was an air of self-indulgence about her, subtle but precise, one was certain she liked time to compose herself. While we sat there she must have gotten up a half-dozen times, to go away for two minutes, come back for three. She had the exasperated impatience of a college girl. One expected her to swear mildly. "Oh, Christ!" or "Sugar!" or "Fudge!" And each time she got up, there was a glimpse of her calves, surprisingly thin, not unfeverish. I was reminded of the legs on those adolescent Southern girls who used to go out together and walk up and down the streets of Fayetteville, North Carolina, in the

Summer of 1944 at Fort Bragg. In the petulant Southern air of their boredom many of us had found something luminous that summer, a mixture of languor, heat, innocence, and stupidity which was our cocktail vis-à-vis the knowledge we were going soon to Europe or the other war. One mentions this to underline the determinedly romantic aura in which one had chosen to behold Jackie Kennedy. There was a charm this other short Summer of 1960 in the thought a young man with a young attractive wife might soon become President. It offered possibilities and vistas, it brought a touch of life. It was thus more interesting to look at Jackie Kennedy as a woman than as a probable First Lady. Perhaps it was out of some such motive, such a desire for the clean air and tang of unexpected montage, that I spoke about her in just the way I did later that afternoon.

"Do you think she's happy?" asked a lady, an old friend, on the beach at Wellfleet.

"I guess she would rather spend her life on the Riviera."

"What would she do there?"

"End up as the mystery woman, maybe, in a good murder case."

"Wow," said the lady, giving me my reward.

It had been my way of saying I liked Jackie Kennedy, that she was not at all stuffy, that she had perhaps a touch of that artful madness which suggests future drama.

Later (on this day), one had a short session alone with Jack Kennedy, and the next day, another. As one had suspected in advance neither interview was satisfactory, they hardly could have been. The hazards of the campaign make it impossible for a candidate to be as interesting as he might like to be (assuming he has such a desire). One kept advancing the argument that this campaign would be a contest of personalities, and Kennedy kept returning the discussion to politics. After a while one recognized this was an inevitable caution for him. What remained after the interview was a passing remark whose importance was invisible on the scale of politics but proved altogether meaningful to my particular competence. As we sat down for the first time,

Kennedy smiled nicely and said that he had read my books. One muttered one's pleasure. "Yes," he said, "I've read . . ." and then there was a short pause that did not last long enough to be embarrassing in which it was yet obvious no title came instantly to his mind, an omission one was not ready to mind altogether since a man in such a position must be obliged to carry a hundred thousand facts and names in his head, but the hesitation lasted no longer than three seconds or four, and then he said, "I've read *The Deer Park* and . . . the others," which startled me, for it was the first time in a hundred similar situations, talking to someone whose knowledge of my work was casual, that the sentence did not come out, "I've read *The Naked and the Dead* . . . and the others." If one is to take the worst and assume that Kennedy was briefed for this interview (which is most doubtful), it still speaks well for the striking instincts of his advisers.

What was retained later is an impression of Kennedy's manners, which were excellent, even artful, better than the formal good manners of Choate and Harvard, almost as if what was creative in the man had been given to the manners. In a room with one or two people, his voice improved, became low-pitched, even pleasant—it seemed obvious that in all these years he had never become a natural public speaker and so his voice was constricted in public, the symptom of all orators who are ambitious, throttled, and determined.

His personal quality had a subtle, not quite describable intensity, a suggestion of dry pent heat perhaps, his eyes large, the pupils gray, the whites prominent, almost shocking, his most forceful feature: He had the eyes of a mountaineer. His appearance changed with his mood, strikingly so, and this made him always more interesting than what he was saying. He would seem at one moment older than his age, forty-eight or fifty, a tall, slim, sunburned professor with a pleasant weathered face, not even particularly handsome; five minutes later, talking to a press conference on his lawn, three microphones before him, a television camera turning, his appearance would have gone through a metamorphosis, he would look again like a movie star, his coloring vivid, his manner rich, his gestures strong and quick, alive with that concentration of vitality a successful actor always seems to radiate. Kennedy had a dozen faces. Although they were not at all similar as people, the quality was reminiscent of someone like Brando, whose expression rarely changes but whose appearance seems to shift from one person into another as the minutes go by, and one bothers with this comparison because, like Brando, Kennedy's most characteristic quality is the remote and private air of a man who has traversed some lonely terrain of experience, of loss and gain, of nearness to death, which leaves him isolated from the mass of others.

> The next day while they waited in vain for rescuers, the wrecked half of the boat turned over in the water and they saw that it would soon sink. The group decided to swim to a small island three miles away. There were other islands bigger and nearer, but the Navy officers knew that they were occupied by the Japanese. On one island, only one mile to the south, they could see a Japanese camp. McMahon, the engineer whose legs were disabled by burns, was unable to swim. Despite his own painfully crippled back, Kennedy swam the three miles with a breast stroke, towing behind him by a life-belt strap that he held between his teeth the helpless McMahon . . . it took Kennedy and the suffering engineer five hours to reach the island.

The quotation is from a book that has for its dedicated unilateral title *The Remarkable Kennedys,* but the prose is by one of the best of the war reporters, the former Yank editor Joe McCarthy, and so presumably may be trusted in such details as this. Physical bravery does not, of course, guarantee a man's abilities in the White House—all too often men with physical courage are disappointing in their moral imagination—but the heroism here is remarkable for its tenacity. The above is merely one episode in a continuing saga that went on for five days in and out of the water, and left Kennedy at one point "miraculously saved from drowning (in a storm) by a group of Solomon Island natives who suddenly came up beside him in a large dugout canoe." Afterward, his back still injured (that precise back injury which was to put him on crutches eleven years later, and have him search for "spinal-fusion surgery" despite a warning that his chances of living through the operation were "extremely limited") afterward, he asked to go back on duty and became so bold in the attacks he made with his PT boat "that the crew didn't like to go out with him because he took so many chances."

It is the wisdom of a man who senses death within him and gambles that he can cure it by risking his life. It is the therapy of the instinct, and who is so wise as to call it irrational? Before he went into the Navy, Kennedy had been ailing. Washed out of Freshman year at Princeton by a prolonged trough of yellow jaundice, he was then sick for a year at Harvard. Do his trials suggest the self-hatred of a man whose resentment and ambition are too large for his body? Not everyone can discharge his furies on an analyst's couch, for some angers can be relaxed only by winning power, some rages are sufficiently monumental to demand that one try to become a hero or else fall back into that death which is already within the cells. But if one succeeds, the energy aroused can be exceptional. Talking to a man who had been with Kennedy in Hyannisport the week before the convention, I heard that he was in a state of deep fatigue.

"Well, he didn't look tired at the convention," one commented.

"Oh, he had three days of rest. Three days of rest for him is like six months for us."

One thinks of that three-mile swim with the belt in his mouth and McMahon holding it behind him. There are pestilences which sit in the mouth and rot the teeth—in those five hours how much of the psyche must have been remade, for to give vent to the bite in one's jaws and yet use that rage to save a life: It is not so very many men who have the apocalyptic sense that heroism is the First Doctor.

from Conversations with Kennedy
by Benjamin C. Bradlee

Journalist Benjamin C. Bradlee and his wife Tony became friendly with Senator and Mrs. John Kennedy when the couples were neighbors in the late '50s. That friendship gave Bradlee an edge over competing reporters when he covered Kennedy's White House—but the roles of journalist and friend sometimes conflicted.

September 14, 1962

I saw the president in Newport briefly this morning, for the first time since I had been banished for my part in the *Look* magazine critique of the Kennedys and the press. We exchanged an absolute minimum of words over an elapsed time of perhaps twenty minutes. I was greeted with "Oh, hi. How've you been?" In the middle of the "conversation," he said "That's fine" a couple of times. And at the end, he asked after Tony and said, "See you later."

I had been nervous about seeing him again—after three months in the doghouse. In a strange way, I understood why he was sore . . . it was hard to make new friends once those White House doors had closed behind you, and if old friends wanted to be friends *and* reporters, maybe the two couldn't mix. I wanted to be friends again. I missed the access, of course, but I missed the laughter and the warmth just as much. What I couldn't and wouldn't do was send a message over the stone wall, saying I had learned my lesson. Anyway, the freeze is obviously still on.

The occasion for this brief encounter was the sequel, at last, of the case of "John's Other Wife." Most Washington correspondents, or at least most of those with any involvement in covering the White House, had been familiar with the broad outlines of the case for months. And yet no responsible newspaper or magazine had written one word about it.

Some anti-Semitic, racist hate sheets had published stories, however, ("Kennedy's Divorce Exposed! Is Present Marriage Valid? Excommunication Possible"), and I felt *Newsweek* could be first with the story if we backed into it by writing about the hate sheets themselves in the Press section, how they were spreading the story, and who was financing them. I approached Salinger with the idea, but told him I would need some solid FBI documentation about the character of the organizations and people involved in spreading the Blauvelt story.

A couple of days later, Salinger called me with the following proposition: If I agreed to show the president the finished story, and if I got my tail up to Newport where he was vacationing, he would deliver a package of the relevant FBI documents to a Newport motel and let me have them for a period not to exceed twenty-four hours. It was specifically understood that I was not to xerox anything in the FBI files, that I was not to indicate in any way that I had been given access to FBI files (I never had been given such access before, and I have never been given such access since), and that in case of a lawsuit, I would not be given access to these files a second time. I checked with *Newsweek*'s editor, Oz Elliott, and we decided to go ahead, despite a reluctance to give anyone, even the president of the United States, the right of approval of anything we wrote. In effect, we were giving Kennedy what he later said he liked so much "the right of clearance." This is a right all presidents covet, but which they should normally not be given. This one time, the book seemed worth the candle, however, and we decided to strike the deal.

Chuck Roberts, *Newsweek*'s White House correspondent, and I got on the next plane to Newport via Providence, and went right to the motel. The FBI files arrived soon afterwards, late in the afternoon, and we stayed up all night long, first reading everything in the files, then writing the story.

"Ever since the heyday of yellow journalism," the story in the magazine's Press section began, "the sense of responsibility of the American press has been more censured than praised. For political profit or for readers' pennies, sensation has often triumphed over reliability.

"But for the last 16 months, virtually every major newspaper, magazine and wire service in the U.S. has refused to publish a sensational report—familiar to hundreds of thousands of Americans—about the president of the United States. They have spiked the story despite what appears to be 'documentary evidence' and despite scattered publication of it, or hints at it, by hate groups and gossip columnists.

"The 'story' falsely alleges that before he married Jacqueline Bouvier in Newport, R.I., on Sept. 12, 1953, John F. Kennedy was secretly married to a two-time divorcee."

The story went on to describe the organizations that were spreading the story . . . an Alabama hate sheet called "The Thunderbolt"; an Arkansas racist sheet called "The Winrod Letter," which had distributed hundreds of thousands of specially photostated four-page folders entitled "The Blauvelt Family Genealogy"; the Christian Education Association, headed by Condé McGinley, publisher of what the FBI called "the vitriolic hate sheet 'Common Sense'; the "Right Brigade," described by Cleveland police as a "crackpot" organization; and a Holyoke, Mass., paper company whose mailings were handled by an associate of Robert Welch, founder of the John Birch Society.

At eight o'clock the next morning, as planned, I took the finished piece over to Hammersmith Farm, the Auchincloss summer mansion, where the Kennedys were vacationing to watch the America's Cup races, returned the FBI files to Salinger, and got the president's ok. As I was leaving his office with Kennedy, we bumped into the Ormsby-Gores, who were joining the Kennedys to watch the yacht races. The British ambassador smiled politely and asked if I were joining them for the races.

"No," Kennedy answered quickly. "He's not coming." And he meant it.

November 6, 1962

Maybe the exile is ending.

Jackie invited Tony over to the White House to play tennis today, and then invited the children over for movies and supper.

Just before leaving, the whole clan—Tony, Jackie, and a total of seven children—trooped down to the president's office, shouting, screaming, and licking lollipops.

The lollipops were given to Arthur Schlesinger to hold, while Marina and John did their special dance at the request of the president.

November 9, 1962

There was a dance at the White House tonight, smaller than any of the others, about sixty people. This was the one that had been scheduled for June. We had cocktails upstairs in the Oval Room, dinner and dancing downstairs in the Blue Room.

The president and Tony had a long session about the difficulties of being friends with someone who is always putting everything he knows into a magazine.

Everybody loves everybody again.

from President Kennedy:
Profile of Power

by Richard Reeves

Journalist, historian and filmmaker Richard Reeves (born 1936) set out to chronicle Kennedy's three-year administration, not to revile or celebrate it. He offers an unusually clear sense of how Kennedy saw Vietnam during the early phases of America's military build-up in that country.

President Kennedy had met for hours with Taylor and Rostow before they left Washington on October 17 for their inspection tour of South Vietnam. By choosing those two men, the President was making it clear that the United States had no intention of withdrawing from Southeast Asia. These were his tough guys. "The question," in Taylor's words, "was how to change a losing game and begin to win, not how to call it off."

"As we understand your position," Taylor and Rostow said in a formal memo to Kennedy, "you would wish to see every avenue of diplomacy exhausted before we accept the necessity for either positioning U.S. forces on the Southeast Asian mainland or fighting there. . . .Should we have to fight, we should use air and sea power to the maximum and engage minimum U.S. forces on the Southeast Asian mainland."

Kennedy told Taylor about his own experiences in Vietnam, which he had visited for a day in 1951 as a young congressman on an around-the-world tour. He had begun that day in Saigon with the commander of the 250,000 French troops fighting Viet Minh guerrillas. General Jean de Lattre de Tassigny had assured him that his soldiers could not lose to these natives. He had ended the evening on top of the Caravelle Hotel with a young American consular officer named Edmund Gullion. The sky around the city flashed with the usual nighttime artillery and mortar bombardment by the Viet Minh.

"What have you learned here?" Kennedy asked the diplomat.

"That in twenty years there will be no more colonies," Gullion had said. "We're going nowhere out here. The French have lost. If we come in here and do the same thing we will lose, too, for the same reason. There's no will or support for this kind of war back in Paris. The homefront is lost. The same thing would happen to us."*

In Congress, after that 1951 trip, Representative Kennedy had spoken of the $50 million a year the United States was then giving France in aid of its Vietnam operation: "We have allied ourselves to the desperate effort of a French regime to hang onto the remnants of an empire. I am frankly of the belief that no amount of American military assistance in Indochina can conquer an enemy which is everywhere and at the same time nowhere. . . . The forces of nationalism are rewriting the geopolitical map of the world."

But by 1956, Senator Kennedy had helped organize American Friends of Vietnam, saying in a speech then: "Vietnam represents the cornerstone of the Free World in Southeast Asia, the keystone to the arch, the finger in the dike. Burma, Thailand, India, Japan, the Philippines, and obviously Laos and Cambodia are among those whose security would be threatened if the Red tide of Communism overflowed into Vietnam. . . . The United States is directly responsible for this experiment—it is playing an important role in the laboratory where it is being conducted. We cannot afford to permit that experi-

*When they parted, Gullion asked Kennedy: "What are you going to do?" The congressman replied: "Run for senator or governor. Whatever opens up and looks good." Kennedy's trip ended in Japan, where he was hit by a 106-degree fever. He received the last rites of the Catholic Church there, but was brought home finally by his traveling companion, Robert Kennedy, then twenty-five years old. When he became president, Kennedy appointed Gullion Ambassador to the Congo.

ment to fail. . . . If we are not the parents of little Vietnam, then surely we are the godparents."

Now, briefing the ten members of his group before leaving on October 17, Taylor emphasized that the President had asked for his personal views and advice. They would be consulted and could make suggestions, but it was his trip and his report. The four-star general particularly wanted to impress that on the one-star general Kennedy put on the team: Ed Lansdale. But Lansdale could not contain himself. He quickly began offering suggestions, beginning with this one: Recruit two thousand or so young veterans of Chiang Kai-shek's Nationalist Chinese Army in Taiwan, give them weapons and Vietnamese names, then grant them timber concessions in the jungle and "Let them fight their way to the trees," mopping up any Viet Cong in their way. "Human defoliation," Lansdale called it.

Taylor told Lansdale he would not be in the official meeting with President Diem. "But we're friends. . . ," said Lansdale. Taylor was talking to reporters when the American party arrived at Tan Son Nhut Airport on October 18. He did not see Diem's private secretary invite Lansdale to dinner that night at the Presidential Palace. Diem surprised Lansdale by saying that he wanted U.S. combat troops in Vietnam. He was not as direct the next day with Taylor, but the general got the idea. Diem said he had to reconsider his opposition to foreign troops.

"Why have you changed your mind?" Taylor asked.

"Because of Laos," Diem replied. He thought the United States had abandoned the men it supported across the border, though he did not say that to Taylor. Like European leaders, Diem had come to believe that American casualties were the best guarantee that the United States would not go home after any attack. He was telling Lansdale this time that his people needed some sign of formal commitment by the United States, a physical guarantee.

On October 25, after four days in Saigon listening to President Diem, and to ARVN generals complaining about Diem, Taylor spent most of one day flying over rice-growing areas of the Mekong Delta. The fields had been ruined by the worst flooding in years. Back in

Saigon, Taylor sent an "Eyes Only" cable to Kennedy recommending that the flood be used as a pretext for sending in six to eight thousand U.S. troops. He added: "It will be necessary to include some combat troops for the protection of logistical operations and the defense of the area occupied by U.S. forces. Any troops coming to VN may expect to take casualties." Flying home one week later, on November 1, Taylor stopped at the Philippine hill resort of Baguio. He sent two "Eyes Only for the President" cables repeating the call for troops more specifically and citing both advantages and disadvantages of the proposal:

> As an area for the operations of U.S. troops, SVN is not an excessively difficult or unpleasant place to operate. While the border areas are rugged and heavily forested, the terrain is comparable to parts of Korea where U.S. troops learned to live and work without too much effort [and] NVN is extremely vulnerable to conventional bombing. [But] if the first contingent is not enough to accomplish the necessary results, it will be difficult to resist the pressure to reinforce . . . there is no limit to our possible commitment (unless we attack the source in Hanoi).

The next day in Washington, Kennedy told Senate Majority Leader Mike Mansfield that Taylor was going to recommend sending in troops.

"South Vietnam could be a quicksand for us," said Mansfield. He wrote the President a quick note saying he could see only four possible results: "1. A fan-fare and then a retreat. 2. An indecisive and costly conflict along the Korean lines. 3. A major war with China while Russia stands aside; 4. A total world conflict."

On the other hand, Democratic Senator Stuart Symington of Missouri, who was in Saigon, cabled Kennedy at the same time to say: "It seems to me we ought to try to hold this place. Otherwise this part of the world is sure to go down the drain."

Maxwell Taylor and the other members of the commission to Vietnam reported personally to the President on November 3. He and other commission members were shown into the Oval Office at four o'clock in the afternoon, but Kennedy was late coming back from a long lunch with the president of Senegal. Taylor walked around the office, saying his daughter would ask him every detail of what it looked like. Then he sat himself down in the President's rocking chair, trying it out. That's when Kennedy walked in. Taylor snapped to attention, but his hips were too wide for the chair and it came up with him. He wriggled out of the thing and Kennedy pretended not to notice.

The title across the cover page of Taylor's report was "A Limited Partnership." He repeated his call for sending six thousand or more U.S. troops to South Vietnam, arguing: "It is evident that morale in Vietnam will rapidly crumble if the sequence of expectations set in motion by Vice President Johnson's visit and climaxed by General Taylor's mission are not soon followed by a hard U.S. commitment to the ground in Vietnam. . . . In Washington, as well, intelligence and back-up operations must be put on a quasi-wartime footing. . . . The initiative proposed here should not be undertaken unless we are prepared to deal with any escalation the communists might choose to impose.

"There is reason for confidence if the right men are sent to do the right jobs," Taylor said finally, in a phrase tailored for Kennedy. In private, the President asked Taylor and Rostow how long the Diem government could hold on without American help. He was shocked by the answer: "Three months."

Troops in and Diem out were arguments at the crux of the dialogue the President heard. "No one action, not even the removal of Diem, is the key to success in Vietnam," Taylor told Kennedy.

Rostow asked Taylor later what he thought Kennedy would do and the general answered: "I don't know. He's instinctively against introduction of U.S. forces."

The anti-Diem argument was summarized for the President by a member of the Taylor mission, William Jorden of the State Department's Policy Planning Council, who wrote:

There is near paralysis in some areas of administration.

Small decisions that would be handled by minor officials in one of the ministries of most governments are taken to the Presidency. . . . A chance remark in a cafe can produce a jail sentence. Men are held indefinitely without indictment or even the placing of charges. . . . Brother Nhu holds power second only to that of Diem himself. Brother Can rules the northern provinces like an oriental satrapy from his base in Hue. Archbishop Thuc, as the President's elder [brother], is listened to respectfully by the President. . . . Madame Nhu presides over the women of South Viet Nam like an Empress. . . . Even persons long loyal to Diem and included in his official family now believe that South Viet Nam can get out of the present morass only if there is early and drastic revision at the top.

Rusk weighed in with an anti-Diem argument from Tokyo, cabling the President that he thought the South Vietnamese president was "a losing horse."

The number-three man at State, George Ball, had a different take, saying a small number of U.S. troops would have no real impact on events in Vietnam. "Taylor is wrong," he told Kennedy on November 7. Ball knew Southeast Asia relatively well. As a lawyer in private practice, he had once handled French legal matters in Indochina. Vietnam was not a small country, he said, it ran more than a thousand miles from north to south, with a population of over 30 million, more than ten times the population of Laos.

"Within five years, we'll have three hundred thousand men in the paddies and jungles and never find them again," he told the President. "That was the French experience. Vietnam is the worst possible terrain both from a physical and political point of view."

Kennedy didn't like that. "George, I always thought you were one of the brightest guys around here," he said. "But you're just crazier than hell. That just isn't going to happen."

Kennedy was touchy on Vietnam now. Former President Eisenhower had just given two foreign policy speeches, praising the administration for steadfastness in Berlin, but criticizing Kennedy on Cuba and Vietnam. "Indecision and uncertainty," said Ike. The big problem as Kennedy saw it—Vietnam as a domestic issue—was addressed by McNamara and Rusk in a joint memo analyzing Taylor's recommendations: "The loss of South Vietnam would stimulate bitter domestic controversies . . . and would be seized upon by extreme elements to divide the country and harass the Administration."

Kennedy told them to produce a working paper for a National Security Council meeting in the next few days. Then he went off to his eighteenth news conference, in the State Department Auditorium, where there was not a single question about Vietnam.

The President touched, as newspapers say, "on a wide range of concerns." He praised negotiators trying to work out an equitable trade balance with the country's second largest trading partner, Japan. The Japanese were complaining that the difference between exports and imports was running close to $1 billion a year in favor of the United States. He laughed off a question by Mae Craig, of the *Portland Press Herald* in Maine, who asked him what he was doing about campaign promises of equal rights and equal pay for women. He deftly (and untruthfully) dodged a question about his 180-degree turn on the missile gap by saying that during the campaign he was only quoting Eisenhower's concerns. But no reporter asked about Vietnam.

Three days later, on November 11, Rusk and McNamara delivered their NSC working paper, summarizing this way:

> The fall of South Vietnam to Communism would lead to the fairly rapid extension of Communist control, or complete accommodation to Communism, in the rest of mainland Southeast Asia and in Indonesia. The strategic implications worldwide, particularly in the Orient, would be extremely serious. The chances are against, probably sharply against, preventing the fall of South Viet-Nam by any measures short of the introduction of U.S. forces on a

substantial scale—without serious interference with our present Berlin plans. . . . We should be prepared to introduce United States combat forces if that should become necessary for success. Dependent upon the circumstances, it may also be necessary for United States forces to strike at the source of the aggression in North Viet-Nam.

Being "prepared" was a way to meet the President's desire to blur and defer the question of combat troops. But in the end, they concluded: "We now take the decision to commit ourselves to the objective of preventing the fall of South Viet-Nam to Communism and that, in doing so, we recognize that the introduction of United States and other SEATO forces may be necessary to achieve this objective."

Kennedy crossed that out. He did not want to go that far. He received a note that same day from Averell Harriman, who was dealing with the Soviets on a Laos settlement in Geneva: "There are some indications that the Soviet Union would be interested in the establishment of a peaceful and stable situation in Southeast Asia, at least for a time." The CIA was reporting similar small hints from the Chinese and from Viet Cong sources, too. There was no doubt that keeping the Americans out was a principal priority of the North Vietnamese, and perhaps of the Soviets.

Reading Harriman's cable, Walt Rostow, who had a sense of the President's political insecurities, had a countermemo on the way to him in less than an hour: "If we postpone action in Vietnam in order to engage in talk with the Communists, the image of U.S. unwillingness to confront Communism—induced by the Laos performance—will be regarded as definitely confirmed. There will be real panic and disarray . . . . The moves we now make will be examined on both sides of the Iron Curtain with the greatest care as a measure of this Administration's intentions and determination."

Kennedy called his men together in the Cabinet Room on November 15. He sided with Taylor and McNamara—up to a point. He had effectively decided that, operationally, Vietnam was a military issue. But he was not willing to send in U.S. combat troops, he said. Not now. Not yet. He agreed to almost every other recommendation in Taylor's report. More advisers, more pressure on Diem to act less like a Mandarin emperor and more like an American-style democrat, and more helicopters flown by Americans in an attempt to gain control of South Vietnamese troop movement.

Notes on the November 15 meeting were taken for Vice President Johnson by his military aide, Colonel Harold Burris, who caught Kennedy's seeming ambivalence:

> He questioned the wisdom of involvement in Viet Nam since the basis thereof is not completely clear. By comparison he noted that Korea was a case of clear aggression. . . . The conflict in Vietnam is more obscure and less flagrant. The President then expressed his strong feeling that in such a situation the United States needs even more support of allies in such an endeavor as Vietnam in order to avoid sharp domestic partisan criticism as well as strong objections from other nations of the world. The President said that he could even make a rather strong case against intervening in an area 10,000 miles away against 16,000 guerrillas with a native army of 200,000, where millions have been spent for years with no success. . . .

The President also agreed to the use of herbicide defoliants—commercial weedkillers containing cacodylic acid and several kinds of butyl—sprayed from U.S. planes in an operation code-named "Ranch Hand." The idea was to clear underbrush within two hundred feet of roads through ambush country. Then, in a second phase—food denial—the weedkiller would be used to destroy fields of rice, manioc, corn, and sweet potatoes in Viet Cong territory. Presented with three defoliant options, Kennedy, as he almost always did, selected the compromise choice, allocating $10 million for roadside defoliation and then food denial, "with prior consideration and authorization by

Washington." He bypassed the first option, a $75 million Air Force plan to kill anything green over 32,000 square miles of South Vietnam, almost half the country.

At the end of the long meeting, after hearing General Lemnitzer argue again that communism must be stopped in Vietnam or it would engulf most of Asia, Kennedy said again that he was not sure he could justify sending troops around the globe to Vietnam while there was a Communist government ninety miles offshore in Cuba. "Mr. President," Lemnitzer said, "speaking for the Joint Chiefs, we feel we should go into Cuba, too."

Kennedy's decisions that day were executed in instructions to Nolting in Saigon. He was ordered to tell Diem that the United States was prepared to join the government of South Vietnam "in a sharply increased joint effort to cope with the Viet Cong threat." The procedure outlined was a letter from Diem to Kennedy citing efforts at government reform and asking for new U.S. assistance. "The President's reply would be responsive to Diem's request. . . ," Nolting was told. There was a catch, though. "We would expect to share in the decision-making process in the political, economic and military fields as they affected the security situation."

"If this doesn't work," Kennedy said, as he stood up to end the meeting, "perhaps we'll have to try Walt's Plan Six . . . ." He nodded over to Rostow—the "Air Marshal," as Rostow was called, wanted to attack North Vietnam.

As a check on his tough guys, Kennedy also told John Kenneth Galbraith to take a look at Vietnam on his way back to his ambassador's post in India. Galbraith could write reports as fast, as colorful, and as certain as Rostow's. He did not disappoint, cabling the President on November 21 that troops were not the problem. Diem had "a comparatively well-equipped army with paramilitary formations numbering a quarter million men . . . facing a maximum of fifteen to eighteen thousand lightly armed men. If this were equality, the United States would hardly be safe from the Sioux. . . . The only solution must be to drop Diem. . . . While no one can promise a safe transaction we are now married to failure. . . . We should not be alarmed by the army as an alternative. Civilian rule is ordinarily more durable and more saleable to the world. But a change and a new start is of the essence. . . ."

Ambassador Galbraith left a very unhappy colleague in Saigon. "Nolting while not in favor of dumping Diem," Galbraith continued, "has said that a nod from the United States would be influential." Nolting did not know that Galbraith had told Kennedy back in the White House that he should drop Nolting, too, and replace him with Averell Harriman. In his own note to Kennedy a couple of days earlier, Harriman had said: "We must make it clear to Diem that we mean business about internal reform. This will require a strong ambassador who can control all U.S. activities (political, military, economic, etc.) and who is known by Diem to have the personal intimacy and confidence of the President. . . ."

Fighting back for Taylor and those who would send in troops, Rostow read Galbraith's cable and sent Kennedy a memo on November 24: "The Viet-Nam situation confronts us with the question of whether we shall or shall not accept the mounting of a guerrilla war across a frontier as legitimate. I wish it were not so; but the New Frontier will be measured in history in part on how that challenge was met."

Rostow had done it again. "History" was a trigger word for Kennedy. Politics was a mistress, coming by every day, delightful and undemanding, but history was the goddess Kennedy pursued with notes and short calls to Sorensen or Schlesinger: "Get that down for the book." He meant the book he would write after eight years. "There are limits to the number of defeats I can defend in one twelve-month period," he had told Galbraith. "I've had the Bay of Pigs, pulling out of Laos, and I can't accept a third."

He told Rostow he did not need stacks of memos to understand political consequences, that was his business. American withdrawal and Communist triumph would destroy him and the Democratic Party in a replay of the "Who Lost China?" debate that had plagued President Truman in the early 1950s. "Diem is Diem and he's the best we've got," Kennedy told Rusk in frustration, as the South Vietnamese president began ignoring the demands of Washington.

Diem was keeping the U.S. proposals secret, saying of the American conditions that they would make him look like a stooge, handing the nationalism issue to the Communists. At the same time the press in Saigon shifted to an anti-American line, protesting U.S. pressure on Diem with headlines such as "Vietnam Not a Guinea Pig for Capitalist Imperialism to Experiment On."

Despite what he said to Taylor and Nolting, President Diem and his family seemed to have the impression that they could do whatever they wished, and that the United States would go along rather than accept the public humiliation of withdrawing. Rusk agreed that there was no turning back now for Kennedy, not after the President had decided to openly violate the Geneva Accords and their limit of 685 U.S. advisers.

"We will honor our commitments," the Secretary of State told NATO foreign ministers in Brussels, briefing them secretly on the situation in Southeast Asia. "We will not be a virgin in the Atlantic and a whore in the Pacific."

But Kennedy would not yet decide. The domestic political consequences of withdrawal were too much to risk, and he knew what would happen if he gave the military a go-ahead on combat troops. "They want a force of American troops," he told Roger Hilsman, the chief of the State Department's intelligence bureau. "They say it's necessary to restore confidence and maintain morale. But it will be just like Berlin. The troops will march in; the bands will play; the crowds will cheer; and in four days everyone will have forgotten. Then we will be told we have to send in more troops. It's like taking a drink. The effect wears off, and you have to take another."

Kennedy knew all that, but he was sipping. Public letters between the presidents were exchanged on December 15. "Vietnam is not a great power," wrote Diem. "We must have further assistance from the United States if we are to win the war now being waged against us." The President answered: "We are prepared to help the Republic of Viet-

Nam to protect its people and independence. We shall promptly increase our assistance to your defense effort."

That week, two U.S. helicopter companies arrived in Vietnam, thirty-three aircraft and four hundred men. The President did not want them used in combat immediately because of ongoing negotiations over Laos. A system was put in place to allow him to make day-to-day decisions on the use of U.S. combatants without leaving a paper trail. It was outlined in a memo from one of his military advisers on December 19: "If there is no reaction from the White House, Saigon will be given an affirmative answer. Mr. Bundy is aware of this procedure which I gather is an agreed approach to avoid pinning down the President."

By the end of December, there were 2,067 American military advisers in Vietnam. On December 20, they were given the first official authorization to use their weapons—in self-defense. On December 22, 1961, Specialist 4th Class James Thomas Davis of Livingston, Tennessee, was killed in the jungle. He was the first.

from The Dark Side of Camelot
by Seymour M. Hersh

Many Kennedy fans hated Seymour M. Hersh's critical biography of JFK, but the book is a serious and even sensitive take on the late president's flaws. This passage draws upon various sources (not all of them named) to draw intriguing connections between Kennedy's difficult childhood and some of his behavior as a grown man.

J ack Kennedy was a dazzling figure as an adult, with stunning good looks, an inquisitive mind, and a biting sense of humor that was often self-mocking. He throve on adoration and surrounded himself with starstruck friends and colleagues. Women swooned. Men stood in awe of his easy success with women, and were grateful for his attentions to them. Today, more than thirty years after his death, Kennedy's close friends remain enraptured. When JFK appeared at a party, Charles Spalding told me, "the temperature went up a hundred and fifty degrees."

His close friends knew that their joyful friend was invariably in acute pain, with chronic back problems. That, too, became a source of admiration. "He never talked about it," Jewel Reed, the former wife of James Reed, who served in the navy with Kennedy during World War II, said in an interview for this book. "He never complained, and that was one of the nice things about Jack."

Kennedy kept his pain to himself all of his life.

• • •

The most important fact of Kennedy's early years was his health. He suffered from a severe case of Addison's disease, an often-fatal disorder of the adrenal glands that eventually leaves the immune system unable to fight off ordinary infection. No successful cortisone treatment for the disease was available until the end of World War II. A gravely ill Kennedy, wracked by Addison's (it was undiagnosed until 1947), often seemed on the edge of death; he was stricken with fevers as high as 106 degrees and was given last rites four times. As a young adult he also suffered from acute back pain, the result of a college football injury that was aggravated by his World War II combat duty aboard *PT-109* in the South Pacific. Unsuccessful back surgery in 1944 and 1954 was complicated by the Addison's, which severely diminished his ability to heal and increased the overall risk of the procedures.

Kennedy and his family covered up the gravity of his illnesses throughout his life—and throughout his political career. Bobby Kennedy, two weeks after his brother's assassination, ordered all White House files dealing with his brother's health "should be regarded as a privileged communication," never to be made public. Over the years, nonetheless, biographies and memoirs have revealed the extent of young Jack Kennedy's suffering. What has been less clear is the extent of the impact his early childhood illnesses had on his character, and how they shaped his attitudes as an adult and as the nation's thirty-fifth president.

Kennedy's fight for life began at birth. He had difficulty feeding as an infant and was often sick. At age two he was hospitalized with scarlet fever and, having survived that, was sent away to recuperate for three months at a sanatorium in Maine. It was there that Jack, torn from his parents and left in the care of strangers, demonstrated the first signs of what would be a lifelong ability to attract attention by charming others. He so captivated his nurse that it was reported that she begged to be allowed to stay with him. Poor health plagued Jack throughout his school years. At age four, he was able to attend nursery school for only ten weeks out of a thirty-week term. At a religious school in Connecticut when he was thirteen, he began losing weight and was diagnosed with appendicitis. The emergency operation—a family surgeon was flown in for the procedure—almost killed him; he never returned to the school. Serious illness continued to afflict Kennedy at prep school at Choate, and local physicians were unable to treat his chronic stomach distress and his "flu-like symptoms." He was diagnosed as suffering from, among other ailments, leukemia and hepatitis—afflictions that would magically clear up just as his doctors, and his family, were despairing. Once again, he made up for his sickness with charm, good humor, and a winning zest for life that kept him beloved by his peers for the rest of his life.

His loyal friend K. LeMoyne Billings, who was a classmate at Choate, waited years before revealing how much Kennedy had suffered. "Jack never wanted us to talk about this," Billings said in an oral history for the John F. Kennedy Library in Boston. "But now that Bobby has gone and Jack has gone, I think it should be told. . . . Jack Kennedy all during his life had very few days when he wasn't in pain or sick in some way." Billings added he seldom heard Kennedy complain. Another old friend, Henry James, who met Jack at Stanford University in 1940, eventually came to understand, he told a biographer, that Kennedy was not merely reluctant to complain about pain and his health but was psychologically unable to do so. "He was heartily ashamed" of his illness, James said. "They were a mark of effeminacy, of weakness, which he wouldn't acknowledge. I think all the macho stuff was compensation—all that chasing after women—compensation for something that he hadn't got." Kennedy was fanatic about maintaining a deep suntan—he would remain heavily tanned all his adult life—and he once explained, James said, "it gives me confidence. . . . It makes me feel strong, healthy, attractive." A deep bronzing of the skin was, in fact, a symptom of Addison's disease.

Kennedy had few options other than being strong and attractive; his father saw to that. Joseph Kennedy viewed his son's illness as a rite of passage. "I see him on TV, in rain and cold, bareheaded," Kennedy told writer William Manchester in 1961, "and I don't worry. I know nothing can happen to him. I tell you, something's watching out for him. I've stood by his deathbed four times. Each time I said good-bye to him, and he always came back. . . . You can't put your finger on it, but there's that difference. When you've been through something like that back, and the Pacific, what can hurt you? Who's going to scare you?"

Jack was always striving to be strong for his father; to finish first, to shape his life in ways that would please Joe. Jack's elder brother, Joseph Jr., always in flourishing health, had been his father's favorite, the son destined for a successful political career in Washington. With Joe Jr.'s death in 1944 as a naval aviator, Jack became the focus of Joe Kennedy's aspirations. In Jack's eyes, his father could do little wrong. Many of Jack's friends thought otherwise, but learned to say nothing. "Jack was sick all the time," Charles Spalding told me in 1997, "and the old man could be an asshole around his kids." During a visit to the Kennedy home in Palm Beach, Florida, in the late 1940s, Spalding said, he and his wife, Betty, were preparing to go to a movie with Jack and his date, Charlotte MacDonald. Spalding went upstairs with Jack and Charlotte to say good night to Joe, who was shaving. The father turned to Charlotte and said scathingly, "Why don't you get a live one?" Spalding was appalled by the gratuitous comment about his best friend's chronic poor health and couldn't resist making a disparaging remark about Joe Kennedy to Jack. The son's defense of his father was instinctive: "Everybody wants to knock his jock off, but he made the whole thing possible."

Charles Bartlett, another old friend, saw both Joe Kennedy's toughness and his importance to his son. Bartlett, who became friends with Jack in Palm Beach after the war, declared that Joe Kennedy "was in it all the way. I don't think there was ever a moment that he didn't spend worrying how to push Jack's cause," especially as his son sought the presidency in 1960.

"He pushed them all," Bartlett, who later became the Washington bureau chief of the *Chattanooga Times,* told me in an interview for this book. "He pushed Bobby into the Justice Department, and he made Jack do things that Jack would probably rather not have done. He was very strong; he'd done things for the kids and wanted them to do some things for him. He didn't bend. Joe was tough." And yet, Bartlett added, "I just found that, in so many things, his judgment down the road was really enormous. You had to admire him."

Jewel Reed vividly recalled her first visit to a family gathering at Hyannis Port, Massachusetts, and the intense energy Joe Kennedy focused on his children. "The table was dynamic, and Mr. Kennedy was checking up on everybody about whether they had come in first or second or third in tennis or yachting or whatever," she said in an interview for this book. "And he wanted them to be number one. That stuck with me a long time. I remembered how intensely he had focused on their winning."

There was a high cost, Reed added. "His values that he imposed upon his children were difficult. His buying things. I hate to use the word bribery, but there was bribery in his agenda often." During Jack Kennedy's first Senate campaign, in 1952, Reed said, when he stunned the experts by defeating Republican Henry Cabot Lodge, Jr., "the billboards in Massachusetts came to about a quarter of a million dollars. That was a long, long time ago, and a quarter of a million was an awful lot of money." Reed also said that Joe Kennedy purchased thousands of copies of *Profiles in Courage,* Jack's Pulitzer Prize-winning bestseller, published in 1956, "to keep it on top of the bestseller list. I don't know what he did with all those books. That was bribery in a way. He was pushing, and if it cost money, he paid it. I'm sure that the children couldn't have felt comfortable about that."

The point, Reed added, was that Joe Kennedy "loved his family. It was very evident, and I remember Teddy [Edward M. Kennedy, Joe's youngest child] paying tribute to his father in saying that he was always there when they needed him. And that's saying a lot."

It was different with Rose Kennedy. As Jack's friends knew, he was full of misgivings about his mother. Kennedy once said to his aide Kenny O'Donnell that he could not recall his mother ever telling him,

"I love you." Charles Spalding got a firsthand glimpse of a rare flash of Jack's hostility toward his mother. "I remember being down in Palm Beach and she [Rose Kennedy] came by in the middle of lunch and said to Jack, 'Oh, baby, I just hate the idea of your having to go back [to Washington].' Jack just blurted out, 'If you hadn't pushed me to be a success, I could stay here.' "

In an interview in 1990 with British biographer Nigel Hamilton, author of *JFK: Reckless Youth*, a definitive account of Kennedy's early years, Spalding speculated that Jack's craving for women and his compulsive need to shower, as often as five times a day, were linked to a lack of mothering. Kennedy, Spalding said, "hated physical touching—people taking physical liberties with him—which I assume must go back to his mother and the fact that she was so cold, so distant from the whole thing. . . . I doubt if she ever rumpled the kid's hair in his whole life. . . . It just didn't exist: the business of letting your son know you're close, that she's there. She wasn't."

"What *is* touch?" Spalding added. "It must come from some deeper maternal security—arms, warmth, kisses, hugs. . . . Maybe sex is the closest prize there is, that holds the whole thing together. I mean if you have sex with anybody you care about at all, you feel you've been touched. . . . "

In an extraordinary series of interviews, one of Jack Kennedy's lovers has candidly described his strengths and weaknesses as she saw them during a bittersweet relationship that spanned four years during which he campaigned for and won the presidency. The woman, who subsequently married and had a successful career, agreed to share her insights only upon a promise of anonymity. She had met Kennedy, then a U.S. senator, at a fund-raising dinner in Boston in the late 1950s; she was nineteen years old, a student at Radcliffe, and he began flirting with her.

"It was glamorous," she recalled. "It was supposed to be terrific. It was supposed to be just what anybody would want, what any woman would want. During that early time there would be looking at me.

There would be nodding at me. There would be leaning across the table to say something just to me. There would be those signs of special attention. Yes, in public. And of course that was very flattering. I thought, 'Oh, gosh. I really must be quite something.' "

The affair deepened. She fell totally in love with the handsome Kennedy and spent hours, after making love with him, at dinner or in long conversations in bed. "I was absolutely thrilled to the gills," she told me. "Here I was, twenty years old, having dinner in the White House, the Abraham Lincoln bedroom. It seemed very amazing. There was a time when he needed to make a statement about a certain thing that happened in the world. And [he] went off and came back half an hour later and was really thrilled with the fact that he had come up with six declarative sentences that just laid it out." Their relationship, the woman said, "was supposed to be secret, and so I just went along and didn't talk about it." As for Kennedy's seemingly ideal marriage to Jackie, she said, "I did not have the foggiest idea of any consciousness of solidarity with other women. It just did not flicker. I cannot tell you how unevolved as a woman I was, and how it was assumed that women compete with each other for the best men. I just went right along with that. Somehow it didn't register with me at any deep level that what I was doing was absolutely immoral, absolutely atrocious behavior."

Kennedy, while attentive and engaging, rarely talked about his childhood in their time together, the woman told me. But she now understands that his ability to compartmentalize his life, to take the enormous risk—while seeking and occupying the presidency—of being so publicly married and so privately a womanizer, stemmed from his experiences as a child. He was "a boy who was sick frequently, who was frail, in a family where there was a tremendous premium on aggressive, competitive, succeeding, energizing activity. In the class that John Kennedy came from, there's a tremendous emphasis on appearance and how does it look? Well, it's not supposed to look like it's painful. It's not supposed to look like you feel like you don't know something or that you don't understand what's going on in your family or in the world. There's a tremendous premium on being smooth and in charge and in control—you aren't sweaty and nervous. You just sail effortlessly through the trials and tribulations that bring down other people, but not you."

The inevitable result, she explained, was that there were many times when Jack felt the pain of being excluded. "If you are a sickly child who spends a good deal of time in your bed at a young age in a house full of a lot of children, all of whom are in school or playing games or doing whatever they're doing, you could feel left out. It didn't sound like everybody then [in his family] took turns to come and sit with him and chat with him and draw pictures with him." Kennedy could have responded to the experience, the woman told me, by learning to "identify with others in the same situation. Or you can say 'I'm never going to have that feeling again.' " Kennedy chose to shut out the pain. "It was something he did not reflect [on] and didn't want to think about much and hoped it would never happen and went out of his way to make sure it"—talking about his childhood emotions—"didn't happen."

Kennedy spoke to the woman only once, she recalled, about being a trustworthy parent. If his daughter, Caroline, got into any trouble, "He hoped that she would come to him and not feel that she had to hide it from him. His father had always wanted him to have that feeling with him, and that was a really important thing." The woman came to understand that Kennedy's relationship with his father was "the most vibrant relationship he'd ever had—love, fear, palpitations, trying to please him." Asked whether Kennedy felt he could turn to his mother for help, she answered, "I do not know. I never heard him speak about his mother. Never."

Jack Kennedy's delight in his children, and in all children, was profound, and recognized as such by staff aides who knew nothing of his early life. Marcus Raskin, who worked on nuclear disarmament issues for the National Security Council, recalled in an interview for this book that he and his colleagues would ask, in moments of international crisis, "Where are the children?" If Caroline and her younger brother, John, "were in Washington, then there wouldn't be a war. If the children were away, then you weren't sure." The question was not facetious, Raskin insisted. Jerome B. Wiesner, the president's science adviser, told McGeorge Bundy's national security staff, Raskin said, "to watch where the kids are. If they're here [in Washington], then there's going to be no war this week. If the kids aren't here, then we've got to be careful." Wiesner's remark was obviously tongue-in-cheek, Raskin said, but "many things are said ha-ha that have a grain of truth to them." He and his colleagues, Raskin said, looked in moments of crisis "for some sort of human affect to understand the momentous questions that they were dealing with."

If the president's national security advisers understood his love for children, so did the Secret Service. Larry Newman was one of the White House agents assigned to Kennedy on the evening in August 1963 when the president made a visit to his youngest child, Patrick, born prematurely and hospitalized with a lung ailment, who was fighting for his life in Children's Hospital in Boston. Newman, who was in the elevator with the president and Patrick's doctor, listened as Kennedy was told that his newborn son was unlikely to survive. The elevator stopped at the fifth floor, where the pediatric intensive care unit was. The floor had been cleared of all visitors for the presidential visit. The hallway was dark; the patient rooms were illuminated by night-lights. Newman recalled in an interview for this book that while walking with the president to intensive care, "we passed a room where there were two delightful-looking little girls who were sitting up in bed. They were probably about three or four years old, and they were talking and laughing together. The only problem—one girl was bandaged up to her chin. She had severe burns. And the other had burns down her arms and huge pods [of bandages] on the end of her hands. President Kennedy stopped and just looked at these two little girls. He asked the doctor, 'What's wrong with them?' And the doctor explained that one girl may lose the use of her hands. The president stood there. His son was down at the end of the hall in grave to critical condition. We just stood there with him; it was just a small party in the dark. He started feeling in his pockets—it was always a sign he wanted a pen. Someone gave him a pen. He said, 'I'd like to write a note to the children'. And nobody had any paper for the thirty-fifth president of the United States to write a note on. So the nurse scurries to the station and gets the name of the children and their family and Kennedy writes a note to each child. There was no fanfare, no photo-op. There was nothing. The nurse took the notes and said she would see that the family got it. And then we proceeded down the hall to see his son, who of course died the next day. It was something he didn't need to do, but he always seemed to come out of his reserved and Bostonish [ways] with children.

"Nothing was ever said about it. There was no press release or anything. He just went on to do what he had to do—to see his son. This was part of the dichotomy of the man—the rough-cut diamond. You could see so many qualities he had that just glowed; you couldn't see why he wanted to follow other roads that were so destructive. It was truly painful."

The Exner File

by Michael O'Brien

Judith Campbell Exner is famous for claiming that she slept with JFK and (much more outrageously) that she served as his go-between in shady dealings with the Mafia. Historian and JFK biographer Michael O'Brien in 1999 (shortly after Exner's death) offered this lucid summary of her various claims and their reliability.

The death of Judith Campbell Exner on Sept. 24, 1999, reminds us of the enormous impact she had on the reputation of President John Kennedy and on media coverage of the private lives of public figures. Exner had a two-year affair with Kennedy, and because of her gangland connections and Kennedy's CIA connection, their relationship became a public scandal when it was revealed in 1975.

Of all the Kennedy sex scandals, the Exner story may be the one that troubles his admirers most. It is also a tale that remains clouded with uncertainty. Exner changed it several times, amplifying her original confession of an affair into bizarre claims about her role in a conspiracy involving Kennedy and the Mafia. The first accusations were bad enough; the later ones would seriously injure Kennedy's reputation as president, if true. For that reason, it's important to be clear about which of Exner's claims we should believe, and which appear to be fantasy.

The name Judith Campbell Exner burst into the national headlines on December 17, 1975. A month earlier the Senate Select Committee to Study Governmental Operations with Respect to Intelligence Activities (the Church Committee), in its report on CIA assassination attempts, had discreetly stated that a "close friend" of President Kennedy had also been a close friend of mobsters John Roselli and Sam Giancana. After her identity had been leaked to *The Washington Post*, Exner, then 41, called a press conference. Sitting next to her second husband Dan Exner, a golf pro, and hiding behind large sunglasses, she denied any knowledge of underworld activities. Two years later, in her autobiography, *My Story*, Exner recounted her sexual tryst with JFK and her simultaneous relationship with Giancana, plus her friendship with Roselli. That the president would share the sexual favors of a Mafia don's girlfriend was shocking and frightening.

A short, dour, homely Sicilian, Sam Giancana held court at the Armory Lounge in Forest Park, Illinois, ordering murders and managing his crime empire. An extraordinary criminal, Giancana had allegedly been responsible for more than two hundred murders up to 1960. A leading member of the La Cosa Nostra, the national crime syndicate, Giancana was Chicago's Mafia boss, the successor to Al Capone. His crime network ranged from protection rackets to numbers games, loan sharks to bookmakers. He had served time in prison and been arrested more than 70 times, including three times for murder. Giancana's friend and associate, John Roselli, represented the Chicago mob on the West Coast.

Born Judith Immoor, Exner grew up in Pacific Palisades, California, where her father worked as an architect. The family was well off, but when Judith was 14, her mother nearly died in an auto accident. Traumatized, Judith withdrew from high school and was privately tutored. At 18, she married the alcoholic actor William Campbell, but after an unhappy marriage they divorced in 1958. Stunningly beautiful, she resembled actress Elizabeth Taylor and became a regular at Hollywood parties. One evening in 1959 she met singer Frank Sinatra, and they engaged in a brief affair.

Then on the evening of February 7, 1960, Campbell met then-Senator John Kennedy and his entourage at Sinatra's table at the Sands lounge in Las Vegas. After perfunctory introductions, Kennedy conversed with all the women at the table, but focused on Campbell. When he listened to her, she recalled in her autobiography, "it was as if every nerve and muscle in his whole body was poised at attention. As I was to learn, Jack Kennedy was the world's greatest listener." The next day Kennedy invited her for lunch on the patio of Sinatra's suite. Again he seemed to have "an almost insatiable interest in what and who I was." They talked for three hours.

After their Las Vegas encounter, Kennedy phoned her constantly, telling her how much he missed her and wondering when they could meet again. "He called almost every day," said Campbell, "no matter where he was, or how tired." They finally rendezvoused on March 7, 1960, at the New York Plaza Hotel, where they had their first sexual encounter. In Florida in late March, Sinatra introduced Campbell to a man named "Sam Flood". It took a while for Campbell to learn that this new friend was actually Sam Giancana. Was it just a coincidence, critics wondered, that within a two month period Sinatra's introductions had sparked Exner's romances with a future president and a notorious criminal? Was Giancana using Exner because she was Kennedy's girlfriend? In her autobiography Exner dampened such speculation. It "never occurred to me that Sam's interest in me was simply because of my association with Jack Kennedy." She added, "Sam never asked me for anything."

On April 6, 1960, Kennedy invited her for dinner at his Georgetown home while Jackie was away. Exner recalled the visit:

"We wandered through various rooms until we came to the master bedroom, which was upstairs at the front of the house. There were twin beds with pale green spreads, very filmy and delicate. He put his arms around me and we sat on one of the beds. We kissed and he was almost immediately amorous. I went to the bathroom to undress, and when I came back into the room, the lights were very low and Jack was already in bed.

'I've missed you so much,' I said, as I went into his arms. We kissed passionately, and he said, with his lips still on mine, 'Do you think you could love me?'

'I'm afraid I could,' I whispered, and it was so true."

On the evening of Monday, July 11, 1960, the opening day of the Democratic National Convention in Los Angeles, she met him in his hotel suite. Kennedy brought a second woman along and proposed to Exner that they engage in a menage a trois. Exner was furious and refused.

Nonetheless, throughout the fall of 1961 and the winter and spring of 1962, she continued seeing Kennedy in the White House. Their routine seldom varied. The president's secretary, Evelyn Lincoln, made reservations for her at the Mayflower Hotel. In the evening the White House car drove her to the East Gate, the one tourists used in the daytime. "Either Jack would meet me in the entrance hall near the door or an aide would escort me to the little elevator and Jack would be waiting in the family quarters." After her arrival about 7:30 p.m., she and the president usually had frozen daiquiris and then dinner.

By late spring 1962, their romance had cooled off. He phoned her infrequently, and she returned his calls less often. "It happened so gradually that I wasn't really aware that it was over until long after it had ended," she said.

Was it true? By the time Exner wrote her autobiography in 1977, Kennedy, Giancana, and Roselli were all dead. Was she simply telling her story or had she concocted all or most of it in order to sell a book?

Kennedy's advisors Ken O'Donnell and Dave Powers both denied even knowing Exner, then known as Judith Campbell. "The only Campbell I know," Powers told the press in late 1975, "is chunky vegetable soup." But both of them were lying. So was Evelyn Lincoln, who claimed Campbell was merely a campaign volunteer. The dates in the gate logs of Campbell's White House visitations generally coincided with her own recollections. And O'Donnell and Evelyn Lincoln personally authorized some of Exner's visits. During Kennedy's presidency, telephone logs show Exner called Lincoln more than eighty times and there were also calls from Lincoln to Exner. Exner's autobiography convincingly listed fifteen telephone numbers where she had reached both Lincoln and Kennedy from 1960-1962. The evidence she offered— addresses, telephone numbers, descriptions of White House decor— "makes the defensive protestations of the keepers of the Kennedy flame somewhat dubious," said a review in *The New York Times*.

In addition, her claims were limited to the affair. Exner had told the Church Committee that her relationship with Kennedy was only personal and that she had no knowledge of any relationship between Giancana and Kennedy. She made the same denials in her December 1975 press conference and in her autobiography. At her press conference she accused the media of "wild-eyed speculation" for suggesting that she was an intermediary between JFK and Giancana.

But 11 years after her book was published, Exner began telling another, very different story. In 1988 *People* magazine published an article by Kitty Kelley based on the author's interviews with Exner. "I lied when I said I was not a conduit between President Kennedy and the Mafia," Exner told Kelley. "I lied when I said that President Kennedy was unaware of my friendships with mobsters. He knew everything about my dealings with Sam Giancana and Johnny Roselli because I was seeing them for him. I wouldn't have been seeing them otherwise."

Why had she lied before the Church Committee, during her 1975 press conference, and in *My Story*? She needed to protect herself, she said. "If I'd told the truth, I'd have been killed. I kept my secret out of fear." Exner's fear seemed well-founded. Senate investigators were about to call Giancana to testify before the Church Committee when, on the night of June 19, 1975, he was shot seven times in the head in the kitchen of his Oak Park, Illinois residence. The killer was never found, but it was a mafia-style murder. Days later Roselli testified before the Senate committee about the CIA's attempts to kill Castro, including Giancana's role. A year later, Roselli's dead body was found in a 55-gallon oil drum weighted with heavy chains floating in Dumfoundling Bay, near Miami.

Exner claimed that her first assignment as courier was suggested by JFK at the dinner in his Georgetown townhouse on April 6,1960. That evening had not just focused on dinner and lovemaking, as she had stated in her autobiography. A third person, a lobbyist named Bill, was at the table, and he and Kennedy had spent the entire evening discussing strategy for the upcoming West Virginia primary on May 11.

During the conversation Jack turned to her and said, "Could you quietly arrange a meeting with Sam [Giancana] for me?" Pleased to be of help, Exner called her new friend Giancana the next morning and arranged a rendezvous. "I arrived at 8:30 a.m. on April 8th and talked to Sam at a Chicago club," said Exner. "I told Sam that Jack wanted to meet with him because he needed his help in the campaign." Giancana agreed, and the meeting was set four days later at the Fontainebleau Hotel in Miami Beach. "I called Jack to tell him, then I flew to Miami because Kennedy wanted me to be there."

On April 12 Kennedy met with Giancana at the Fontainebleau. "I was not present," Exner said, "but Jack came to my suite afterward, and I asked him how the meeting had gone. He seemed very happy about it and thanked me for making the arrangements." Apparently in gratitude, Kennedy gave her $2,000 in cash. Kitty Kelley speculated that the April 12 meeting concerned the West Virginia primary.

Even after becoming president, Exner contended, JFK continued to use her as a courier. A few days after the bungled Bay of Pigs invasion in April 1961, Kennedy called her in California and asked her to fly to Las Vegas, pick up an envelope from Roselli and deliver it to Giancana in Chicago. Then she was to arrange a meeting between the President and the Mafia boss, one that took place in her suite at the Ambassador East on April 28, 1961.

"It was a short meeting early in the evening," Exner said. "Sam arrived first and then Jack, who put his arms around me and said, 'I'm sorry I can't stay and see you for the evening.'" (He was in town to address a Democratic party dinner.) After the President and Giancana shook hands, JFK asked Exner to stay in the suite while he and Giancana talked.

On April 29, Exner flew to Florida at Kennedy's request, where she met with Giancana and Roselli, picked up another envelope and returned to Washington on May 4th. "We were scheduled to have lunch at the White House on Saturday, May 6," she said, "but [Kennedy] said the envelope couldn't wait, so I took it to him late Friday afternoon." The following day, May 6, she lunched at the White House where Kennedy gave her another envelope for Giancana.

Meanwhile the FBI was hounding Exner and Giancana; she was terrified, but when she told Kennedy, he seemed unconcerned. "Don't worry," he told her. 'They won't do anything to you. And don't worry about Sam. You know he works for us." According to Exner "He told me that over and over. 'Don't worry. Sam works for us'."

For 18 months in 1960 and 1961, Exner claimed she served as the president's link with the Mob. She crisscrossed the nation carrying envelopes between the president and Giancana, and arranged about 10 meetings between the two, one of which, she thought, took place inside the White House. "They were sealed but not taped," Exner said of the plain 9" by 12" manila envelopes. "They weighed about as much as a weekly magazine and felt as if they contained papers, but I don't know for sure because I never looked inside. It never occurred to me to do something like that. I didn't know what they contained."

In 1997, 20 years after the publication of *My Story*, Exner significantly changed her account again. In separate interviews with journalists Liz Smith (for her article in *Vanity Fair*) and with Seymour Hersh (for his book, *The Dark Side of Camelot*) Exner unveiled new sensational allegations.

On April 6, 1960, at the dinner and lovemaking session at JFK's Georgetown home, JFK not only asked her to deliver an envelope to Giancana, he revealed to her the contents of the envelope. "I want you to know what's in it," Kennedy told her. He opened it and showed her the money, perhaps as much as $250,000 in hundred-dollar bills. To buttress his story that Exner delivered money to Giancana in Chicago, Hersh produced a witness: Martin Underwood, a former political operative for Mayor Richard Daley, and a Kennedy campaign worker in 1960. According to Hersh, in April 1960 Kenny O'Donnell asked Underwood to take the overnight train from Washington to Chicago and keep an eye on Exner. Underwood claimed he watched her on the train and saw her deliver the envelope to the waiting Sam Giancana.

JFK also revealed to Exner the contents of envelopes she subsequently delivered to Giancana and Roselli. "I knew what [the documents] dealt with. I knew they dealt with the 'elimination' of Castro and that Sam and Johnny had been hired by the CIA. That's what Jack explained to me in the very beginning."

For the first time Exner implicated Robert Kennedy in the CIA-Mafia-Castro story. "I used to be at the White House having lunch or dinner with Jack, and Bobby [Kennedy] would often come by," she told Liz Smith. "He'd squeeze my shoulder solicitously and ask, 'Judy, are you O.K. carrying these messages for us to Chicago? Do you still feel comfortable doing it?' "

Exner also told Hersh that she was a conduit for payoffs to Kennedy from a group of California businessmen desperate for defense contracts. Her close friend Richard Ellwood, a neighbor and vice president of a small electronics company in Culver City, California, introduced her to "two senior Pentagon procurement officials." She began socializing with all of them during her frequent trips to Washington. Eventually, Exner told Hersh, "I took payoffs" from the California businessmen to Kennedy in the White House. "I didn't want to go to Jack" with the payoff money, she said. But "I asked Jack about it and he thought it was a good idea." She recalled three separate contract proposals for which she brought payoffs into the White House.

"What I want to tell you is my very last secret, an extremely personal one," Exner dramatically told Liz Smith in 1997. The secret was the abortion she had as a result of her last sexual encounter with the President. She was "too ashamed" to tell it earlier. "But now, before I die, I think the Camelot myth should also be demystified, and the Kennedy legend examined for its reality. I don't have a single, solitary thing to hide."

Kennedy, she said, had begged her to come back and talk, to try again. She went to see him one last time in late December 1962. "I said I wouldn't see him anymore; it was too painful. But we were intimate that one last time, in the White House." Shortly afterward she realized she was pregnant. "I hadn't been with anyone but Jack—not ever during the whole time." By her calculations she was "almost two months" pregnant. Because abortion was then illegal, the President said, "Do you think Sam would help us? Would you ask Sam? Would you mind asking?" Giancana agreed to assist her.

The same evening she told Giancana she needed an abortion she was sexually intimate with him. "It was the one time with Sam and it was an emotional response to his loving-kindness and caring for what I was going through. But I would hardly say that that was having a simultaneous affair with two men." Exner claims she had her abortion at Chicago's Grant Hospital, and left the hospital on January 28, 1963.

Exner's autobiography had been convincing because her key contentions could be documented with FBI reports, Secret Service logs, White House telephone records, witnesses, and evidence in her own possession. The same is not true for her later revelations. Her supporters, mainly Liz Smith and Seymour Hersh, have tried to bolster her recollections but their evidence is not compelling. The sensational charges—that money and documents were directly exchanged between JFK and Giancana; that Robert Kennedy also colluded with Giancana; that the President welcomed payoffs from California defense contractors; and, finally, that Exner aborted a child conceived by JFK—all rely primarily on Exner's testimony.

Exner's post-1977 observations defy logic. Why would JFK select Exner as his courier to the Mafia? She thought she was the perfect choice because Kennedy didn't trust the CIA. She was the "one person around him who didn't need anything from him or want anything. He trusted me." But John Kennedy had plenty of aides—and Joe Kennedy plenty of retainers—who could have performed the role of courier far more safely and capably. When Kennedy supposedly selected Exner to be his courier to Giancana, he had known her for only two months, and she had been introduced to "Sam Flood" less than two weeks earlier.

Secret Service agents who candidly testified about the President's womanizing do not confirm any of Exner's contentions about JFK's relations with Giancana. Moreover, Hersh's account of the train ride Campbell took on Kennedy's behalf in April 1960 to deliver money to Giancana has unraveled, because the key witness recanted his original story. Martin Underwood denied that he followed Judith Campbell on the train, and claims he had no knowledge about her alleged role as a courier.

If the FBI "hounded" Exner and Giancana, wouldn't the G-men have trailed or wire-tapped Giancana when he supposedly had all these meetings with Kennedy in Chicago, Florida, and the White House? Finally, why did Exner wait until 1997 to reveal that she had met Robert Kennedy and that he colluded with the President and Giancana? She would not have risked her life by mentioning that fact a decade earlier.

Those who have examined the record carefully claim that Exner's post-1977 stories are impossible to believe. As the historian Garry Wills notes, "Ms. Exner has, like all of us, read about the CIA's attempt to use Giancana to assassinate Castro, so—sure enough—Kennedy relied on her to send messages and documents to Giancana dealing with this explosive matter. What documents? Hersh might have asked himself at this moment."

Evan Thomas, for many years *Newsweek*'s Washington bureau chief and author of a forthcoming book on Robert Kennedy, asked why JFK would have used a "none-too-bright girlfriend to handle something so incredibly sensitive as passing bribes to the Mafia? Surely Father Joe taught his sons a few tricks about keeping secrets. Using emotionally fragile lovers as bagmen could not have been one of them. . . . It also stretches credulity to suggest that Giancana, the all-powerful don, would have been waiting around on a station platform in Chicago to meet the train."

Even conservative critics, who might have been expected to treat Exner's later revelations more favorably, were unimpressed. After reading Exner's 1977 autobiography, columnist William Safire severely criticized Kennedy. But her subsequent assertions left him cold. "She's changed her story too often over the decades," Safire concluded.

So why did Exner concoct her story? First, she had a long history of instability, making her an exceptionally unreliable witness. She admitted to lying repeatedly and changed her story several times. She had been addicted to alcohol and amphetamines, suffered from depression and paranoia, seriously contemplated suicide, endured two divorces (one from an alcoholic). She was hounded and harassed by the FBI, feared death at the hands of the Mafia, and was told her cancer was terminal. Her background and problems do not inspire confidence in her veracity.

Moreover, Exner deeply resented critics of *My Story* who portrayed her as a vapid party girl, the mistress of the President and a Mafia don. She referred to it as her "stupid" book. She wasn't a "tramp, a slut," she said. "I was never anybody's kept woman." Probably to counter her image as simply a scarlet woman who sexually serviced two celebrities, she invented a role, concocted fanciful tales, trying to recreate her image into a serious, sympathetic and important person.

She reveled in the drama and intrigue of her post-1977 stories. She was dying of cancer, she dramatically told Kelley, Smith and Hersh. "For that reason, I must now tell the truth." As if she had just tumbled out of a spy novel, she breathlessly explained her techniques for arranging contacts between Kennedy and Giancana. "As a rule I would just call Sam," she said. "I learned to almost speak in a kind of code. I would usually say, 'Have him call the girl from the West! And if something was happening in Florida, it was, 'Can you meet him in the South?' Sam always knew that 'him' was Jack. I really became very adept. I think that I was having a little bit of fun with this also." The $50,000 *People* magazine paid Exner in 1988 for telling her amplified story to Kitty Kelley may also have stimulated her imagination.

Historians may never prove or disprove Exner's assertions. Scholarship on the Mafia and on the Presidents' private lives, observes historian Michael Beschloss, "is not subject to the same precision as the study of diplomatic history, for which there are official documents drafted and preserved according to professional standards in public archives." Perhaps evidence will emerge in the future to bolster Exner's recent contentions. Until then, we should assume that the first story regarding the affair was true, because it was supported by White House logs and other evidence; but that her later claims about her role in an alleged Giancana-Roselli-Kennedy triangle, because they are not supported by other sources, are fantasy.

The Conspiracy Theories

by Pamela Colloff and Michael Hall

Who killed JFK? The assassination of the 35th President spawned dozens of conspiracy theories, some ridiculous and some with disturbingly convincing elements. Most people who write on the subject have axes to grind, but this 1998 Texas Monthly *article by Pamela Colloff and Michael Hall offers objective reviews of the most popular theories, with discussions of each theory's strongest and weakest links.*

There is never an ordinary day at Dallas' Dealey Plaza, where personal revelations and quiet mourning are as familiar as the downtown rush-hour traffic. But this August afternoon is stranger than usual: A dark blue 1961 Lincoln Continental convertible limousine is sitting in the center lane of Elm Street, which has been blocked off. Stills of the Zapruder film line the sidewalk, serving as the storyboard for the day's activities: a restaging of the century's most famous murder, the assassination of John F. Kennedy, for a television documentary that will try to determine, with the help of lasers, where the shots came from. Three men in white shirts are huddled around the convertible, bending and shifting the limbs of its foam rubber passengers. A gray dummy sits in the back seat, just as Kennedy did, while another—in John Connally's place—rests on the jump seat in front of him. "His arm has got to come over more," insists one man, pulling the president's left arm farther across his spongy torso. A film crew circles the scene, while tourists, ballistics experts, conspiracy buffs, and reporters watch the goings-on. "But shouldn't his other hand be over the chrome line?" asks one observer. The men in the white shirts mull this over, glancing first at the film stills and then at the mannequins, before resuming their work. The heat is oppressive, but the comparing and tweaking continues late into the day.

Of course, they will never get it right: the precise slant of a wave, the tilt of a head, the trajectory of a bullet. Elm Street has been closed several times for such reenactments, but there is still no consensus on exactly what happened. There are too many shifting perspectives, inexplicable details, and active imaginations, all aching to make sense of a senseless act. Over the past 35 years, countless theories have evolved, but they discount the overwhelming proof, both physical and circumstantial, that Lee Harvey Oswald was the man who shot Kennedy. "I have sent men to the electric chair with less evidence," said Henry Wade, Dallas County's district attorney in 1963.

In 1964 the Warren Commission concluded that Oswald was Kennedy's assassin, and that he had acted alone. But the official story had troubling inconsistencies: Conflicting eyewitness accounts, discrepancies in the autopsy reports, and the unlikely paths and precision of Oswald's shots all suggested more than one gunman had been at Dealey Plaza. The first cries of foul play came from across the Atlantic, most notably from English writer Bertrand Russell, but it wasn't until 1966, with the publication of Mark Lane's *Rush to Judgment* and Edward Jay Epstein's *Inquest*, that the Warren Commission's findings were challenged at home. *Life* magazine, which had purchased the Zapruder film soon after the assassination, launched a new investigation of the case. The magazine's consultant, former Navy lieutenant Josiah Thompson, argued the following year in *Six Seconds in Dallas* that a close examination of the film showed the president being shot from several directions, hence a conspiracy.

New Orleans district attorney Jim Garrison stepped into the fray in 1967, using the loose ends of Oswald's life—he had defected to the Soviet Union and sought asylum in Cuba and had tenuous connections to anti-Castro militants—to speculate that the CIA had somehow been involved. For the most part, the public ignored such cynical talk, but as first Vietnam and then Watergate wore on, its distrust grew. Interest in a more thorough investigation of the Kennedy assassination reached critical mass in 1975, when the Zapruder film was first shown on TV and Senate hearings revealed that the CIA had conspired with the Mafia to kill Fidel Castro in the early sixties. The following year, the House Select Committee on Assassinations (HSCA) was formed, and in 1979 it concluded that while Oswald was indeed the gunman, he had had an accomplice, who shot, and missed, from the grassy knoll. The existence of a conspiracy was confirmed—by the federal government, no less. The HSCA also hinted at involvement by Cuban exiles or members of the mob, a theory that remained in vogue throughout the eighties. Since 1991, when Oliver Stone's controversial movie *JFK* used Garrison as its hero and pointed fingers at the CIA, the FBI, Cuban exiles, military intelligence, and munitions profiteers, the specifics of the various theories have been lost, replaced by a sense of overall complicity: Everyone was in on it.

What follows is an overview of the conspiracy oeuvre, though it is hardly exhaustive. We haven't included some of the shadowy figures— Umbrella Man, the Babushka Lady, Badge Man—that populate the fringes of conspiracy-think. Nor do we examine the more far-out theories: that Joe DiMaggio, angered at Kennedy's treatment of his ex-wife, Marilyn Monroe, got his Italian friends to knock him off; or that the president, who was already suffering from Addison's disease, staged his own death, ensuring a glorified place in history; or that Frank Sinatra's drummer, Franklin Folley, was somehow involved. Instead, we present the ones that have endured over the years. They are as intriguing as they are implausible, and they raise as many questions as the Warren Commission failed to answer. Underlying all of them are uncanny coincidences, convergences of terrible knowledge, and most important, a desire to believe that there was a grand design—some kind of meaning and purpose—behind Kennedy's murder. Thirty-five years later, these narratives have become more appealing than the banal alternative: a lone nut, a good shot, an utterly vain death.

• • •

The CIA Theory

When Kennedy assumed the presidency in January 1961, he inherited a federal agency that had spun out of control. The CIA had pursued its own objectives during the Eisenhower administration—instigating coups, inciting rebellions, trying to assassinate foreign leaders—generally without White House supervision. When the 1961 Bay of Pigs invasion (which the CIA had orchestrated) proved to be a disaster as well as an enormous political liability for Kennedy, he fired the director and his deputies, threatening to "smash the CIA into a thousand pieces and scatter it to the winds." Rogue agents, fearful he would do just that, struck first, either by placing CIA sharpshooters at Dealey Plaza or by enlisting former Marine and spy wannabe Lee Harvey Oswald to do the job.

Believers

Authors Mark Lane (*Plausible Denial*), John Newman (*Oswald and the CIA*), and Anthony Summers (*Conspiracy*).

Strange Details

CIA director Allen Dulles, whom Kennedy had fired in 1961, later served on the Warren Commission. CIA deputy director Charles Cabell, whom Kennedy had also fired, was the brother of Earle Cabell, Dallas' mayor in 1963. One of Kennedy's alleged mistresses, Mary Pinchot Meyer, was married to a CIA official and was murdered in 1964. Richard Nixon—who oversaw the CIA's original plan to take back Cuba from Castro when he was Eisenhower's vice president—was in Dallas on the day of the assassination.

Reasons to Believe

If anybody could have planned and concealed a plot as intricate as the Kennedy assassination, power-hungry CIA agents could; they had already helped oust heads of state in Guatemala and Iran. The agency had little congressional oversight in 1963 and was full of furtive cells, subgroups, and enthusiastic spooks who acted with impunity and whose modus operandi was "plausible deniability." Indeed, as Kennedy's motorcade was making its way through Dallas, a CIA operative in Paris was—unbeknownst to most of his higher-ups—giving a poison fountain pen to Cuban turncoat Rolando Cubela, who had volunteered to hand it to Fidel Castro. While in the Marines in 1957 and 1958, Oswald was stationed at Atsugi Air Base in Japan, the home of the largest CIA station in the Pacific.

During the Warren Commission's investigation, the CIA withheld untold amounts of information, notably that the agency and the mob had jointly tried to kill Castro.

Reasons Not to Believe
There is no evidence that Oswald was ever a CIA operative; at Atsugi he was a low-level officer who was court-martialed twice and displayed erratic behavior, once shooting himself in the arm. Just because the CIA would lie, cheat, steal, overthrow governments, and try to assassinate other countries' leaders does not mean that it would kill its own.

Recent Developments
Speculation about the CIA's involvement has always centered on one of the most intriguing assassination riddles: the identity of the three tramps, a trio of men arrested in the rail yard behind Dealey Plaza immediately after the assassination. Photos showed them being led through the downtown streets by Dallas police officers, yet there was no record of their arrest. Conspiracy theorists have long believed that they looked suspiciously like CIA bogeymen E. Howard Hunt and Frank Sturgis (as well as Charles Harrelson, the assassin of federal judge John Wood and the father of actor Woody Harrelson). According to the three tramps theory, these CIA operatives killed Kennedy; after they were arrested, they were whisked away by unidentified federal agents who destroyed all records of the incident. But in 1992 Dallas researcher Mary La Fontaine searched through Dallas Police Department files and found overlooked arrest records from November 22,

1963. The three tramps were, in fact, three tramps: Harold Doyle, Gus Abrams, and John Forrester Gedney.

The Mafia Theory

The mob felt betrayed in 1963. Chicago godfather Sam Giancana had helped Kennedy win the 1960 election through skullduggery, and Miami mobster Santos Trafficante had aided the CIA in its assassination attempts on Castro. But rather than pledging their loyalty, the Kennedys launched an all-out campaign against organized crime. Attorney General Robert Kennedy first went after Teamster boss Jimmy Hoffa and then deported New Orleans syndicate boss Carlos Marcello to Guatemala. Pushed around long enough, and angry at the president for going soft on Castro—who had shut down its lucrative Cuban casinos—the mob made someone an offer he couldn't refuse. Oswald was either its hit man or its patsy. Upon his arrest, the mob dispatched Jack Ruby to silence him.

Believers

Authors John H. Davis (*The Kennedy Contract*) and David Scheim (*Contract on America*) and veteran journalist Jack Anderson.

Strange Details

In 1975 and 1976, during the course of congressional investigations of the mob and the CIA, Sam Giancana was gunned down in his kitchen, Jimmy Hoffa "disappeared," and Las Vegas mobster Johnny Roselli—who had told Jack Anderson that Ruby was ordered to silence Oswald—was dismembered, stuffed into an oil drum, and tossed off the coast of Florida. Kennedy and Judith Exner, one of Giancana's molls, were introduced in 1960 by Frank Sinatra and carried on an affair for more than two years; Exner says she often carried envelopes from the president to the mobster.

Reasons to Believe

In 1979 the HSCA concluded that Hoffa, Marcello, and Trafficante all had the "motive, means, and opportunity" to assassinate Kennedy. Hoffa had told a federal informant that he would like to kill RFK but that his brother was the more desirable victim because "when you cut down the tree, the branches fall with it."

Marcello—according to Las Vegas promoter Edward Becker—once coolly explained why it was better to target JFK than RFK: "If you cut off a dog's tail, the dog will only keep biting. But if you cut off its head, the dog will die." An FBI informant testified before the HSCA that Trafficante told him in 1962 that the president "was going to be hit." In 1992 Frank Ragano, a longtime lawyer for Hoffa and Trafficante, told the *New York Post* that the two mobsters and Marcello had agreed to kill the president. Ragano claimed that Trafficante said on his deathbed: "Carlos f-ed up. We shouldn't have gotten rid of Giovanni [John]. We should have killed Bobby." Oswald's uncle and surrogate father, Dutz Murret, was a bookie in the Marcello organization, and his mother, Marguerite, dated members of Marcello's gang. When Ruby was a teenager in Chicago, he ran errands for Al Capone. As an adult, he had ties to members of the Giancana, Hoffa, Marcello, and Trafficante families. In 1959 he visited Trafficante in his Cuban jail cell, where Castro had thrown the mobster after the revolution. Two days before the assassination, a prostitute and heroin addict named Rose Cheramie told a Louisiana state policeman that she had been en route to Dallas with two men "who were Italians or resembled Italians" and were planning to kill Kennedy. After the assassination, she told Dr. Victor Weiss at East Louisiana State Hospital that "the word in the underworld" had been that Kennedy was going to take a mob bullet. She also said that Oswald and Ruby "had been shacking up for years . . . They were bedmates."

Reasons Not to Believe
The HSCA was ultimately "unable to establish any direct evidence" of mob complicity. Chicago FBI agent William Roemer, who spent hours listening to wiretaps of mobsters after the assassination, said they were "gleeful" but did not talk of a conspiracy. There is no proof that Ruby

was anything more than a small-timer on the periphery of the Dallas underworld. Hoffa, Trafficante, and Marcello were cautious men, yet killing JFK was a rash solution—one that would only have brought on more heat from RFK. And why would a bunch of seasoned killers rely on a loser like Oswald? Cheramie—who had spent time in mental hospitals and who had a history of providing the FBI with false leads—was in the throes of heroin withdrawal when she told her story. After the assassination, she said that she had once worked as a dancer for Ruby, whom she knew as Pinky, but there is no evidence that she did. Nor is there reliable evidence that Oswald and Ruby ever knew each other.

Recent Developments
In 1993 Illinois cop killer James Files confessed to Kennedy's murder. Claiming to have been an Army paratrooper in Laos, a trainer of Cuban exiles for the Bay of Pigs invasion, and the personal driver for Chicago mobster Charles Nicoletti, Files said that he fired from the grassy knoll while Nicoletti shot from the Dal-Tex Building. In 1994 the *New York Post* ran a story on Files titled "Call This JFK Tale Knoll and Void."

Et Tu, Lyndon?
The LBJ Theory
By 1963 Lyndon Johnson had grown weary of the obscurity of his office and was concerned that the scandals surrounding his cronies Bobby Baker and Billie Sol Estes would ruin his hopes for the presidency. When rumors circulated that JFK was going to drop him from the 1964 ticket, LBJ worked to stage an elaborate coup on home turf, enlisting loyal Texas oilmen who feared losing the oil depletion allowance and warmongers who wanted to step up involvement in Vietnam. One of their foot soldiers was an angry young man named Lee Harvey Oswald.

Believers
Authors David Lifton (*The Texas Connection*) and Harrison Edward Livingstone (*Killing Kennedy*)

• • •

Strange Details
John Connally, LBJ's longtime friend and colleague, roomed in college with Dallas County district attorney Henry Wade, whose November 24, 1963, press conference made the definitive case against Oswald. Eugene Locke, the deputy ambassador to Vietnam under LBJ, once served as the attorney for Marie Tippit, the wife of Dallas police officer J. D. Tippit, whom Oswald shot soon after the assassination.

Two days after the assassination, deputy attorney general Nicholas Katzenbach pushed for the creation of a federal investigatory commission, partly out of concern that the public might suspect Johnson's involvement: Historically, assassinations of heads of state have been carried out by their successors. Soon after becoming president, Johnson, a hawk, pressed the House and Senate for passage of the Gulf of Tonkin resolution, initiating a period of increased involvement in Vietnam. Johnson sealed certain assassination records until 2039, ordered that Kennedy's limousine be refurbished rather than entered into evidence, and handpicked each member of the Warren Commission, which answered ultimately to him.

Reasons Not to Believe
LBJ was fiercely ambitious but not depraved; to believe that he would order Kennedy's murder requires an extraordinary leap of logic. Despite years of speculation—beginning, most memorably, with Barbara Garson's popular 1967 play, *MacBird!*, and amplified in Oliver Stone's *JFK*—there is not one shred of evidence to support the idea that LBJ had a hand in the assassination.

Recent Developments
The newly released LBJ tapes show that Johnson was by no means the puppet of warmongers; he clearly agonized over Vietnam and sought resolution to the conflict. They also reveal a man of more depth, and of greater conscience, than his detractors have ever given him credit for—hardly the portrait of a Judas waiting in the wings.

The Red Scare
The KGB Theory
Humiliated by Kennedy in the Cuban Missile Crisis, Soviet premier
Nikita Khrushchev decided to punish him. Scenario 1: Oswald, who
lived in the Soviet Union from 1959 to 1962, was trained in espionage
there and then ordered to make the hit. Scenario 2: Oswald was the
patsy in Khrushchev's game, set up by an Oswald double and KGB
operatives who fired the fatal shots at Dealey Plaza. Scenario 3: Oswald
returned home from the Soviet Union an unwitting assassin, programmed a la The Manchurian Candidate to carry out the orders of
those behind the Iron Curtain.

Believers
CIA counterintelligence chief James Angleton and author Michael
Eddowes (*Khruschev Killed Kennedy*)

Strange Details
Russian baron and suspected spy George de Mohrenschildt, who
helped introduce Oswald to the Russian emigre community in Dallas
and was his closest friend before the assassination—fatally shot himself in 1977, before he was set to testify before the HSCA. The uncle of
Marina Nikolayevna Prusakova, Oswald's Russian-born wife, was a
ranking officer in the Soviet Ministry of Internal Affairs.

Reasons to Believe
In January 1960 Oswald was given a rent-free apartment in Minsk,
where an espionage training academy was located. Recently declassi-
fied files show that up to twenty KGB agents shadowed him and may
have manipulated his behavior. ("Maybe they did drop a few tablets
in his glass," a high-ranking KGB official told the Russian newspaper
Izvestia, "but only to make him let down his guard and be a little more
talkative.") The Russians, who had never before captured a U2 spy
plane, suddenly managed to do so a scant six and a half months after
the defection of Oswald, who had worked as a Marine radar operator

in Atsugi, Japan, where the U2 was based. On a trip to Mexico City on September 27, 1963, Oswald visited the Soviet embassy and spoke to KGB agent Oleg Maximovich Nechiporenko who was expelled from Mexico in 1970 for conspiring to overthrow the government—and Valeriy Vladimirovich Kostikov, an agent in "wet affairs": sabotage and assassination.

Reasons Not to Believe
Secret agents usually keep a lower profile than did Oswald, whose pinko leanings—such as addressing his fellow Marines as "comrades" in the midst of the cold war or reading *Das Kapital* in the barracks—earned him the nickname Oswaldskovich. It seems unlikely that the KGB would have recruited someone as unstable as Oswald—who attempted suicide five days after arriving in Moscow—for such a covert operation, since a Soviet-backed plot to kill Kennedy would have resulted in certain nuclear retaliation if uncovered. At Atsugi, Oswald was a low-level soldier with little exposure to the U2. A 1981 exhumation of Oswald's body revealed that it was indeed he who was buried, not his Soviet-trained double, as some conspiracy theorists suspected. Marina later recanted her testimony and professed her husband's innocence, saying that she had been threatened with deportation if she did not cooperate. Why would Khrushchev want to get rid of Kennedy in favor of Johnson, a more zealous anti-communist with closer ties to the military?

Recent Developments
In 1992 the KGB released dossier #31451: the Oswald file. It contained few revelations other than the KGB's own suspicions that the American defector was a CIA operative. There was, however, one tantalizing detail: After spying on several of Oswald's hunting trips, KGB operatives concluded that he was a poor shot.

Hoover' Endgame
The FBI Theory
By the fall of 1963, J. Edgar Hoover had anticipated that his long

tenure as FBI director was coming to an end. Federal law required the 68-year-old to step down on his seventieth birthday, and he knew that Kennedy was eager to be rid of him. But rather than fading quietly into the background, Hoover orchestrated an early transfer of power to his ally LBJ, who, as president, could—and did—exempt him from mandatory retirement, allowing him to lord over the bureau until his death in 1972. Scenario 1: Hoover knew of various plots to kill Kennedy but took no action, failing to inform the Secret Service of threats to the president's life and taking an uncharacteristically hands-off approach to investigating possible conspirators. Scenario 2: Oswald was an FBI informant who killed Kennedy on orders from the bureau. Scenario 3: Oswald warned the FBI of plots to kill Kennedy, only to find himself framed and then silenced by fellow informant Jack Ruby.

Believers
Authors Mark North (*Act of Treason*) and George O'Toole (*The Assassination Tapes*)

Strange Details
Ruby briefly worked as an FBI informant in 1959. The FBI's number Three man, William Sullivan, who had overseen the "internal security aspects" of the assassination investigation, was fatally shot in 1977 on a hunting expedition before testifying before the HSCA. When Oswald was a child, his favorite television show was *I Led Three Lives*, the story of an FBI counterspy.

Reasons to Believe
The FBI had been keeping tabs on Oswald since at least 1960 but did not inform the Secret Service that he worked in a building along the motorcade route. Ten days before the assassination, Oswald dropped off a handwritten note at the FBI's Dallas field office for James Hosty, a special agent who had been trailing him for several months. Hosty destroyed the note on orders from his superior the day Oswald was shot but never acknowledged its existence until 1975, when he

explained that it had merely warned him to "stop harassing" Oswald's wife, Marina. (He had questioned her twice in early November.) Some speculate that the note really contained violent threats; others think it was a warning from Oswald that someone in Dallas was going to kill the president. Texas attorney general Waggoner Carr told the Warren Commission he had information that Oswald was an undercover FBI agent, prompting a top-secret emergency meeting of the commission in January 1964. Eyewitness accounts of varying reliability placed Oswald in New Orleans fraternizing with, and even receiving envelopes from, FBI agents. The sole investigatory body for the Warren Commission was the FBI, which intimidated witnesses, suppressed and destroyed evidence that cast an unflattering light on the bureau, and conducted a shoddy investigation, even declining to take Abraham Zapruder's super-8 footage when he offered it after the assassination. According to Hale Boggs, a Warren Commission member: "Hoover lied his eyes out to the commission—on Oswald, on Ruby, on their friends, the bullets, the gun, you name it."

Reasons Not to Believe
The HSCA could never establish that Oswald had worked as an FBI informant. Carr's speculations were partly based on a 1964 *Houston Post* article whose source, Dallas County assistant district attorney Bill Alexander, later admitted to having concocted the story because he distrusted the feds. Why would Hoover—whose personal files on politicians' indiscretions filled four rooms of FBI headquarters—have preferred murder to blackmail as a means of furthering his own ambitions?

Recent Developments
In his 1996 memoir, *Assignment: Oswald*, Hosty said he found notes he took during Oswald's twelve-hour interrogation at Dallas police headquarters—notes that he told the Warren Commission he had destroyed. Although they shed little new light on Oswald, their sudden appearance raises questions about what else the FBI has withheld over the years.

The Cuban Connection
The Castro Theory
Fidel Castro had survived dozens of attempts on his life by agents of the U.S. government (some involving poisoned cigars, lethal powders, and exploding seashells) as well as the botched Bay of Pigs invasion and other CIA-orchestrated raids. After one too many bazooka attacks, the dictator said, "Basta!" in the fall of 1963 and struck back. He found a willing assassin in Oswald, a known communist sympathizer.

Believers
Lyndon Johnson (eventually) and anti-Castro activist Carlos Bringuier.

Strange Details
Oswald admired Castro, often referring to him as Uncle Fidel. In the summer of 1963 Oswald was planning to relocate his family to Havana.

Reasons to Believe
In a September 1963 interview with the Associated Press, Castro called Kennedy a "cretin" and threatened to retaliate against him: "U.S. leaders should think that if they are aiding terrorist plans to eliminate Cuban leaders . . . they themselves will not be safe." On September 27, 1963, Oswald visited the Cuban consulate in Mexico City, ostensibly to obtain a visa. Eager to ingratiate himself with Cuban bureaucrats, he presented himself as "a friend of the Cuban revolution" and, some speculate, offered his services as an assassin. Autulio Ramirez Ortiz, a hijacker who claimed to have infiltrated Cuban intelligence in the early sixties, testified before the HSCA that he saw a file labeled "Osvaldo-Kennedy" at a Cuban intelligence facility. The file, Ortiz said, contained a photo of Oswald, a KGB recommendation, and this conclusion: "Oswald is an adventurer. Our embassy in Mexico has orders to get in contact with him. Be very careful."

• • •

Reasons Not to Believe

Castro had to have known that the U.S. would strike back if his plot were discovered. Oswald's visa request at the Cuban consulate was turned down.

Recent Developments

According to National Security Agency documents released last year, the usually unflappable Castro was terrified the U.S. would retaliate against Cuba in the first hours after the assassination. The NSA intercepted messages going in and out of Cuba, including one from a foreign agent who saw Castro's televised speech on the evening of November 23: "Fidel, emotional and uneasy, tried . . . to refute the accusations which were then appearing and to twist them so that the assassination would appear as the work of the Ultra Reaction, of the extreme racists of the Pentagon, who are fanatical supporters of war against Cuba and the Soviet Union. Although it was only the third time I had witnessed a speech by Fidel, I got the immediate impression that on this occasion he was frightened, if not terrified."

Cuba Libre: The Cuban Exiles Theory

In the early days of the Kennedy administration, Cuban exiles reserved their contempt for Castro, who had taken away their homeland. But after the Bay of Pigs invasion, they felt equally betrayed by Kennedy, who had withheld air support during the operation, leaving 1,500 Cuban soldiers stranded and at the mercy of Castro's army. After Kennedy thwarted subsequent plans to invade, enraged exiles orchestrated the president's murder with help from their CIA associates, either in retaliation for the deaths of their brothers-in-arms or to frame Castro for Kennedy's murder, thereby forcing a full-scale U.S. invasion. Oswald, who had tried to infiltrate the anti-Castro movement in New Orleans, was either the exiles' agent or their patsy.

Believers

HSCA investigator Gaeton Fonzi, authors Bernard Fensterwald (*Coinci-*

dence or Conspiracy?) and Sylvia Meagher (*Accessories After the Fact*), and CBS newsman Peter Noyes.

Strange Details

In August 1963 Oswald approached Carlos Bringuier, a New Orleans shopkeeper active in the anti-Castro movement, and asked to join his organization. Four days later Oswald was arrested for disturbing the peace while passing out pro-Castro leaflets—an elaborate scheme, some say, to deflect attention from his involvement in the anti-Castro conspiracy.

Reasons to Believe

Cuban exile Sylvia Odio told the HSCA that in late September 1963, three men showed up at her Dallas apartment and convinced her and her sister that they were members of the cause. Two of the men, "Leopoldo" and "Angelo," were Cubans, while the third, "Leon Oswald," was an American, described later as a former Marine, a man who thought Kennedy should be assassinated because of the Bay of Pigs, a good shot, and "kind of nuts." Two months later Odio and her sister were shocked when they recognized the president's assassin: Leon was Lee Harvey Oswald. The HSCA later termed Odio a "credible" witness. Cuban exiles viewed the Bay of Pigs as nothing less than unforgivable treachery on Kennedy's part. At the end of 1962 he added fuel to the fire when he shut down Operation Mongoose (a CIA program that was preparing Cuban pilots and soldiers for another invasion) in exchange for Khrushchev's dismantling of Russian missiles on the island. By 1963 the Kennedy administration was cracking down on Cuban exiles, raiding their paramilitary training camps in Louisiana and Florida.

Reasons Not to Believe

Oswald was in Mexico City on the day Odio says he visited her. Why would virulent anti-communists trust Oswald, a known Red?

Recent Developments

In 1994 Florence Martino told writer Anthony Summers that on the morning of November 22, 1963, her husband, John—an anti-Castro activist—said, "Flo, they're going to kill him. They're going to kill him when he gets to Texas." Then, she said, John got a bunch of phone calls from Texas. "I don't know who called him, but he was on the phone, on the phone, on the phone. . ." John Martino, who had once worked for Santos Trafficante, had been imprisoned by Castro from 1959 to 1962. (He later wrote a book, *I Was Castro's Prisoner*.) After his release he threw in with Cuban exiles and later claimed that they had framed Oswald. He died in 1975.

Friendly Fire: The Secret Service Theory
Secret Service agents were pawns in a grand scheme to kill the president. Working on orders from higher-ups—the FBI or the vice president—they (a) provided lax security in Dallas so that sharpshooters would have a clear shot and/or (b) hijacked the body as part of an elaborate scheme to alter the corpse, scuttle the autopsy, and cover up the whole affair.

Believers
Authors David Lifton (*Best Evidence*) and Bonar Messinger (*Mortal Error*)

Strange Details
Into the wee hours on the morning of the assassination, Secret Service agents drank Everclear at the Cellar, a rowdy beatnik club in Fort Worth whose owner, Pat Kirkwood, was an acquaintance of Jack Ruby's. Secret Service agents Winston Lawson and Forrest Sorrells, who chose the motorcade route, rode in a covered sedan in front of the president's convertible.

Reasons to Believe
Although plans for a presidential motorcade in Miami four days before the assassination were scrapped when a right-wing extremist told a police informant that Kennedy would be shot "from an office building with a high-powered rifle," few precautions were taken in Dallas: Build-

ings along the motorcade route were not secured, lookouts were not posted, and the presidential limousine's "bubble top" was removed. Against regulations, the Secret Service chose a motorcade route that required a 120-degree turn, an angle that forced Kennedy's limousine to slow to a crawl as it passed the book depository building and turned onto Elm Street. Rather than having four motorcycles stationed on each side of the president's limo, as Dallas police chief Jesse Curry had suggested, Agent Lawson ordered that only two motorcycles be on each side and that they remain by the rear bumper. After the first two shots were fired, Agent William Greer, Kennedy's driver, briefly applied the brake rather than the accelerator, allowing the presidential limousine to come to a near stand still right before the third and fatal shot was fired. At Parkland Hospital on the afternoon of the assassination, agents forced their way past Dallas medical examiner Earl Rose with the president's coffin in hand, insisting that the autopsy would be performed not in Dallas, as required by state law, but in Washington, D.C.

Reasons Not to Believe
Could all of the seventy Secret Service agents assigned to protect the president in Dallas have turned against him—and kept silent about such a conspiracy for 35 years? Since the president's coffin was never left unattended on Air Force One, the corpse could not have been tampered with.

Recent Developments
Interest in the Secret Service's possible connection to the assassination was revived by Menninger's 1992 book, *Mortal Error*, which claims that Agent George Hickey fired the third and fatal shot while riding in the presidential follow-up car. According to Menninger's thesis, when Hickey reached for his AR-15 upon hearing shots, he slipped off the safety, lost his balance, and accidentally pulled the trigger.

Saigon Surprise: The Vietnam Theory
On November 2, 1963, after South Vietnamese president Ngo Dinh

Diem began negotiations with North Vietnamese communists, he was shot at point-blank range, along with his brother and political adviser, Ngo Dinh Nhu, during a U.S. backed coup. Seeking revenge, the wealthy and powerful Diem family—perhaps led by the widowed Madame Nhu, Saigon's "Dragon Lady"—settled the score three weeks later in Dallas.

Believers
Lyndon Johnson (initially)

Strange Details
In 1950, when Diem was forced into exile by Ho Chi Minh, he fled to a Catholic seminary in New York, where he became friendly with then-senator John Kennedy. Kennedy had approved the coup but was assured that an attempt would be made to evacuate Diem and Nhu from Saigon; he was appalled to learn that they had been murdered. Eight years later, CIA operative Howard Hunt doctored State Department files so that researchers of the Pentagon Papers might "discover" that Kennedy had arranged Diem's murder. Allen Dulles, who created the Saigon Military Mission and staffed it with men who would later help orchestrate the Saigon coup, was a member of the Warren Commission.

Reasons to Believe
The Diem regime showed no mercy to its foes. Immediately after her husband's murder, Madame Nhu told American reporters, "Such a cruel injustice against a faithful ally cannot go unnoticed, and those who indulge in it will have to pay for it."

Reasons Not to Believe
If the South Vietnamese were wily enough to pull this off, why didn't they kill Ho Chi Minh first?

Recent Developments
In 1997 Seymour Hersh's *The Dark Side of Camelot* alleged that

Kennedy not only knew Diem would be murdered but also personally asked Air Force general Edward Landsdale, a CIA man, to do the job himself.

Conspiracy A-Go-Go: The Shadow Government Theory
There is a secret government within our government, a cabal that in 1963 ordered the murder of a popular president, set up a patsy, installed its own puppet, and orchestrated an elaborate cover-up that included tampering with the corpse, destroying and suppressing evidence, and killing witnesses. Heading the cabal were some of the world's most powerful men: rich and corrupt industrialists, generals, and right-wing politicians. Down below was an eclectic group of mobsters, spooks, lowlifes, and anti-Castro extremists, many of whom were headquartered at 544 Camp Street in New Orleans, including Oswald, former FBI agent Guy Banister, soldier of fortune David Ferrie, and suspected CIA informant Clay Shaw. Together, in the summer of 1963, they plotted Kennedy's demise.

Believers
New Orleans district attorney Jim Garrison, filmmaker Oliver Stone, and former chief of special operations for the Joint Chiefs of Staff Fletcher Prouty

Strange Details
Theorists enjoy playing an elaborate parlor game of Six Degrees of Assassination. One version goes like this: As a teenager, Oswald had been in the Civil Air Patrol with Ferrie, who had done private investigative work for mobster Carlos Marcello, whose close associate Santos Trafficante had been the main mob boss in prerevolution Cuba, where in 1959 he was imprisoned by Castro, visited by Ruby, and then bailed out by Cuban turncoat Rolando Cubela, who, on November 22, 1963, was being briefed in Paris on killing Castro by an agent of the CIA, whose former director (and future Warren Commission member), Allen Dulles, had been forced out by Kennedy following the Bay of Pigs

invasion, as had his deputy, Charles Cabell, whose brother Earle was the mayor of Dallas, which had been papered on November 22 with "Wanted for Treason" leaflets published by Robert Surrey, an aide to Major General Edwin A. Walker, who had been the target of an assassination attempt in April 1963, the chief suspect of which, according to the Warren Commission, was Oswald. Surrey also played bridge with James Hosty, the FBI agent who had been shadowing Oswald, whose wife, Marina, often mocked her husband's lovemaking and told him how attracted she was to Kennedy, who had had an affair with Judith Exner, girlfriend of mafioso Sam Giancana, who had helped steal the 1960 election for Kennedy by stuffing ballot boxes in Chicago, where Ruby had run errands for Al Capone as a teenager and Banister had helped ambush John Dillinger.

Reasons to Believe

Pressed for time, obsessed with secrecy, and embarrassed by their awareness of Oswald's existence, both the FBI and the CIA withheld critical information and did little to investigate possible links between their own organizations and Oswald, between the CIA and Cuban paramilitary organizations, between the Mafia and various assassination players, and between Ruby and the mob, Cubans, and the Dallas police force.

Reasons Not to Believe

How could such a labyrinthine plan with so many participants never be exposed? How could a bunch of inefficient, bungling bureaucracies work so well and with such determination and unanimity? Notwithstanding Kevin Costner's noble portrayal of him in *JFK*, Garrison—the chief proponent of this theory—was a lying, attention-grabbing megalomaniac with McCarthyite tendencies who had been dismissed from the National Guard for mental problems. He tried to prove his theory by taking businessman Clay Shaw to court in 1969 for conspiring to kill the president. The resulting trial was nothing less than a circus. Garrison sought to prove his case with an array of peculiar characters, including a man in a toga identifying himself as Julius Caesar, a heroin addict, and a New York accountant who said he often fingerprinted his daughter to make sure she was not an impostor. The prosecution mischaracterized evidence and bribed, intimidated, and even had witnesses hypnotized. He ultimately said that there were sixteen assassins at Dealey Plaza, including the three tramps and a man who popped out of a sewer. Though he presented plenty of intriguing suspicions, he had few facts, and it took the jury only 45 minutes to find Shaw innocent of all charges. The *New York Times* later called Garrison's crusade against Shaw "one of the most disgraceful chapters in the history of American jurisprudence."

Recent Developments

JFK's release forever changed the way Americans view the assassination. Oliver Stone provided the seamless—albeit wildly inventive and historically inaccurate—story line that lawyer Garrison had always coveted. If we vaguely believed in a conspiracy before, by late 1991, 73 percent of Americans were sure of it, while 35 percent thought the CIA was directly involved. In response, Congress created the Assassination Records Review Board, whose mandate was to obtain assassination-related files from often-reluctant agencies like the FBI and the CIA, declassify them, and make them available to the public. The upshot was the release of thousands of important items, including the personal papers of Warren Commission members, a presidential aide's amateur film of the motorcade, and notes from Oswald's interrogation at Dallas police headquarters, as well as an archive of more than four million pages of secret records. Nothing earth-shattering was ever discovered (the board was shut down in September), though many documents still remain hidden from view. According to the act that created the board, all relevant documents must be released to the public by 2017. except for ones deemed worthy for further postponement by any sitting President.

from The Last Brother: The Rise and
Fall of Teddy Kennedy
by Joe McGinniss

Two Kennedy siblings—Joe, Jr. and Katherine—already had died in planes when Ted Kennedy had his closest brush with death. It came in 1964, less than seven months after JFK's assassination. Joe McGinniss' controversial biography of the senator includes this account of the accident.

The Massachusetts Democrats were holding their 1964 nominating convention in West Springfield. Unlike 1962, for Teddy the event was to be not a competition but a coronation—indeed, the climax to one of the most rewarding days of his public life.

That Friday, June 19, the Senate was finally to vote on the civil rights bill. The outcome was not in doubt. The legislation, which even in its final, tempered version was of historic importance, would be approved by a wide margin. But the vote held enormous symbolic significance for Teddy. As the brother of the assassinated President who had introduced the bill, he intended to remain on the Senate floor until its passage.

Then, as soon as the final vote was tallied, he would fly to Massachusetts by private plane to accept his renomination by acclamation at the convention.

He could not use the family plane, the *Caroline,* because Bobby was flying to Hyannis Port for the weekend and Bobby, as the older brother, always had first call on the *Caroline.*

But the family had a friend in Andover named Dan Hogan, president of a company that manufactured liquid detergent and owner of a twin-engined Aero Commander 680 that he frequently flew himself for both recreational and business purposes.

In the less than three weeks since Teddy had returned from Europe, Hogan had already flown him to three separate speeches. But he explained that Friday morning to Teddy's administrative assistant, Ed Moss, he would not be able to fly Teddy from Washington to Springfield because this was the weekend of his twenty-fifth reunion at Yale.

His plane, of course, remained at Teddy's disposal. In fact, Hogan told Moss, he'd arranged to have Ed Zimny, an experienced professional pilot whom he knew well, fly the aircraft to Washington and then take Teddy to Springfield as soon as the Senate vote was cast.

If the Senate stayed on schedule, Teddy would arrive at the auditorium in early evening. As was so often the case, however, the Senate did not stay on schedule. Throughout the day, as delays mounted, Moss, who had begun to accompany Teddy on almost every trip he made, was on the telephone repeatedly, rearranging travel arrangements and scheduling for the evening.

Teddy, never a patient man when it came to travel schedules, grew more and more irritated as the Senate slogged slowly through the multitude of procedural details that had to be disposed of before the final vote on the civil rights bill was taken.

The pilot, Zimny, had arrived at 4:00 p.m. and was waiting at the private air terminal at Washington's National Airport. He was eager to leave for Springfield as soon as possible because, as he told Moss several times, the weather, while fine in Washington, was quickly deteriorating to the north.

But there was nothing Ed Moss, or Teddy himself, could do to hurry the tedious pace at which the country's most august deliberative body conducted its business.

Not until 7:00 p.m. did it appear that the vote was finally drawing near. Teddy was supposed to have been in West Springfield already. The delegates had long since assembled inside the convention hall.

Knowing he'd be arriving hours later than expected, Teddy arranged to speak briefly to the delegates through a telephone-and-loudspeaker hookup.

As in 1962, more than seventeen hundred of them, obscured by cigarette smoke and slick with sweat, greed and their own private fears, were packed into the hot, humid auditorium. The evening had already turned loud and raucous. The only contest was between Governor Endicott "Chub" Peabody—whose two-year term had been widely viewed as unsuccessful—and his challenger, Lieutenant Governor Francis X. Bellotti, who was supported by Eddie McCormack.

The Kennedys had chosen Peabody two years earlier because they'd wanted Teddy's ticket to have ethnic balance, and now they were stuck with him. Teddy had put vast personal distance between himself and Peabody, but so great was Teddy's popularity that the mere implication that he still favored the incumbent was enough to doom Bellotti's chances.

By the night of the balloting it had become obvious that the bland and ineffectual Peabody would easily win the convention's endorsement. Thus, the only spark of excitement the delegates could hope for would be the triumphal entrance of Teddy, however delayed he might be.

As it was announced that he was on a phone line from Washington, the hall fell silent. His voice crackled through the auditorium's loudspeaker system. It was now almost 7:30 p.m. and it seemed he might not actually reach the convention hall until almost 11:00.

"I just want everyone to know," he said, "that I am a candidate this year, even though I am hundreds of miles away." Then he added, "We are now fifteen minutes away from the vote for civil rights." The crowd inside the convention hall cheered. This was Jack's bill and, as such, even to those Massachusetts Democrats personally unstirred by the plight of the blacks, it had acquired the status of sacred writ.

Teddy said he would be with them in person as soon as possible, and closed by adding, "And I ask you not to get so impatient that you decide to nominate Joan instead."

The crowd laughed and cheered. But Joan herself, who detested these sorts of events almost as intensely as Jacqueline had, was not even at the convention hall. She was spending the evening with friends at a private home in Springfield. She planned to wait there for Teddy and travel to the hall only when he arrived.

The Senate finally began to vote at 7:40 p.m. The process took only ten minutes. The final tally was 73—27. Gratified but somber, Teddy hurried back to his office from the floor. Birch Bayh, a Democratic senator from Indiana, accompanied him. Bayh had agreed to deliver the keynote speech at the Springfield convention. He and his wife, as well as Ed Moss, would be flying to Massachusetts with Teddy.

Moss called Zimny at the airport, saying they'd be there within half an hour. Again, the pilot urged Moss to hurry. The weather in western Massachusetts was worsening steadily.

Moss was forty-one years old, married and the father of three. Being that much older than Teddy—as well as being highly competent, affable and discreet—he'd come to occupy a special place on the senatorial staff. An administrative aide, yes, but more than that: like Joey Gargan, somebody with whom Teddy could relax. One of the few who still saw him as a man and not a myth; as Teddy rather than as the reincarnation of Jack.

But even Moss occasionally misjudged the temper of the moment. Anticipating that Teddy would be elated by the wide margin by which the bill had passed, he joked that, to cap off the night, "You should make some kind of spectacular entrance at the convention."

"What do you want me to do," Teddy said tartly, "crack up the airplane?" Beset by many conflicting emotions, he was not in a frivolous mood.

Moss, already recognizing his mistake, suggested that Teddy might at least parachute out of the plane as it flew over the convention hall. The Senator was not amused. With no further comment, he hurried to a waiting car, Moss and the Bayhs trailing behind.

As they started for the airport, Moss mentioned for the first time that the pilot had reported the Massachusetts weather to be less than ideal and that he'd seemed in a hurry to get started.

Teddy himself was always in a hurry. Still, tonight there was a stop he had to make. This had been Jack's bill. On this, the night of its passage, he needed to spend a few private moments at Jack's grave.

He told the driver to stop at Arlington. He got out of the car and knelt, alone, head bowed, at the base of the eternal flame.

Meanwhile, in western Massachusetts, the valleys began to fill with fog.

As expected, Peabody had trounced Bellotti, 1,259—377, but no one except for Peabody, Bellotti and maybe Eddie McCormack seemed to care. Teddy was to be the star of this show. Until he arrived, there was no show. It was now after 11:00 p.m. An announcement was made that Teddy's plane had been delayed but was en route and that he would arrive at the hall before midnight.

But midnight came and Teddy didn't. Delegates mingled aimlessly, fatigue and liquor now blurring their sense of anticipation. Suddenly, and somewhat frantically, the chairman of the convention gaveled for silence. He said he had just received word that the plane bearing Senator Kennedy had crashed while trying to land near Springfield but that the Senator was reported to be alive.

In shock and horror, disbelieving delegates pushed toward the press section of the auditorium, desperate for further information. Already, many were in tears. This could not be. This was too much. No God could permit yet another tragedy to befall this star-crossed family.

And Teddy . . . Teddy, who now filled their hearts with pride as Jack had done . . . it could not be that something had happened to Teddy.

Within minutes, the chairman again gaveled the hall to silence. In his other hand, he held up what appeared to be a wire service news bulletin. To the enormous relief of nearly two thousand stricken listeners, he said the first report had apparently been in error. There had been a crash in the vicinity of Springfield, but it had not involved Teddy's plane. "The Kennedy plane is still aloft," he announced.

The hall erupted with the wildest cheers of the night. Oh, what a triumphant moment it would be when Teddy—after all this unexpected turmoil—finally arrived.

But then, for a third time, the gavel sounded. Again, the chairman stepped to the microphone. For those close enough to see his face, no words were necessary.

"It now appears that the first announcement was correct," he said. "Senator Kennedy is hospitalized but still alive."

He asked for a moment of silent prayer. Then, at 12:20 a.m., he pounded his gavel for the last time, declaring the convention adjourned. Delegates, many crying openly, poured out of the hall in chaos, running through mist and drizzle toward the nearest car radio, the nearest television set.

Jack Crimmins, a former state policeman who lived in South Boston and served as Teddy's primary chauffeur within Massachusetts, had been waiting for the plane at tiny Barnes Municipal Airport in the town of Westfield, seven miles from the West Springfield convention hall.

Bradley Field, the larger commercial airport that served Springfield, was located south of the city, over the state line in Connecticut. Though far better equipped to handle air traffic in bad weather, Bradley was almost a forty-five-minute drive from the convention hall. Teddy was already too late. He decided, despite the weather and the pilot's concerns, that he would fly into Barnes. Ed Moss had told Crimmins to be there, waiting with the car, by 11:00 p.m.

At 11:05, the dispatcher in the Barnes control room told Crimmins he'd just been in radio contact with Teddy's pilot and, due to poor weather, the flight would be slightly delayed.

Crimmins could see the weather for himself: thick fog, light drizzle, seemingly no visibility at all.

Five minutes later, the dispatcher told Crimmins that because of the fog Teddy's pilot must have decided not to try a landing at Barnes after all, that he must have diverted to Bradley. At least, he'd broken off radio contact.

Crimmins called the convention hall to report this to Teddy's chief aide there. If the plane landed at Bradley, no one would be there to meet him and it would be at least another hour before Teddy arrived at the convention. Crimmins left the Barnes airfield to make the short drive to the convention hall, hoping that by the time he got there somebody who knew what the hell was going on might deign to tell him.

Under the best of circumstances, Jack Crimmins was a man with a low irritation threshold, and all these delays and changes of plans had left him fuming. Crimmins liked to take a drink or two in the evening, a pleasure that thus far he'd had to forgo. Now, if he was going to have to drive halfway to Hartford and back again, it would be 2:00 a.m. before he was finally off the road and able to unwind.

As he left Barnes and turned onto the main road, he saw several police cruisers racing past, lights flashing, heading north, which was not the direction he was going.

He turned on his car radio and heard the bulletin immediately. Teddy's plane had crashed while trying to land at Barnes. Teddy, believed to be alive but badly injured, was being rushed by ambulance to a nearby hospital.

"Sonofabitch!" Crimmins said. He turned and headed not toward the convention hall but back to the private home where he knew Joan was waiting.

The plane had left Washington at 8:35. Normally, in the twin-engined, six-seat Aero Commander, the flight would take an hour and twenty minutes.

They'd be on the ground by ten, Teddy said. He had a car waiting. It would take less than half an hour to pick up Joan and get to the convention hall. A 10:30 arrival, then. That wouldn't be too bad.

Birch Bayh joked that it wouldn't be too good, either. That from his limited knowledge of Democratic politics in Massachusetts he doubted there would be a delegate left still standing by 10:30 p.m. and he was certain that even if there were, they'd be in no condition to hear a belated keynote speech delivered by a senator from Indiana.

Teddy assured Bayh that he would give him such an introduction that the crowd would think they were about to hear Lincoln at Gettysburg. Bayh jokingly warned Teddy not to overdo it: he said the speech his staff had prepared was good, but not that good.

Once they were airborne, Teddy had seemed to relax a bit. He was sitting directly behind the pilot, Zimny, facing the rear of the plane. Ed Moss was in the front seat, next to Zimny. Bayh and his wife were sitting side by side at the rear, facing Teddy and able to converse with him.

Teddy turned to ask Zimny about the report of bad weather in Springfield. The pilot said there were numerous pockets of thunderstorms from New York City north, and drizzle spreading across western Massachusetts. By the time they reached the hills around Springfield, visibility could pose a problem, but he assured Teddy that the Aero Commander was equipped for instrument landings. He did warn, however, that the flight would take longer than expected because he'd be detouring around the worst of the turbulence associated with the thunderstorms.

At forty-eight, Zimny was the oldest man aboard the plane. Both Bayh and his wife were in their thirties. Zimny had been flying since the 1930s and had, in fact, been a combat pilot in World War II, just like Joe Junior.

Teddy joked that it was probably a good thing that Dan Hogan had his Yale reunion. He said that as an amateur pilot himself, he always felt better with a professional—especially if the weather was iffy. But then he stressed that he was already hours late and would appreciate it if Zimny could get them to the Barnes airfield as quickly as possible, even if it meant a bit of turbulence.

As the small plane jounced through the darkness, Teddy, with increasing impatience, kept glancing at his watch. His surface affability was wearing thin. Birch Bayh was one of the brightest and nicest members of the Senate and Teddy liked his wife, Marvella, too, but it had been a long week for all of them, finally pushing the civil rights bill through, and they were tired.

Teddy would take pleasure in the hero's welcome he knew he'd receive at the convention. Just two years ago, Eddie McCormack had actually thought he could deny Teddy the delegate's endorsement. He'd failed in embarrassing fashion, just as tonight, Teddy knew, he was failing again as Peabody routed Bellotti.

But this business of being treated as the personification of Jack every waking minute caused internal strains at many levels. To Bayh, who was immensely fond of Teddy and who'd been an ardent admirer of Jack's, it seemed obvious that the demands of the past six months had extracted a high price from the youngest brother. Teddy seemed brittle; stretched taut.

Bayh sensed that Teddy had been comforted by the cloak of invisibility he'd worn throughout his first ten months in the Senate. It had been almost a security blanket. Suddenly and tragically—and having had no time whatever to prepare—he'd become the least invisible man in America, perhaps in the world. The demands and expectations now seemed infinite. As much as he respected Teddy, Bayh sometimes wondered how, in the years ahead, he would ever manage to meet them all.

They were falling farther and farther behind schedule as Zimny wove his way around the thunderstorms. Teddy's mood was turning dark as the night. It would be at least 11:00 p.m., probably later, before the pilot had them on the ground. It might be midnight before Teddy reached the convention. His great day of triumph threatened to turn into one more insufferable marathon.

Then Zimny, who'd been in frequent radio contact with air controllers, turned to report that the weather had worsened beyond his most pessimistic expectations.

Conditions at the tiny Barnes airfield were now marginal even for an instrument landing. By far the more prudent course would be to divert to Bradley Field. Not only was the airport itself much larger and better equipped, but the terrain around it was not nearly so treacherous as the fog-draped hills that surrounded Barnes.

Absolutely not, Teddy said. Goddamnit, they were late enough already. This was an Aero Commander equipped for an instrument landing, Zimny was an experienced pilot licensed to make instrument landings and Teddy expected him to land at Barnes. He had no intention of diverting to Bradley.

Zimny was not a squeamish man. He was also not lacking in confidence. It was annoying to have an amateur pilot with limited experience looking over his shoulder and second-guessing his every move, but this was, after all, Teddy Kennedy, and Zimny knew both how important the occasion of his renomination was and how late they were for it.

If the Senator wanted to try for Barnes in the fog, with only an eight-hundred-foot ceiling and even that falling fast, well, Zimny would try for Barnes in the fog.

He was five miles from the runway at 11:00 p.m., descending at a rate of five hundred feet per minute. He banked sharply and turned for his final approach. The fog was so dense, Bayh said later, "it was like flying through a black void."

Bayh also could sense Teddy's heightened tension as the plane continued its blind descent. Teddy apparently had unfastened his seat belt and was half standing, twisted in his seat, looking closely at the instrument panel. Bayh suggested that maybe that bigger airport in Connecticut wasn't such a bad idea, after all.

"Let's give the pilot every chance," Teddy replied. He himself had never had a fear of flying, though as a pilot he had often inspired stark terror in his passengers. Reckless and heedless, Teddy flew a plane the way he drove a car: as if no harm could ever come to him, or else as if he simply didn't care whether or not it did.

With the altimeter showing the plane at eleven hundred feet, Zimny lowered his wing flaps and landing gear. The instrument approach called for him to fly to a predesignated point beyond the runway, maintaining an altitude of at least eight hundred feet, and to notify ground control when he was over it.

But Zimny apparently wanted to get lower. He may not have been entirely comfortable with the instrument approach he'd been instructed to use. He may have wanted to get below the fogbank and see the runway himself before finally committing to a landing.

Still half standing, his jaw now clenched, Teddy looked at the altimeter. Zimny was continuing to descend. He did not level off at eight hundred feet as instructed; he went lower. Zimny had apparently chosen to trust his instincts, not the instruments.

They came out of the fog at six hundred feet, still three miles short of the runway. But the ground was not where it was supposed to be. The ground—or at least the tops of trees—had reached up to meet them.

Bayh saw a momentary flash of what appeared to be white clouds just outside the window of the plane. Later, he realized they must have been apple blossoms. For the fog had obscured an apple orchard covering the ridge of a hill that was three hundred feet higher than the landing strip. A hill and an apple orchard that Zimny had not known about, had not expected to be there.

"I could see the trees," Teddy said later. "We seemed to be riding along the tops of them. It was like a toboggan ride. I knew we were going to crash."

Too late, Zimny pulled back on the stick and threw full power to the engines, hoping to regain altitude. But the plane was already in the trees. Nose down, it plunged toward the ground, tree branches shearing off parts of both wings. As the plane struck the earth, its momentum caused it to cartwheel forward, then plow seventy-five yards farther through the orchard as the roof of its cabin was torn off.

The Aero Commander 680 finally came to rest with its crumpled cockpit smashed against one apple tree and its largely intact tail section pressing against another.

Bayh was first to speak. He turned to his wife, asking how she was.

"I'm all right," she said, but in a very weak voice. Then Bayh became aware of the ominous odor of gasoline and realized that the plane might explode at any moment.

He called to Teddy. There was no answer. Teddy, half standing at the moment of impact, had been thrown about the cabin like an oversized rag doll.

Now he was sprawled across the floor of the plane. "He lay there inert and motionless," Bayh said later. "I was sure he was gone."

Bayh could not even see into the crumpled cockpit but he heard no sounds of motion, no sounds of life. His own left side felt numb and his right hip hurt badly but, smelling the gasoline, he knew he had to get himself and his wife out of the plane and away from it before it exploded.

He pushed Marvella out through a shattered rear window. Then, with her help, he managed to pull himself out. The two of them stumbled down the hillside in fog and drizzle.

They were perhaps fifty yards from the plane when Bayh realized he would have to do something about Teddy. Maybe Teddy was not dead but only unconscious. Bayh could see the red taillight of the plane still spinning and blinking in the darkness. He knew this meant that at least a portion of the plane's electrical system was still functioning. Electricity—perhaps sparks—and a smashed and leaking fuel tank were the most dangerous combination imaginable.

The last thing in the world Birch Bayh wanted to do was return to that airplane, which might explode like a keg of dynamite at any moment. But he did not hesitate. Teddy was in there, perhaps still alive. Bayh had to help him. Bayh had to try to save him, even at the risk of his own life.

In pain and considerable shock, leaving Marvella at what he considered a safe distance from the plane, he struggled back up the wet and slippery hillside in the dark.

A quick check of the cockpit showed that, whether dead or alive, both Zimny and Moss, their heads covered with blood, were trapped by the twisted metal all around them. It would not be possible to pull them free.

Slowly, however, and with great difficulty, Bayh managed to extricate Teddy's massive, limp body from the crumpled midsection of the plane. Teddy was alive but barely conscious and obviously in terrible pain. Also, he was not able to walk and had no feeling in his legs.

Barely able to walk himself, but half carrying, half dragging Teddy, Bayh staggered down the hillside, away from the plane, which he still feared might explode at any moment. Both the air and the ground all around them seemed filled with white apple blossoms, their sweet scent mingling with the stink of leaking gasoline.

Marvella came back up the hill to meet them. Bayh laid Teddy on the ground. He was groaning, still barely conscious. Marvella put her raincoat over him to keep him warm. This was something she knew you were supposed to do when a person was going into shock. Then they left him there, pleading for water, saying he thought he was paralyzed, and they stumbled toward the road at the bottom of the hill, hoping to flag down a passing motorist and get help.

Zimny was already dead by the time the first state police and ambulances arrived. Moss died seven hours later, during brain surgery, without ever regaining consciousness.

Teddy was taken ten miles by ambulance to Cooley Dickinson Hospital in Northampton, not arriving there until after midnight. Doctors at first did not expect him to survive. It was difficult even to assess the nature and extent of his injuries, but it was obvious that he was in shock; that his back had been badly damaged, probably broken; that a lung had been punctured and that he was suffering from massive internal bleeding.

He was only semiconscious, his face gray, his pulse erratic, his blood pressure, one doctor said, "almost negligible." In the emergency room, he was immediately given blood transfusions and antishock treatment.

As soon as they could, they took X rays. At least two ribs were clearly broken but, worse, three vertebrae on his lower spine appeared to be fractured, with one, a doctor said, "crushed pretty completely." What they could not yet determine was whether or not the spinal cord itself had been injured. If it had, in all probability Teddy would be a paraplegic for the rest of his life.

In those first hours, however, it did not seem likely that the rest of his life would amount to much. The doctors were still not at all sure he would last through the night. He remained in deep shock, his blood pressure still dangerously low, suggesting some sort of internal hemorrhage. They could not tell if his liver, kidneys or spleen might be ruptured. He was also finding it extremely difficult to breathe.

During his first hour in the emergency room, Teddy received three units of whole blood through transfusion to replace what he was losing internally. Through intravenous injection and nasal tube he was also given saline solution and glucose in an attempt to bring him out of shock. Then a tube was inserted in his chest to ease his breathing. All the while, he was kept inside an oxygen tent.

Aware of how serious the injuries to his back were, the emergency room doctors quickly immobilized Teddy on a stretcherlike orthopedic frame. He was in terrible pain, but until they were sure he was no longer in shock, until his breathing improved, and until they could identify the source of the internal bleeding, doctors could not administer painkillers or sedatives.

Within the hour, the press was storming the emergency room door. Another Kennedy had died, or might die at any moment! Joan arrived in the company of Jack Crimmins, looking dazed, wandering around saying repeatedly, almost chanting, "He's going to be all right. I know that he'll be all right."

A phone call was made to Hyannis Port. Bobby was awakened and given the news. By 2:00 a.m. he was in a state police cruiser, speeding west on the Massachusetts Turnpike. Joan made sure that Cardinal Cushing was informed. Teddy's sisters were told. It was decided not to awaken either the crippled Ambassador or Rose. There was no need for them to be told until morning. This was a drill that seemed much too familiar. The reflexes of November still functioned all too well.

Bobby reached the hospital at 4:00 a.m. and immediately demanded to know whether Teddy would be paralyzed. The doctors explained that at this point possible paralysis remained low on the list of concerns. Even by dawn, it was not clear that Teddy would survive.

The internal bleeding continued and doctors were unable to locate the source. If it was the kidney, liver, spleen or bowel, surgery would be required, but Teddy's condition remained so unstable that it seemed unlikely he could survive an immediate operation.

By midmorning, twenty members of the Kennedy family had gathered at the hospital. Cardinal Cushing was on his way from Boston. Jacqueline would be arriving on Sunday. Teddy remained semiconscious, his overall condition still grave. Later, the director of the Cooley Dickinson emergency room would say, "I worked on him for two and a half days. But it was a week before we were sure he was going to live."

from In His Steps: Lyndon Johnson
and the Kennedy Mystique

by Paul R. Henggeler

JFK's stature as a glamorous and tragic figure made him a hard presidential act to follow. Lyndon Johnson, torn by competing needs—to use the Kennedy legacy and to build an independent power base—often felt snubbed and abused by the surviving Kennedys. Historian Paul R. Henggeler here recounts LBJ's delicate maneuverings with the family—particularly RFK and Jackie—before and after President Kennedy's death.

Upon the assassination of John Kennedy on November 22, 1963, Lyndon Johnson became the thirty-sixth president of the United States. Although he had achieved his lifelong ambition, he assumed office not through electoral victory but through the murder of his predecessor, a popular president whose glamour, wit, and style had captivated millions of Americans. Following in the footsteps of a martyred president, he correctly anticipated that much of the public would view him as an interloper. "I took the oath," he told Doris Kearns:

> I became President. But for millions of Americans I was still illegitimate, a naked man with no presidential covering, a pretender to the throne, an illegal usurper. And then there was Texas, my home, the home of both the murder and the murder of the murderer. And then there were the bigots and the dividers and the Eastern intellectuals, who were

waiting to knock me down before I could even begin to stand up. The whole thing was almost unbearable.

Few experiences evoked Johnson's anxiety more than the deaths of his political mentors. When Franklin Roosevelt died, William S. White found Johnson standing in the corridor of the Capitol building with "tears in his eyes," a "shaking jaw," and "a white cigarette holder" in his hand. "He was just like a daddy to me always," he told the reporter. Sam Rayburn's death in 1961 was also a moving experience, especially occurring in the midst of his unhappy tenure as vice president. "Every death was hard on him," one friend noted. "He was more sober. Death hurts him. . . ."

Older than "Jack," Johnson did not share the son-father relationship with him that he had with Roosevelt and Rayburn. Nor was their relationship as lengthy or as intense. Nevertheless, Kennedy had given him access to power, and their relationship, as far as Johnson was concerned, had grown courteous and respectful. So Kennedy's death prompted customary depression. What's more, Johnson had been traveling just two cars behind the president when he was murdered. As vice president he was among the first to be informed of Kennedy's death. "The greatest shock that I can recall," he noted, "was one of the men saying, 'He's gone.' "

Returning to Washington, Johnson was solemn. Undersecretary of State George Ball met the new president at Andrews Air Force Base and perceived him as "near a state of shock." "He moved erratically," Ball wrote, "and I saw twitches in his face." That evening at his Washington home, when a local television station aired a retrospective of Kennedy's life, Johnson covered his eyes. "Turn it off," he said. "It's all too fresh. I can't watch it." Although he was surrounded by friends, he felt alone. Raising a glass of orange juice to a portrait of Rayburn, he seemed at a loss: "Oh, Mister Sam, I wish you were here now. How I need you." He insisted that his entourage stay at his home that night. Horace Busby recalled sitting in the president's bedroom as he tried to fall asleep. Each time that he thought Johnson had finally drifted off to sleep, Busby started to leave the room. But the president would awaken and summon him back.

Johnson's sadness and fears may have been tinged with guilt. In retrospect he claimed that as vice president he had always been highly conscious of Kennedy's mortality. "Every time I came into John Kennedy's presence," he recalled, "I felt like a god damn raven hovering over his shoulder." He was disturbed by rumors that soon surfaced that he had conspired in the murder. Circumstantial evidence made him suspicious to those who searched for a larger explanation for Kennedy's death: Johnson's unsavory political past; his well-known yearning for power; the widespread gossip that he might be dropped from the 1964 ticket; the disrespect he showed for Kennedy at the 1960 convention; and the location of the murder.

Although Johnson was emotionally burdened, aides and scholars have judged the transition period to be his finest hour. Years of pent-up political energy seemed released by his sudden acquisition of power. He worked immediately with Kennedy's cabinet and advisers to assess foreign and domestic policy matters. In the days surrounding the funeral he conferred with major heads of state. Working sixteen-hour days he reviewed the budget and plotted his strategy to break through the congressional stalemate that had burdened Kennedy's legislative initiatives. By August 1964 his accomplishments included passage of the tax reform bill, a reduced budget, a civil rights bill, the wheat-cotton bill, the wilderness bill, a $375 million bill to improve the nation's mass-transit system, and, finally, Johnson's own $948 million anti-poverty package. Perhaps most important, he projected an image of able leadership which was heralded by the press for conveying stability. Appearing frequently on television during his first months in office, Johnson seemed humble but confident.

After guiding the nation through the transition, Johnson reflected on his actions. "We were like a bunch of cattle caught in the swamp . . ." he told Kearns. "I knew what had to be done. There is but one way to get the cattle out of the swamp. And that is for the man on the horse to take the lead, to assume command, to provide direction. In the period of confusion after the assassination, I was that man." He refused to be overwhelmed by emotion. He consciously worked to convey control, aware of public scrutiny and the apprehension that some people felt about him. "Any hesitation or wavering, any false step, any sign of self-doubt, could have been disastrous," he wrote. "The nation was in a state of shock and grief. The times cried out for leadership."

The leadership that Johnson offered, however, was linked to the past and tied to Kennedy's incomplete presidency. As an accidental president, Johnson needed to respond to the public's failed expectations and to be mindful of his surrogate role. If he intended to win the Democratic nomination and remain in power, if he wanted to win the public's trust and lessen his image of illegitimacy, his actions and attitudes needed to appear congruous with the perceived intentions of the martyred president. Trying to move the nation forward and secure his own position, he often reached backwards, embracing the image and substance of his predecessor.

A significant part of Johnson's effort to woo public support involved the cultivation of the two most tangible remnants of the past, John Kennedy's brother and his widow. Should they express dissatisfaction with his presidency, Robert and Jacqueline Kennedy had the potential to jeopardize Johnson's leadership and his future ambitions. From the very beginning the new president sensed there would be "real problems" in dealing with surviving Kennedys. In the interest of continuity he sought reconciliation. "[W]hat can I do, I do not want to get into a fight with the family," he told a cabinet member. "The aura of Kennedy is important to us all."

Few people reflected John Kennedy's charismatic aura more conspicuously than his widow, Jacqueline. Her beauty, eloquence, and extravagant taste made her the perfect counterpart to her husband's "princely" image. After the assassination she displayed remarkable courage and strength during four days of public mourning. As a popular First Lady and a surviving link to the martyred president, she was a powerful symbol of the past and fundamental to Johnson's image of continuity. Johnson was drawn to her both politically and emotionally.

With her qualities of femininity, beauty, wealth, intelligence, and culture, she often evoked his sentimentality and softer qualities.

During his vice presidency Johnson had seemed genuinely fond of Jacqueline. Like many people in Washington, he was impressed with her charm and poise and shared satisfaction in her success. "You continue to get good press," he wrote after a public appearance in 1962, "and I'm always glad to be there to see it happen!" He sent with his letter some press clippings and a pun noting that her speech before the Rural Electrification Administration had "electrified" America. Once, Johnson received a piece of mail addressed, "The Vice-President & Mrs. Kennedy." The error amused him, and he kept the envelope in order to humor others. No matter how minor the chore, the vice president went out of his way to assist the First Lady. During her renovation of the White House, she asked him to help retrieve a chandelier that had been a part of the original mansion. One of them hung in the vice president's office in the Capitol building. Johnson cheerfully returned it to the White House.

Johnson's demeanor toward women was in marked contrast to his behavior toward men. In the company of women he was gracious, warm, vulnerable, and charming. So Kennedy women in general were more attracted to him than Kennedy men. During his vice presidency, for example, Johnson developed a close relationship with President Kennedy's younger sister Jean, traveling with her during his trip to India in 1962. They exchanged numerous casual letters in which she referred to herself as "Baby Sister," and Johnson responded in kind. President Kennedy's wife, sisters, and sisters-in-law "were fairly sympathetic with Johnson for a long time," Harry McPherson recalled. "[W]omen *qua* women find him an attractive man. And I think that sustained him with the Kennedy women for some time."

Like many women, Jacqueline found Johnson charming and recalled being impressed with his "expansive personality." At White House parties she made it a point to dance with him and recalled that he was "very gallant, courtly." The day after her husband's funeral she wrote him a heartfelt letter which fondly recalled their relationship.

"[M]ost of all, Mr. President," she wrote, "thank you for the way you have always treated me . . . before, when Jack was alive, and now as President." She remembered the lack of "strain" in the relationships between the presidential and vice-presidential families. She complimented him for his political courage in accepting the vice presidency and for serving as "Jack's right arm." "But more than that," she affectionately wrote, "we were friends, all four of us. All you did for me as a friend and the happy times we had." "You give so much happiness," Johnson responded in a handwritten letter, "you deserve more. We think of you—pray for you and grieve with you. Would say more but you would have to read it and I fear want to answer it—don't."

The qualities associated with Jacqueline Kennedy were similar to those of important women in Johnson's life, especially his own mother, Rebekah, when she was young. Throughout his adult life he seemed to have an affinity for women who were intelligent, cultured, and wealthy. His affections, however, were seldom reciprocated. In high school and in college he was spurned by wealthy women because their parents disapproved of Lyndon's impoverished background. After college he dated Claudia Taylor, the daughter of a successful businessman. Proposing to her on their first date, he married her a short time later. Wealthy, cultured, a graduate of the University of Texas, Lady Bird was typical of the women in Johnson's life.

Some biographers have accused Johnson of courting women of wealth and status in order to further his own political ends. There was, however, one important exception. During the late 1930s and early 1940s, after his marriage to Lady Bird, Johnson had an intense romantic affair with Alice Glass. A young, attractive woman, she was the common-law wife of Charles Marsh, a wealthy but considerably older man who was instrumental to Johnson's career. Johnson's affair with Glass involved enormous political risk, prompting one friend to conclude that it demonstrated Johnson's capacity to love selflessly, to place another person above his own self-interest. Jacqueline Kennedy bore a remarkable resemblance to Glass. They were both wealthy, elegant, intelligent, witty, and independent. They also shared many of the same interests—horseback riding, fox hunting, art, fashion, and architectural design. Both women were also strikingly beautiful. Both were of similar age when they entered Johnson's life. Both were attracted to men of wealth and power. Jacqueline seemed to inspire an element of selflessness in Johnson as well.

Years after the assassination, Johnson remained moved by the widow. "It was a tragic thing to observe Mrs. Kennedy," he recalled. "Here was this delicate, beautiful lady, always elegant, always fastidious, always the fashion plate," now soiled with her husband's blood. As president he did much to comfort her. Aboard Air Force One, Jacqueline had accidentally referred to him as "Lyndon" and quickly apologized, promising not to make the error in protocol again. "Honey," Johnson replied, "I hope you'll call me that for the rest of your life." He rejected Secret Service advice that he immediately occupy the White House, noting it would be "presumptuous" of him to do so. He sent word to Jacqueline that she should take all the time she desired in leaving the White House. He did not move into the presidential mansion until two weeks later."

Although Johnson, like many Americans, had previously been awed by Jacqueline's public image, it was her courage during the crisis that most impressed him. "I have never seen anyone so brave," he noted on the night of the assassination. Four months later he was asked during a television interview to discuss the most memorable event of the Kennedy assassination. He recalled Jacqueline's "greatness, her gallantry, her graciousness, her courage, and it will always be a vivid memory, and I will always appreciate the strength that came to me from knowing her. . . ." According to Pierre Salinger, after the assassination Johnson often became "highly emotional" when reflecting on her generosity during his vice presidency. "She always made me feel at home," he told his press secretary.

Emotionally partial toward the former First Lady, Johnson worked with her to build a lasting tribute to her husband's memory. She had a "terrible fear then that [John Kennedy would] be forgotten," she acknowledged, and asked the new president's help in renaming Cape

Canaveral and the space center in Florida in his honor. Johnson met her request immediately, calling the governor of Florida within the hour and arranging for Cape Canaveral to be renamed Cape Kennedy. In late November 1963 he wrote to "Jackie," sending her a copy of the executive order establishing the Kennedy Space Center. "It is clear that once again you have hit with unerring taste on the right thing to do," he wrote, signing his letter, "Love, Lyndon."

On the same day she asked for the renaming of Cape Canaveral, Jacqueline also requested that Johnson approve the Pennsylvania Avenue Renovation Commission which had been initiated by President Kennedy. Her long-time concern for the historic preservation of the White House was also met, and her frequent thank-you notes expressed appreciation for Johnson's help in fostering her husband's memory. "It is so important to me that we build the finest memorial," she wrote, after his donation to the Kennedy Library, "so no one will ever forget him—and I shall always remember that you have helped the cause closest to my heart."

Some fifteen years later, Jacqueline still appreciated Johnson's kindness and generosity. She recalled that Lyndon and Lady Bird "were wonderful to me." "Lyndon Johnson was extraordinary," she remarked. "He did everything he could to be magnanimous, to be kind. It must have been very difficult for him." She was especially touched by his allowing her so much time to leave the White House, much more time, she felt, than was socially acceptable—"a great courtesy to a woman in distress." "The man had incredible warmth . . . ," she concluded. "I was really touched by the generosity of spirit . . . I always felt that about him."

The affection between Jacqueline Kennedy and Johnson was, however, mixed with opportunism on both sides. According to journalist Charles Bartlett, Jacqueline's relationship with Johnson entailed a degree of political gamesmanship. In the weeks after her husband's death she initiated various efforts to ensure that the public would fondly remember the Kennedy presidency. Johnson was part of that process. She told Bartlett that she had "always liked Johnson" and felt he was "very generous." But she also acknowledged that her brother-in-law Robert encouraged her "to put on my widow's weeds and go down to his office and ask for tremendous things . . . and he has come through on everything."

Johnson's response to Jacqueline suggested more than political self-interest. Some actions were highly personal. Jacqueline was touched that he would call her "quite a lot in the beginning." At Christmas his daughter delivered presents for John Jr. and Caroline Kennedy, and he remembered their birthdays with presents and cards. When Jacqueline moved to her own Georgetown home in early February, he attended a housewarming party. "The President came to that," Jacqueline recalled, "completely by surprise. He just went out of his way to do everything like that."

It is difficult, however, to determine where Johnson's compassion for Jacqueline ended and his own self-interest began. He had little choice but to respond to her requests, for he would have appeared callous had he refused her. Furthermore, he had a clear interest in constructing the Kennedy myth. By elevating John Kennedy's memory, he contributed to an emotional environment that, if properly tapped, could inspire public support for pending legislation which awaited passage by Congress."

Johnson's sympathy for Jacqueline never prevented him from understanding her value in smoothing his transition to power. Immediately after the assassination he was intent on identifying himself with her. Aboard Air Force One in Dallas, discussions about camera angles and lenses made the late president's aides fearful that Jacqueline would be a party to the swearing-in ceremony. She was similarly taken aback when she saw fresh clothes laid out for her in the cabin of the plane. Johnson insisted upon waiting for Jacqueline before taking the oath of office. "I want her here," he explained to Judge Sarah Hughes. He grew visibly impatient with her delay but, in the end, obtained a prized photograph. One of the most powerful images of that fateful day was the somber president with his hand on the Bible, flanked by his wife and Jacqueline.

Johnson's political intentions for Jacqueline became increasingly apparent during the transition year. Several weeks after the assassination, he raised with Salinger the possibility of naming her ambassador to France or Mexico. In February the *Washington Post* reported that she was being considered as a Special Adviser on the Arts. Also in February Johnson made his first public appearance with the widow since the funeral. After signing John Kennedy's prized tax reform bill, he went to her Georgetown home, presenting her with the ceremonial pens.

The 1964 campaign provided further opportunities to link himself with Jacqueline. In late September a Johnson aide noted the "tremendous advantages" of using her during the campaign's "final stages": "Mrs Kennedy's support and expression of her knowledge of the faith and confidence that JFK held for Mr. Johnson can be our homerun ball even if the going doesn't get rough." The suggestion was passed on to Johnson, but Jacqueline was never approached. Two weeks later the president made a surprise but well-publicized visit to her Manhattan apartment. The occasion won him an above-the-fold, front-page photograph in the *New York Times* of himself and Jacqueline smiling outside her apartment building. They did not meet again for two and a half years."

In general, Johnson had difficulty persuading Jacqueline to link herself publicly to his presidency. He invited her to every state dinner at the White House, but she refused. She also declined an invitation to attend a ceremony that dedicated a White House garden in her name. Returning to those familiar surroundings, she explained, would be too painful, but her absence nevertheless fueled press reports that she was distancing herself from the new president. Jacqueline believed that "the press did blow it up an awful lot" but that Johnson understood her reasons. She conceded, however, that she appeared inconsiderate. "I wouldn't blame [the Johnsons] at all," she noted, "if they thought sometimes, 'Listen, couldn't the girl just . . . .'" Indeed, there were occasions when it appeared that she deliberately intended to undercut Johnson. On election day she abstained from voting, later explaining that it was too emotional for her not to be able to vote for her husband. She was aware that her action generated adverse publicity and "hurt" Johnson.

Jacqueline genuinely liked Johnson and was grateful for his generous treatment, but emotional and political boundaries prevented her from returning affection to a man who had replaced her husband as president and who stood in the way of her brother-in-law's future ambitions. Salinger recalled that Johnson was sometimes "bitter" about his inability to woo Jacqueline.

"He couldn't understand, after all his kindnesses to her, why she wouldn't come down." Throughout his life he had expected personal and public gifts to be reciprocated through gratitude and affection. Observed Doris Kearns, who herself was the recipient of Johnson's favors: "It was as if the exchange somehow created a magic bond that linked the recipient to the giver, a bond compounded, in Johnson's mind, of dependence, interest, even love. . . ." Johnson perceived Jacqueline's behavior as a statement against himself. His generosity was expected to produce dividends, and her rejection reaffirmed his image as an interloper. He nevertheless continued to reach out. During the Christmas following his landslide victory in 1964, he wrote to her: "Time goes by too swiftly, my dear Jackie. But the day never goes by without some tremor of a memory or some edge of a feeling that reminds me of all that you and I went through together." Two weeks later she declined his personal invitation to attend his inauguration, breaking a long-standing tradition where wives of former presidents were in attendance. In later years Johnson continued to grant her generous favors while receiving little in return. Had she been a man, Johnson's personal bitterness and political resentment would likely have manifested itself more actively.

After John Kennedy's death, Robert became the head of the family and a recipient of much displaced affection. "You have inherited the leadership as spokesman for the Kennedy family and the Kennedy team,"

Dean Markham, an old and close football friend from Harvard, wrote Robert a week after the assassination. "It is not a mantle that can be set aside or passed on to another." Robert keenly understood that the initial effectiveness of the Johnson presidency was in part contingent on his approval. "We're important to Johnson," he told Richard Goodwin. "I'm the most important because my name happens to be Kennedy." He also knew that the semblance of unity was going to be difficult. Since the 1960 Democratic convention, the tension between Johnson and him had been relentless and personal. "They were very unalike, anyway," Clark Clifford recalled. "I doubt under the best of circumstances they would have developed much of a friendship." "[T]heir temperaments," Jacqueline Kennedy noted, "were different."

John Kennedy's death altered the context of their rivalry; *President* Johnson was no longer vulnerable to the attorney general's authority. The man who once felt mistreated and threatened by Robert now had significant control over his abuser. But Johnson's authority over Kennedy was limited. Robert possessed formidable assets that were important, if not indispensable, to the president's ambitions in 1964. Johnson's only attempt to run for national office had ended in humiliation, and Robert had been vital in organizing his brother's victory. Furthermore, Johnson could not afford to alienate the Kennedy faction of the party. If he fired Robert or pressured him to resign, the Kennedy forces might regroup before the August convention and challenge the nomination. Johnson therefore considered it essential that he and Robert at least appear to be on amiable terms.

John Kennedy's death generated no sudden feelings of affection between the two rivals. "He skipped the grades where you learn the rules of life," Johnson remarked. "He never liked me, and that's nothing compared to what I think of him." Robert, meanwhile, viewed Johnson as a usurper and was irritated by the sight of him as president. When he met Air Force One at Andrews Air Force Base after its return from Dallas, he was determined that Johnson would not exploit the occasion. He swiftly boarded the plane, shuffled past the new president without acknowledging him, and proceeded to the cargo section. He and Jacqueline Kennedy then quickly departed from the back of the plane with the casket, preventing Johnson from appearing before television cameras with the widow.

Tensions increased the next day. Several Kennedy cabinet officials advised Johnson that, for the appearance of order and control, he should move into the Oval Office as soon as possible. Johnson was uncomfortable with the suggestion. He spent the first night working out of the vice president's office in the Executive Office Building. Acting as the chief liaison with the Kennedys, national security adviser McGeorge Bundy discussed with Kennedy the symbolic necessity for Johnson to occupy the White House offices. Robert became annoyed but agreed that Monday morning would be an appropriate time. Bundy wrote the president a memorandum detailing the arrangements, but Johnson never saw it.

On Saturday morning Johnson walked into the Oval Office and, according to Kennedy, informed the secretary that she was to "clear your things out of your office by [9:30] so my girls can come in." The incident, according to Robert, was one of "four or five matters" during Johnson's first week in office "which made me bitterer, unhappy at least, with Lyndon Johnson." Consequently, Kennedy was reluctant to attend Johnson's first cabinet meeting scheduled for the Saturday morning after the assassination. "I was rather fed up with him," he recalled, prompting Bundy to again intercede on Johnson's behalf.

Kennedy arrived at the meeting late. According to Agriculture Secretary Orville Freeman, his "countenance was cold and scornful." When he entered, several cabinet officials stood up, but Johnson remained seated. The attorney general's presence immediately shifted attention away from the president, and, as the meeting progressed, an unacknowledged strain became apparent. Kennedy grew bitter over pledges of support to Johnson. "What he wanted," Kennedy recalled, "is declarations of loyalty, fidelity from all of us." Johnson, meanwhile, was convinced that Robert was intentionally late in order to destroy the meeting's mood. "There was real bitterness in Lyndon's voice on this one," wrote one official.

During the next few days Johnson and Kennedy continued to bicker. Johnson wanted to make a plea for unity through a nationally televised address before Congress on Tuesday. John Kennedy's burial was set for Monday. Robert disapproved. "I thought we should just wait one day," he recalled, "—at least one day after the funeral." Bundy argued on Johnson's behalf, much to Robert's irritation. "Why do you ask me about it?" he snapped at Bundy. Johnson delivered the address on Wednesday.

Johnson pursued a variety of strategies to win Robert's favor. In late November he tried to explain the incidents aboard Air Force One and to clarify his move into the Oval Office. "People around you are saying things about me," Johnson told him. "You can't let your people talk about me and I won't talk about you and I need you more [than your brother did]." Robert gave the president little encouragement, prompting him to rely on Kennedy's aides as a conduit. Kennedy heard from them that Johnson "thought I hated him, and what he could do to get me to like him, and why did I dislike him . . . and whether he should have me over for a drink or have some conversation with me." The president later sent a message through Arthur Schlesinger: "[I]n effect, that President Johnson loves you, wants to be friends with you, that the door at the White House is always open to you." "Your brother would have been very proud of the strength you have shown," Johnson wrote Kennedy on New Year's Day. "As the New Year begins, I resolve to do my best to fulfill his trust in me. I will need your counsel and support."

Kennedy remained with the administration due less to Johnson's pleas than his own political sagacity. Markham had warned that, if he resigned, his decision could "boomerang": "Public sentiment will be on his side, and the feeling will be that he tried to cooperate and work with you, but you didn't want to." Kennedy might have resigned in such a fashion as to gain public understanding. He could have cited overwhelming grief and his inability to transfer loyalties. Instead he remained despite his displeasure, viewing himself as a link between his brother's legacy and Johnson's policies. The emotional difficulty of the task, however, heightened ill feelings. It was, Robert recalled, a "difficult time between the two of us." Johnson was "able to eat people up," and a working relationship with him remained "difficult unless you want to 'kiss his behind' all the time." He was particularly irked by perceived slights to his dead brother and contended that the new president was not properly attributing his legislative achievements to John's earlier efforts."

Johnson's aides were keenly aware of Kennedy's restlessness. Eric Goldman observed that Kennedy "walked through the White House halls, his manner nervous, staring straight ahead, so indrawn he sometimes neglected to say hello to men he knew well." His emotional strain was punctuated by angry outbursts. Disturbed by newspaper reports about his unhappy relationship with Johnson, he verbally accosted Jack Valenti: "I don't appreciate the leaks coming from the White House and from you. I suggest you cut it out." Valenti was "stunned" by the accusation

Johnson's patience with Kennedy was limited. Once, Kennedy complained that his brother would have handled a particular situation differently. "President Kennedy is no longer President," Johnson tersely reminded him. He further alienated Robert through an imprudent conversation with Pierre Salinger. Discussing Texas folklore, he noted the myth that cross-eyed people in general were punished by God for being bad. Elaborating on the notion of "divine retribution," he then expounded that John Kennedy may have been murdered in connection with his involvement in the Trujillo and Diem assassinations. Salinger relayed the conversation to Kennedy. According to Schlesinger, the remark "made the gulf [between Johnson and Kennedy] ultimately impassable . . . ."

Throughout the winter and spring of 1964 Johnson was successful in maintaining a public semblance of a united front. But his callous slip-ups showed that the task of deferring to Robert was personally troublesome. The "aura of Kennedy" was important to Johnson, but it could not compensate for his deep-seated hostility toward the man who had tried to dump him from the 1960 presidential ticket. In aligning himself with the "heir apparent," Johnson did more than merely place himself in a personal bind. Politically he was in the process of creating a dilemma which he would find increasingly difficult to remedy. By linking himself to Robert and thus paying homage to John Kennedy's memory, Johnson inadvertently contributed to a legacy that would ultimately serve Robert's interests more than his own. Lyndon Johnson was slowly becoming wedged between two Kennedys—one a reminder of an illusory past, the other promising the fulfillment of a mythical future.

The 1964 election offered Johnson a chance to establish independence from the "aura of Kennedy." "To achieve greatness," Stewart Alsop wrote in January 1964, "Johnson must first achieve election in his own right." If he could be elected without the aid of the Kennedys, his power would hinge less on the memories of his predecessor and more on his own distinct leadership. As the August Democratic convention neared, Robert Kennedy's future role in the administration became the subject of considerable speculation. Those who hoped for a Kennedy restoration looked toward Johnson to choose the attorney general as his running mate. Johnson's aides knew it would never happen. "I don't want to get elected because of the Kennedys," the president explained privately. "I want to get elected on my own. That's a perfectly normal feeling, isn't it?" Normal or not, his desire for legitimacy created a problem. He needed to move forward toward independence without alienating those who yearned to restore the past.

Johnson's dilemma was in part contingent on Robert Kennedy. Did he expect to be offered the vice presidency? Would he accept it? If he were not asked, would he try to prevent Johnson's nomination? Kennedy was becoming increasingly restless. In January he told reporters that he was committed to the administration only until the November election. In March he announced that he would resign before the next inauguration. Stories soon circulated about the formation of a "government-in-exile" composed of former New Frontiersmen. Its purpose was to complain about the unfairness of an abbreviated Kennedy presidency and to plan for remedying the situation. Stories of an impending challenge from Robert Kennedy contributed to Johnson's "razor-edge sensitivity" about the family. "To him, they were ever present and ever active," Eric Goldman recalled, "pestering everything he tried to do."

Although Johnson had pleaded with Kennedy to remain with the administration, he clearly did not wish Robert to exert real authority. The president did not see or speak with him during the entire month of December 1963. Kennedy rarely attended cabinet meetings, and Johnson seldom solicited his advice. Upon Kennedy's return from the Far East in January, for example, the president gave him only a cursory greeting. Robert withdrew further, believing correctly that Johnson was interested only in his symbolic value.

Johnson, meanwhile, was preoccupied by speculation about Kennedy's political intentions. "Every day, as soon as I opened the papers or turned on the television, there was something about Bobby Kennedy," he recalled. "There was some person or group talking about what a great Vice President he'd make." Some aides thought he was obsessed by the issue, so much so they labeled it the "Bobby Problem." Several Kennedy holdovers encouraged his fears by keeping Robert's plans ambiguous. "The pulling and tugging of the Kennedy partisans," Valenti recalled, "the tiptoeing around the subject that was the staff ballet in the West Wing, the grim, unsettling political climate it was creating, all these pushed and shoved against the daily schedule."

Interested in a spot on the ticket, Kennedy put pressure on Johnson. In February Paul Corbin, a party leader from Buffalo, New York, and a Democratic National Committee staffer, created a well-organized write-in campaign for Kennedy's vice-presidential nomination. The effort was intended to force Johnson's hand by demonstrating popular support for a Johnson-Kennedy ticket during the New Hampshire primary. Whether Corbin acted independently of Kennedy was speculative. At the time, however, many reporters were convinced that Corbin was following Kennedy's direction. Kennedy mildly disavowed Corbin's actions, but it came too late to halt campaign momentum and was not taken seriously by his close associates. "He's much closer now [to actively seeking the vice presidency]," *Newsweek* quoted one Kennedy confidant."

During an interview with the three major networks, Johnson denied being upset with Corbin's activities and considered Kennedy's renunciation "a good one." "I take his word," Johnson said, "that he has done nothing to encourage those efforts, and all of this stuff that you read about is newspaper talk." Privately, however, Johnson was irate. Meeting with Kennedy, he demanded that Corbin leave New Hampshire and resign from the DNC. Kennedy pleaded innocence and assured him of Corbin's upright intentions. "He was loyal to President Kennedy," Robert argued. "He'll be loyal to you." "I know who he's loyal to," Johnson replied. "Get him out of there." Kennedy recalled being taken aback by Johnson's response. It was "a bitter, mean conversation. The meanest tone that I heard anybody take. . . . I said . . . I don't want to have that kind of conversation with you." After the meeting Johnson called Kennedy, informing him that Corbin had been fired from the DNC. "I'll tell you one thing," Kennedy responded to an aide, "this relationship can't last much longer."

The Corbin episode was one of several incidents in which Kennedy was suspected of "floating trial balloons" about his political future. During the month before the convention, Ben Bradlee, the Washington bureau chief for *Newsweek* and a close friend of the late president, spent sixteen hours one day with Robert while he traveled around the country. His subsequent article on July 6 was a virtual advertisement for a Johnson-Kennedy ticket. Bradlee prefaced his interview by noting politically influential people who "argue that the so-called Kennedy cult is part of the new American fabric and electorate," and that Robert was not only qualified for the vice presidency but a logical choice. Kennedy, meanwhile, implied that Johnson had somehow mismanaged his brother's legacy. "I don't want any of that to die," he told Bradlee. "People are still looking for all that idealism." He acknowledged that he had become a "symbol" of the past and was looking for some way to "keep all that alive." Kennedy speculated about the advantage to the party of his presence on the ticket, convincing Bradlee that he was seeking some means to "satisfy his deep—almost religious—desire" to fulfill the Kennedy legacy. "Kennedy himself obviously wants the [vice presidency]," Bradlee concluded, "but not without reservations and not to the exclusion of other jobs."

Kennedy's activity during the remainder of July generated still more speculation. During his four-day visit to Poland he was greeted by large, emotional crowds, receiving wide coverage in the press and reminding the American people of the late president's popular visits to Europe. In West Berlin he repeated the famous "Ich bin ein Berliner" declaration that John had made in 1963. "I am not a candidate for the Vice Presidency," he told students at Warsaw University, "but if you were in America and could vote for me, I would be." Kenneth O'Donnell later boasted that Kennedy's European tour "added to Johnson's anxieties and deepened his suspicions of Bobby's intentions."

White House aides monitored Kennedy's efforts. After Marguerite Higgins published a piece noting Horace Busby's opinions on the vice-presidential nomination, Busby wrote Walter Jenkins to assure that he had not talked to Higgins and advised that others avoid her. Busby characterized her as "a No. 1 Bobby fan" who "seemingly has some sources close to us." In late July a memorandum of unknown origin was sent to Johnson detailing Kennedy's recent visit to Chicago. Its author had it on good authority that Mayor Richard Daley favored Kennedy for vice president but would not push the matter if Johnson did not want him. Johnson was warned that because of Daley's close personal relationship with Kennedy, they were likely to be sharing information."

Of special interest to Johnson was Robert's scheduled Atlanta appearance at the convention. A film tribute to John Kennedy and a speech by Robert were planned for the first day of the convention, before the nomination of the vice president. According to Clark Clifford, Johnson was "afraid" that Robert "might very well stampede the convention and end up being . . . the vice presidential nominee." The White House therefore gave orders to Wolper Productions that no pictures of Robert should appear in the film. The final edited version contained only two obscure images of Robert. Johnson then met with the convention's arrangements committee and convinced its members to reschedule the tribute. The film and Robert's tribute were moved to the end of the convention, the day *after* the vice presidential nominee would be chosen. Officially the White House explained that Johnson did not wish to begin the convention on such a dark note.

Johnson also tried to alter the vice presidential selection process. In mid-April Senator Scott Lucas of Illinois convinced all nine county Democratic chairmen from his downstate congressional districts to sign a pledge giving Johnson a "free choice" in picking his vice-presidential running mate. Lucas was acting with the knowledge of Johnson's political associate and friend Cliff Carter, who informed the president of the effort. When Carter sent the pledge to other delegates in New Jersey, however, they balked, arguing that a blank check would demean the entire convention process. The ploy was subsequently abandoned.

Johnson discussed with his aides a number of alternative nominees who would satisfy the Kennedy faction of the party without blatantly overshadowing his presidency. He considered nominating a Catholic intellectual for the ticket, such as Minnesota Senator Eugene McCarthy. Kennedy's brother-in-law Sargent Shriver, who was Catholic and currently the director of the War on Poverty, was also discussed. "But in another way," Bill Moyers recalled, "Shriver was not acceptable, and that was *because* he was a member of the family. The message that filtered through from the family was that if you are going to take a Kennedy, it's got to be a *real* Kennedy, which Shriver isn't." Moreover, the choice of Shriver was too obvious a ploy to appease the Kennedys. Johnson would have been making the public concession he was trying to avoid.

By late July Johnson sensed that he was losing control of events when, among other things, Nancy Dickerson filed an alarming story.

Dickerson reported for NBC radio a meeting of Kennedy personnel at Hyannis Port and cited "rumors" that Robert and Jacqueline Kennedy had discussed plans to attend the Democratic convention; they anticipated an outpouring of emotion which, they felt, could be harnessed on Robert's behalf to secure the vice presidency. Jacqueline's desire to "help" her brother-in-law upset Johnson. After the broadcast, Lady Bird's press secretary, Liz Carpenter, called Dickerson to obtain a transcript of her report. Upon reading it, Johnson allegedly remarked, "If Nancy says such a thing on the air, then Jackie and Bobby really are behind the build-up."

Marguerite Higgins was one of several journalists who reported that Dickerson's information was responsible for prompting Johnson to make a public statement about Kennedy's vice-presidential chances. In a memorandum to Johnson, Busby heightened the conspiratorial nature of events by alleging that Higgins had been "sold" the story by the Kennedy faction. He had heard through another reporter that she was "the victim of someone trying to foster an image of bad blood between the Johnsons and Mrs. Kennedy." Busby informed Johnson that "obviously it was in the interest of the Kennedys to cultivate her and they have done so."

In reality, Dickerson's story merely hastened Johnson's decision. Johnson already had numerous objections to nominating Kennedy. Reminiscent of his criticism of John Kennedy four years earlier, he told his aides that a man who might be president should have "a little gray in his hair." Robert neither understood the mechanisms of Congress nor appreciated that the United States was "a big place, with lots of different kinds of people and different thoughts and interests, who are not brought together by playing the game of royal family." A Harris poll revealed that 33 percent of the Southern Democrats would bolt the ticket if Kennedy were chosen. Once the Republicans nominated Barry Goldwater in July, his extremism virtually assured Johnson a victory in November. "Look't here," he told his brother Sam. "I don't need that little runt to win. I can take anybody I damn please."

The real motive behind Johnson's decision was not lost on those involved. Valenti knew that Johnson removed Robert to escape the "looming shadow of the Kennedys" which threatened to "engulf him and probably strangle him." Even Kennedy knew that Johnson's decision rested more on who he was than on whom he would alienate. "Actually," he told *Newsweek*, "I should think I'd be the last man in the world he would want [as vice president] . . . because my name is Kennedy, because he wants a Johnson Administration with no Kennedys in it, because we travel different paths. . . . " "I think he's hysterical," Robert added privately, "about how he's going to try to avoid having me."

In later years, after retiring from politics, Johnson discussed with Kearns the decision to "dump" Kennedy. He described powerful feelings that had haunted him at the time but that he never dared to confess publicly. "Somehow it just didn't seem fair," he said:

> I'd given three years of loyal service to Jack Kennedy. During all that time I'd willingly stayed in the background; I knew that it was *his* Presidency, not mine. If I disagreed with him, I did it in private, not in public. And then Kennedy was killed and I became the custodian of his will. I became President. But none of this seemed to register with Bobby Kennedy, who acted like *he* was the custodian of the Kennedy dream, some kind of rightful heir to the throne. It just didn't seem fair. I'd waited for my turn. Bobby should've waited for his. But he and the Kennedy people wanted it now. A tidal wave of letters and memos about how great a Vice President Bobby would be swept over me. But no matter what, I simply couldn't let it happen. With Bobby on the ticket, I'd never know if I could be elected on my own.

Johnson's recollection was revealing. There was some hint of political revenge; he was going to do to Robert in 1964 what Robert wanted to do to him at the 1960 convention. More important, he revealed a paradox that plagued his thinking for the next four years. On the one hand, he had to legitimize his power "no matter what." Otherwise he would never know if he was truly worthy without Kennedy. Yet he was binding himself to the past through John by reaffirming his rights to the Kennedy legacy. As the "custodian of [John Kennedy's] will," Johnson implied that he, not Robert, was the dream-keeper and the "rightful heir to the throne."

Determined to put an end to the mounting rumors, Johnson arranged for a "summit" between himself and Kennedy at the White House on July 29. Kennedy met with O'Brien before seeing the president and was fully aware of the meeting's purpose. "He wanted the vice-presidential nomination," O'Brien recalled, "but we both realized there wasn't much chance that he'd get Johnson's support. Johnson didn't need him, and he didn't want him." Johnson, however, was reluctant to break completely with the past.

Before the meeting Clark Clifford prepared for the president a memorandum detailing five points Johnson wanted conveyed to Kennedy about his role in the upcoming campaign. Titled "The President's Campaign Objectives," it sought to mask Johnson's animosity with carefully worded flattery and compensation. The first point noted the president's desire to "win a victory as clear and sweeping as possible, in vindication of the Administration of President Kennedy and President Johnson." Johnson acknowledged that he wanted to justify his own achievements. But a victory was also "the most important service he can give to the memory of the man who put him on the ticket. Everything the President does will be done in the light of this overreaching purpose."

The second point noted that the Democratic party had many people well qualified to serve as vice president, but it was necessary to choose someone in sharp contrast to William Miller, the Republican party's vice-presidential nominee. The third point noted that, though Kennedy was qualified, Goldwater's nomination and the need to appeal to the South eliminated him as a potential nominee. Johnson wanted Kennedy's help nonetheless. Three reasons were offered:

> a. Only his help can sustain the full effectiveness of the original Kennedy/Johnson partnership.
>
> b. The Attorney General's support will be decisive with very large numbers of American Catholics, and with the younger people of all faiths too.
>
> c. The Attorney General has an unequaled talent for the management of a campaign.

The fourth point of the memorandum stated that the "best possible means" of achieving these goals was for Kennedy "to be the campaign chairman, and the President would like to draft him for this service." The final point noted that, after the election, Johnson would like Kennedy to "accept a most senior post in the new Administration." Cloaking his rejection of Robert in terms of political expediency and pragmatism, Johnson implied that Kennedy's presence on the 1964 ticket might hinder the achievement of his brother's goals.

In anticipation of the "summit," Johnson had a written text prepared which he then read to Kennedy. There were discrepancies between the information contained in Clifford's memorandum and Johnson's three-and-a-half-page statement. Like the memorandum, the text outlined the political conditions leading to his decision and underscored his reasons for eliminating Kennedy. After much consideration, he had concluded that it was "inadvisable" for Kennedy to be his running mate. The "decisive factor" was Goldwater's nomination and its regional implications. The statement reiterated Johnson's responsibility to the Kennedy legacy: "I have an obligation to lead the Democratic Party to victory in this election and to carry out the program started by President Kennedy and continued by me. I must use the best judgment 1 have . . . in making decisions of this kind."

Unlike Clifford's memorandum, the prepared statement was vague about Robert's future role in the administration. He was told that he had a "promising future" and reminded that his distinguished name was "associated with the highest ideals in American public service." Johnson hoped that Robert, after the election, would accept "important governmental assignments and missions," or replace Adlai Stevenson as United States Ambassador to the United Nations. Kennedy was also asked obliquely to "help" during the campaign. The text concluded by noting that their mutual honesty about the matter "constitutes the basis upon which you and I can build a lasting relationship that would prove valuable to both of us and to our country."

Johnson had intended his three-and-a-half-page text to be the "official" record of his meeting. Mindful of the occasion's historical implications, he sent a copy to Valenti with a note reading, "Give these to Vicky. They're very important for my memoirs." The differences between the memorandum and subsequent text were subtle but important. Absent from the text was Johnson's request that Kennedy manage his campaign. The offer of "a most senior post in the new Administration" was also missing. Johnson's proposal of the UN ambassadorship was bogus, since the job was generally perfunctory and would have served to distance him from his rival. Sometime between the preparation of the memorandum and the writing of the text, Johnson had become unwilling officially to acknowledge his need for Kennedy.

Kennedy's own account of the meeting depicted Johnson as more conciliatory and deferential. He noted that after Johnson read his statement, they engaged in a forty-minute conversation. Johnson made compromises and promises absent from his written statement. According to Kennedy, Johnson claimed that he "thought that I had high qualifications to be President; that he wanted to work toward that end." After flattering Kennedy, he assured him that "if I wished to go around the country and speak he would never be jealous of me. . . ." Further, he urged Kennedy to continue serving as attorney general or to assume another post in the administration if he desired. He lauded Kennedy's staff in the Justice Department and expressed admiration for the remaining New Frontiersmen. "He said he really could not count on his own people," Robert recalled. Johnson then asked him to run his campaign. Kennedy rejected the offer, arguing that he was "reluctant" to serve as both attorney general and as campaign manager. The remainder of the conversation centered on Johnson's continued efforts to distance himself from the Bobby Baker scandal which was gaining increasing attention that summer.

Johnson wanted Kennedy's help, but he did not want anyone to know it. Consequently, he sought to mislead others about the content of their conversation. After his meeting with Kennedy he lied to Kenneth O'Donnell, claiming that Robert had asked *him* for the job as campaign manager. It took greater effort to fool the public. On Johnson's advice, McGeorge Bundy spoke with Kennedy and suggested that Kennedy leak to the press that he was pulling out of the race for the vice presidency. Kennedy angrily opposed the idea, arguing that it would be presumptuous of him to withdraw his candidacy when he had never declared it. Robert's aides condemned Bundy as "a Machiavellian turncoat." After Johnson consulted with his eldest and most experienced aides, Clark Clifford, Abraham Fortas, and James Rowe, he devised a strategy intended to obscure the fact that the president had arranged the meeting specifically to remove Kennedy from contention.

Speaking to reporters on July 30, Johnson said it was "inadvisable" for cabinet-level officials or those who frequently participated in cabinet meetings to be considered as vice-presidential nominees; their important duties should not be distracted by politics. The decision eliminated not only the attorney general but also such less likely candidates as Robert McNamara, Adlai Stevenson, Dean Rusk, Sargent Shriver, and Orville Freeman. Years later, Johnson continued to insist that Kennedy was a victim of political circumstance. Kearns, who was instrumental in preparing his memoirs, noted that he persisted in reversing the order of events. According to Johnson, he had first decided to remove the entire cabinet from contention and then summoned Kennedy to explain his reasoning.

Johnson's aides were divided about the effectiveness of the smokescreen. The news media were not fooled. The *New York Times* noted that Johnson and Kennedy had "never been on close terms" and cited party leaders who felt that the decision showed that Johnson wanted to win on his own, "with no hint of having relied upon the Kennedy name to put him into office." *Newsweek* described Johnson's maneuver as a "coldly calculated decision." "It was still a Johnson-Kennedy party until yesterday," one aide told the magazine. "You even had some Kennedy people going along on the basis that if anything happened to Johnson, they'd have a Kennedy as President. Now Johnson has cleared the air."

The public posturing may have appeared contrived, but Johnson was relieved of Kennedy. "Now that damn albatross is off my neck," Johnson told an aide. Goldman recalled that he acted like a man who had "exorcised his devil." His delight became reckless. The day after his announcement, he gloated during a White House lunch with Ed Folliard of the *Washington Post*, Tom Wicker of the *New York Times*, and Douglas Kiker of the *New York Herald-Tribune*. Recounting the "summit," Johnson said he watched Kennedy "like a hawk watching chickens." As he told him that he would not be the nominee, Robert's "face changed, and he started to swallow. He looked sick. His Adam's apple bounded up and down like a yo-yo." Johnson mimicked Kennedy's "funny voice" and re-enacted Kennedy's gulp "like a fat fish."

Johnson's insulting account soon circulated around Washington. Angered by the breach of confidence, Kennedy confronted Johnson, who denied having spoken with *anyone* about their meeting. Kennedy was incredulous, and Johnson vainly promised to check his calendar. "He tells so many lies," Kennedy remarked about a week later, "that he convinces himself after a while he's telling the truth. He just doesn't recognize truth from falsehood." Johnson's lie suggested that the Kennedy albatross had been lightened, not removed.

Consistent with Johnson's chronic insecurities, no degree of precaution was adequate in his struggle to deny Robert Kennedy the vice-presidential nomination. Aware of the unpredictability of conventions, he soon worried that his personal elimination of Kennedy did not necessarily guarantee that the delegates would not nominate him against the president's wishes. So Johnson worked to cement the decision by further orchestrating people and events.

Two Kennedy holdovers, Lawrence O'Brien and Kenneth O'Donnell, had been instrumental in John Kennedy's political campaigns since 1952. Johnson had convinced them to remain with his administration, hoping to use their connections with big-city political leaders during the fall campaign. At the same time he worried that they might engineer Robert's nomination for the vice presidency. Consequently, during the convention Johnson literally isolated the two aides, placing them in a remote motel on the outskirts of Atlantic City. He also used the Federal Bureau of Investigation to monitor Kennedy's activities. Since coming into office Johnson had developed an amiable relationship with FBI Director J. Edgar Hoover, who sent the new president "material" on Robert and replaced an FBI liaison close to the Kennedys with Cartha DeLoach, an old friend of Johnson's. Several weeks before the convention Johnson ordered DeLoach and a team of thirty FBI officials to Atlantic City, ostensibly to collect information about possible civil disruptions. According to William Sullivan, a former director of the FBI, their actual purpose was to gather data useful to the president, "particularly in bottling up Robert Kennedy." DeLoach instructed agents not to disclose the existence of the FBI team to the Secret Service or the attorney general. They eventually sent to the White House forty-four pages of information acquired through the use of informants, wiretaps, and the infiltration of political groups. The amount of material specifically pertaining to Kennedy is unknown.

Also of concern in terms of circumventing Robert Kennedy was the timing of the release of the Warren Commission Report. After the murder of Lee Harvey Oswald, Johnson had issued an executive order creating a special commission headed by Chief Justice Earl Warren to investigate the assassination of John Kennedy. He hoped that the report would quiet rumors that Kennedy had been the victim of a conspiracy. One far-flung theory speculated that Johnson had the president killed in order to prevent the investigation of Bobby Baker. Johnson wanted the commission to issue its report before the Democratic convention. As long as the public entertained the remote possibility that he had somehow engineered the assassination, Robert stood to benefit. McGeorge Bundy met with the commission's chief counsel, who agreed to issue the report about two weeks before the convention. Bundy did not want it published too close to the convention because it would be "bad for President Kennedy's memory, bad for the administration, and confusing to the country." It soon became clear, however, that the commission could not finish its report by the first week in August and thus meet Johnson's needs. He decided to delay its publication until September 24, one month after the convention.

Relatively confident that Robert could not ambush the convention, Johnson next worried that the attorney general's mere appearance there might overshadow his own presence and triumph. On the one hand, Johnson wanted to exploit the emotional power that his relationship with John Kennedy had accorded him. But he also wanted the convention to be a celebration of himself. He therefore undertook the delicate task of paying homage to the Kennedy past while building his own distinct image. He specified that two forty-foot portraits of himself flank the convention platform. He planned for delegates to sing renditions of "Hello Lyndon" to the tune of "Hello Dolly." Initially he insisted that the White House approve all convention speeches. The White House then sought ways to minimize John Kennedy's "presence" without appearing callous. In the weeks preceding the convention, for example, Douglass Cater, a special assistant to the president, expressed alarm that Johnson might be upstaged by the film tribute to President Kennedy. He had previewed the film and considered it "well done" but was disturbed by its closing "tear-jerker" music from the Broadway show *Camelot*. Cater acknowledged that the song was "highly schmaltzy" but nonetheless predicted "the delegates will be left weeping." He had "mixed feelings about its propriety at a convention." "It would be less dramatic but probably less risky to show that film sequence without the music," Cater wrote. "I have a vague unrest about engaging in such an emotional bender just before the Johnson acceptance speech."

To remedy the situation, Cater suggested that Johnson himself consider giving the tribute to John Kennedy. An alternative solution would be to insert a filmed tribute by the president at the end of the Kennedy film and "make it known that you are viewing the proceedings from your convention suite." The possibility of having Johnson himself pay tribute to Kennedy alarmed other aides. "If the President appears for the memorial before accepting the nomination," James Rowe warned, "it will make his speech 'one hell of an anti-climax.'" Later it was decided that Robert Kennedy would give the tribute to his brother. But the potential impact of his appearance demanded caution. The White House resisted pressure from the television networks that they reschedule the event earlier in the week when audience interest would be highest."

Johnson and his staff made additional scheduling adjustments to prevent the tribute from overshadowing the acceptance speech. A lull was created between the Kennedy tribute and Johnson's speech in order to allow the delegates ample opportunity to regain their composure. Plans were arranged so that Robert would speak on behalf of his late brother and introduce the film tribute. Next there would be memorial tributes to Eleanor Roosevelt and Sam Rayburn, followed by Hubert Humphrey's acceptance speech for the vice-presidential nomination. The elapsed time between the Kennedy tribute and Johnson's speech was approximately an hour and a half.

Despite safeguards against Robert Kennedy's nomination, despite efforts to minimize John Kennedy's shadow, and despite enjoying enormous popularity, Johnson remained pessimistic. In a manner similar to his earlier campaign behavior, he threatened to quit rather than face a strong challenger. "If they try to push Bobby Kennedy down my throat for Vice President," he warned, "I'll tell them to nominate him for the *presidency* and leave me out of it." Just days before the convention he told aides that he was going to withdraw his nomination. "Nobody, he said, really wanted him," George Reedy recalled. "The heart and soul of the Democratic Party was with Bobby Kennedy." There was "something terribly convincing" about Johnson's concerns. Reedy pleaded with Johnson to reconsider, raising the threat of a Goldwater victory. "[H]e said that was preferable to four years of internecine warfare between himself and Bobby Kennedy.

Those who best knew Johnson understood what was at the heart of his depression. By rejecting the convention before it could reject him, Johnson sought to protect his self-esteem. "He wasn't just playing games with his intimates," his long-time friend Abraham Fortas recalled. "He was playing games with himself, too." Fortas speculated about Johnson's thought process: "This is not the right thing to do. Maybe I won't do it after all. Maybe something will happen; the convention won't really want me, and even if they do want me, I shouldn't have it, shouldn't do it." Lady Bird Johnson, who had often witnessed her husband's erratic moods, wrote a reassuring letter:

> *Beloved—*
> You are as brave a man as Harry Truman—or FDR—or Lincoln. You can go on to find some peace, some achievement amidst all the pain. You have been strong, patient, determined beyond any words of mine to express. I honor you for it. So does most of the country.
>
> To step out now would be *wrong* for your country, and I can see nothing but a lonely wasteland for your future. Your friends would be frozen in embarrassed silence and your enemies jeering.
>
> I am not afraid of *Time* or lies or losing money or defeat.
>
> In the final analysis I can't carry any of the burdens you talked of—so I know it's only *your* choice. But I know you are as brave as any of the thirty-five [previous presidents].
>
> I love you always.
> *Bird*

Lady Bird suspected that her husband was reluctant to run for the presidency because "he knew how hard it was going to be and that it was going to get worse." She could not "describe his feelings and why," but she sensed he was worried "how some of those lowering clouds that were on the horizon might rise up to storm proportions."

Johnson went on to capture the Democratic nomination. Hubert Humphrey was nominated as his vice president, partially appeasing Kennedy supporters. Until the last day of the convention, John Kennedy's "presence" was generally underplayed. A portrait of the late president hung above the podium, along with Truman's and Roosevelt's, and a banner proclaiming "Let Us Continue." Occasionally a speaker in the hall would recall John Kennedy, bringing a roar of approval from the delegates. Outside the convention hall, however, a wellspring of emotion seemed anxious to erupt. Kennedy souvenirs saturated the commercial districts. Memorabilia from the Kennedy Library were displayed on the boardwalk, and a bronze bust of the late president with a flame in front of it was on exhibit in Kennedy Plaza, across the boardwalk from the entrance to the convention hall. All week long, when Robert and Jacqueline Kennedy entered and exited hotels in Atlantic City, they attracted huge and enthusiastic crowds.

The tone of the convention shifted markedly on the night of the Kennedy tribute. Although the attorney general was scheduled to give a two-minute introduction to the film, he was greeted by a sixteen-minute ovation. The meaning of the applause was "for each individual to assess or deduce on his own," Chet Huntley reported for NBC. "And questions arise as [to whether] the ovation is on behalf of the Attorney General himself . . . a living symbol of the late President. . . . Did the convention want him as vice-president?" Regardless, the reception surprised reporters and television audiences alike.

Throughout the ovation Robert smiled and looked teary-eyed. Attired in a familiar black suit and tie which he had worn almost continuously since the assassination, he spoke humbly and tentatively. His speech had been carefully crafted and edited by numerous Kennedy personnel and friendly journalists. On the advice of Theodore Sorensen, he had memorized the speech and now spoke informally and quietly into the microphone. His first mention of John Kennedy brought expected cheers from the delegates. He recalled his brother's dedication to help the mentally ill, the aged, and various minorities. The Cuban missile crisis and Test Ban Treaty were cited as part of John's foreign policy legacy. The Democratic party and the people were praised as the source of his brother's strength. The undertone of the speech made clear that Robert would do his best to fulfill John's dreams. Meanwhile, the delegates should transfer their commitment and energy to Johnson and Humphrey. Unknown to the audience, Robert had twice deleted from his final text the assertion that "President Kennedy would feel his life was worthwhile . . . if the same effort and support that was given to him is given to President Johnson and Senator Humphrey . . . ." Instead he inserted a quote from *Romeo and Juliet* given to him by Jacqueline.

> [W]hen he shall die,
> Take him and cut him out in little stars,
> And he will make the face of heaven so fine
> That all the world will be in love with night,
> And pay no worship to the garish sun.

Criticism emerged over the implication of the quote; John Kennedy's presence in the heavens would always be more brilliant than the common appearance of the "garish" Johnson. Kennedy's defenders claimed that it was not intended to disparage Johnson. Only his hypersensitivity, they argued, would allow for such a negative interpretation.

Following Robert's speech, delegates were shown the twenty-minute Kennedy film, *A Thousand Days.* It contained intimate images of John Kennedy plucking a flower and playing with his son. The soundtrack of Richard Burton singing *Camelot* over pictures of Kennedy brought thousands of delegates to tears. The event caused some people to acknowledge Johnson's astuteness in rescheduling it after the vice president was selected.

Johnson did not attend the memorial tribute. Nor did he watch the film. According to his diary entry, he took a nap. Was he afraid to face the emotion of the moment? Aides contended that he simply did not wish to intrude on the occasion. Standing in for her husband, Lady Bird watched the film from the presidential box with Robert and Ethel

Kennedy. Johnson came to the box after the film, inspiring the crowd to sing another rendition of "Hello Lyndon." Robert and his wife tried moving toward the rear of the box. Johnson motioned them forward where they sat uncomfortably together in the front row. Sitting restlessly, Johnson watched the succeeding ceremonies and prepared for his acceptance speech—an address upstaged by John Kennedy's memory.

Johnson's speech had been crafted to balance homage to John Kennedy with his own identity. Aides had suggested that he mention his predecessor and possibly quote the late president. One suggested that he emphasize a "highly desirable" theme of sacrifice that underscored Kennedy's inaugural address. So Johnson called for the nation to "rededicate ourselves to keeping the golden torch of promise which John Fitzgerald Kennedy set aflame." Invoking Kennedy's name six times, he asked the nation not to rest "until we have written into law of the land all the suggestions that made up the John Fitzgerald Kennedy program. And then let us continue to supplement that program with the kinds of laws that he would have us write." As he strained to assert his independence, he found himself looking backwards.

The Holy Family
by Gore Vidal

His family ties to Jacqueline Kennedy (they shared a stepfather) didn't stand in the way of Gore Vidal's (born 1925) jaded view on the Kennedy phenomenon. This essay, which appeared in Esquire 1967, bears witness to his belief that Camelot was a fraud.

The Gospel according to Arthur, Paul, Pierre, and William and several minor apostles

From the beginning of the Republic, Americans have enjoyed accusing the first magistrate of kingly ambition. Sometimes seriously but more often derisively, the President is denounced as a would-be king, subverting the Constitution for personal ends. From General Washington to the present incumbent, the wielder of power has usually been regarded with suspicion, a disagreeable but not unhealthy state of affairs for both governor and governed. Few Presidents, however, have been accused of wanting to establish family dynasties, if only because most Presidents have found it impossible to select a successor of any sort, much less promote a relative. Each of the Adamses and the Harrisons reigned at an interval of not less than a political generation from the other, while the two Roosevelts were close neither in blood nor in politics. But now something new is happening in the Republic, and as the Chinese say, we are living "in interesting times."

In 1960, with the election of the thirty-fifth President, the famous ambition of Joseph P. Kennedy seemed at last fulfilled. He himself had come a long way from obscurity to great wealth and prominence; now his eldest surviving son, according to primogeniture, had gone the full distance and become President. It was a triumph for the patriarch. It was also a splendid moment for at least half the nation. What doubts one may have had about the Kennedys were obscured by the charm and intelligence of John F. Kennedy. He appeared to be beautifully on to himself; he was also on to us; there is even evidence that he was on to the family, too. As a result, there were few intellectuals in 1960 who were not beguiled by the spectacle of a President who seemed always to be standing at a certain remove from himself, watching with amusement his own performance. He was an ironist in a profession where the prize usually goes to the apparent cornball. With such a man as chief of state, all things were possible. He would "get America moving again."

But then mysteriously the thing went wrong. Despite fine rhetoric and wise commentary, despite the glamour of his presence, we did not move, and if historians are correct when they tell us that Presidents are "made" in their first eighteen months in office, then one can assume that the Kennedy administration would never have fulfilled our hopes; much less his own. Kennedy was of course ill-fated from the beginning. The Bay of Pigs used up much of his credit in the bank of public opinion, while his attempts at social legislation were resolutely blocked by a more than usually obstructive Congress. In foreign affairs he was overwhelmed by the masterful Khrushchev and not until the Cuban missile crisis did he achieve tactical parity with that sly gambler. His administration's one achievement was the test-ban treaty, an encouraging footnote to the cold war.

Yet today Kennedy dead has infinitely more force than Kennedy living. Though his administration was not a success, he himself has become a world touchstone of political excellence. Part of this phenomenon is attributable to the race's need for heroes, even in deflationary times. But mostly the legend is the deliberate creation of the Kennedy family and its clients. Wanting to regain power, it is now necessary to show that once upon a time there was indeed a Camelot beside the Potomac, a golden age forever lost unless a second Kennedy should become the President. And so, to insure the restoration of that lovely time, the past must be transformed, dull facts transcended, and the dead hero extolled in films, through memorials, and in the pages of books.

The most notorious of the books has been William Manchester's *The Death of a President.* Hoping to stop Jim Bishop from writing one of his ghoulish *The Day They Shot* sagas, the Kennedys decided to "hire" Mr. Manchester to write their version of what happened at Dallas. Unfortunately, they have never understood that treason is the natural business of clerks. Mr. Manchester's use of Mrs. Kennedy's taped recollections did not please the family. The famous comedy of errors that ensued not only insured the book's success but also made current certain intimate details which the family preferred for the electorate not to know, such as the President's selection of Mrs. Kennedy's dress on that last day in order, as he put it, "to show up those cheap Texas broads," a remark not calculated to give pleasure to the clients of Neiman-Marcus. Also, the family's irrational dislike of President Johnson came through all too plainly, creating an unexpected amount of sympathy for that least sympathetic of magistrates. Aware of what was at stake, Mrs. Kennedy tried to alter a book which neither she nor her brothers-in-law had read. Not since Mary Todd Lincoln has a President's widow been so fiercely engaged with legend if not history.

But then, legend making is necessary to the Kennedy future. As a result, most of the recent books about the late President are not so much political in approach as religious. There is the ritual beginning of the book which is the end: the death at Dallas. Then the witness goes back in time to the moment when he first met the Kennedys. He finds them strenuous but fun. Along with riotous good times, there is the constant question: How are we to elect Jack President? This sort of talk was in the open after 1956, but as long ago as 1943, as he tells us in *The Pleasure of His Company,* Paul B. Fay, Jr., made a bet that one day Jack would be JFK.

From the beginning the godhead shone for those who had the eyes to see. The witness then gives us his synoptic version of the making of the President. Once again we visit cold Wisconsin and dangerous West Virginia (can a young Catholic war hero defeat a Protestant accused of being a draft dodger in a poor mining state where primary votes are bought and sold?). From triumph to triumph the hero proceeds to the convention at Los Angeles, where the god is recognized. The only shadow upon that perfect day is cast, significantly, by Lyndon B. Johnson. Like Lucifer he challenged the god at the convention, and was struck down only to be raised again as son of morning. The deal to make Johnson Vice-President still causes violent argument among the new theologians. Pierre Salinger in *With Kennedy* quotes JFK as observing glumly, "The whole story will never be known, and it's just as well that it won't be." Then the campaign itself. The great television debates (Quemoy and Matsu) in which Nixon's obvious lack of class, as classy Jack duly noted, did him in—barely. The narrowness of the electoral victory was swiftly erased by the splendor of the inaugural ("It all began in the cold": Arthur M. Schlesinger, Jr., *A Thousand Days*). From this point on, the thousand days unfold in familiar sequence and, though details differ from gospel to gospel, the story already possesses the quality of a passion play: disaster at Cuba One, triumph at Cuba Two; the eloquent speeches; the fine pageantry; and always the crowds and the glory, ending at Dallas.

With Lucifer now rampant upon the heights, the surviving Kennedys are again at work to regain the lost paradise, which means that books must be written not only about the new incarnation of the Kennedy godhead but the old. For it is the dead hero's magic that makes legitimate the family's pretensions. As an Osiris-Adonis-Christ figure, JFK is already the subject of a cult that may persist, through the machinery of publicity, long after all memory of his administration has been absorbed by the golden myth now being created in a thousand books to the single end of maintaining in power our extraordinary holy family.

The most recent batch of books about JFK, though hagiographies, at times cannot help but illuminate the three themes which dominate any telling of the sacred story: money, imagemaking, family. That is the trinity without which nothing. Mr. Salinger, the late President's press secretary, is necessarily concerned with the second theme, though he touches on the other two. Paul B. Fay, Jr., (a wartime buddy of JFK and Under Secretary of the Navy) is interesting on every count, and since he seems not to know what he is saying, his book is the least calculated and the most lifelike of the ones so far published. Other books at hand are Richard J. Whalen's *The Founding Father* (particularly good on money and family) and Evelyn Lincoln's *My Twelve Years with John F. Kennedy,* which in its simple way tells us a good deal about those who are drawn to the Kennedys.

While on the clerical staff of a Georgia Congressman, Mrs. Lincoln decided in 1952 that she wanted to work for "someone in Congress who seemed to have what it takes to be President"; after a careful canvass, she picked the Representative from the Massachusetts Eleventh District. Like the other witnesses under review, she never says *why* she wants to work for a future President; it is taken for granted that anyone would, an interesting commentary on all the witnesses from Schlesinger (whose *A Thousand Days* is the best political novel since *Coningsby*) to Theodore Sorensen's dour *Kennedy.* Needless to say, in all the books there is not only love and awe for the fallen hero who was, in most cases, the witness's single claim to public attention, but there are also a remarkable number of tributes to the holy family. From Jacqueline (Isis-Aphrodite-Madonna) to Bobby (Ares and perhaps Christ-to-be) the Kennedys appear at the very least as demigods, larger than life. Bobby's hard-working staff seldom complained, as Mr. Salinger put it, "because we all knew that Bob was working just a little harder than we were." For the same reason "we could accept without complaint [JFK's] brisling temper, his cold sarcasm, and his demands for always higher standards of excellence because we knew he was driving himself harder than he was driving us—despite great and persistent physical pain and personal tragedy." Mrs. Lincoln surprisingly finds the late President "humble"—doubtless since the popular wisdom requires all great men to be humble. She refers often to his "deep low voice" [*sic*], "his proud head held high, his eyes fixed firmly on the goals—sometimes seemingly impossible goals—he set for himself and all those around him." Mr. Schlesinger's moving threnody at the close of *his* gospel makes it plain that we will not see JFK's like again, at least not until the administration of Kennedy II.

Of the lot, only Mr. Fay seems not to be writing a book with an eye to holding office in the next Kennedy administration. He is garrulous and indiscreet (the Kennedys are still displeased with his memoirs even though thousands of words were cut from the manuscript on the narrow theological ground that since certain things he witnessed fail to enhance the image, they must be apocrypha). On the subject of the Kennedys and money, Mr. Fay tells a most revealing story. In December, 1959, the family was assembled at Palm Beach; someone mentioned money, "causing Mr. Kennedy to plunge in, fire blazing from his eyes. 'I don't know what is going to happen to this family when I die,' Mr. Kennedy said. 'There is no one in the entire family, except Joan and Teddy, who is living within their means. No one appears to have the slightest concern for how much they spend.' " The tirade ended with a Kennedy sister running from the room in tears, her extravagance condemned in open family session. Characteristically, Jack deflected the progenitor's wrath with the comment that the only "solution is to have Dad work harder." A story which contradicts, incidentally, Mr. Salinger's pious "Despite his great wealth and his generosity in contributing all of his salaries as Congressman, Senator and President to charities, the President was not a man to waste pennies."

But for all the founding father's grumbling, the children's attitude toward money—like so much else—is pretty much what he wanted it to be. It is now a familiar part of the sacred story of how Zeus made each of the nine Olympians individually wealthy, creating trust funds which now total some ten million dollars per god or goddess. Also at the disposal of the celestials is the great fortune itself, estimated at a hundred, two hundred, three hundred, or whatever hundred millions of dollars, administered from an office on Park Avenue, to which the

Kennedys send their bills, for we are told in *The Founding Father,* "the childhood habit of dependence persisted in adult life. As grown men and women the younger Kennedys still look to their father's staff of accountants to keep track of their expenditures and see to their personal finances." There are, of course, obvious limitations to not understanding the role of money in the lives of the majority. The late President was aware of this limitation and he was forever asking his working friends how much money they made. On occasion, he was at a disadvantage because he did not understand the trader's mentality. He missed the point to Khrushchev at Vienna and took offense at what, after all, was simply the boorishness of the marketplace. His father, an old hand in Hollywood, would have understood better the mogul's bluffing.

It will probably never be known how much money Joe Kennedy has spent for the political promotion of his sons. At the moment, an estimated million dollars a year is being spent on Bobby's behalf, and this sum can be matched year after year until 1972, and longer. Needless to say, the sons are sensitive to the charge that their elections are bought. As JFK said of his 1952 election to the Senate, "People say 'Kennedy bought the election. Kennedy could never have been elected if his father hadn't been a millionaire.' Well, it wasn't the Kennedy name and the Kennedy money that won that election. I beat Lodge because I hustled for three years," (quoted in *The Founding Father*). But of course without the Kennedy name and the Kennedy money, he would not even have been a contender. Not only was a vast amount of money spent for his election in the usual ways, but a great deal was spent in not so usual ways. For instance, according to Richard J. Whalen, right after the pro-Lodge *Boston Post* unexpectedly endorsed Jack Kennedy for the Senate, Joe Kennedy loaned the paper's publisher $500,000.

But the most expensive legitimate item in today's politics is the making of the image. Highly paid technicians are able to determine with alarming accuracy just what sort of characteristics the public desires at any given moment in a national figure, and with adroit handling a personable candidate can be made to seem whatever the Zeitgeist demands. The Kennedys are not of course responsible for applying to politics the techniques of advertising (the two have always gone hand in hand), but of contemporary politicians (the Rockefellers excepted) the Kennedys alone possess the money to maintain one of the most remarkable self-publicizing machines in the history of advertising, a machine which for a time had the resources of the Federal government at its disposal.

It is in describing the activities of a chief press officer at the White House that Mr. Salinger is most interesting. A talented image maker, he was responsible, among other things, for the televised press conferences in which the President was seen at his best, responding to simple questions with careful and often charming answers. That these press conferences were not very informative was hardly the fault of Mr. Salinger or the President. If it is true that the medium is the message and television is the coolest of all media and to be cool is desirable, then the televised thirty-fifth President was positively glacial in his effectiveness. He was a natural for this time and place, largely because of his obsession with the appearance of things. In fact, much of his political timidity was the result of a quite uncanny ability to sense how others would respond to what he said or did, and if he foresaw a negative response, he was apt to avoid action altogether. There were times, however, when his superb sense of occasion led him astray. In the course of a speech to the Cuban refugees in Miami, he was so overwhelmed by the drama of the situation that he practically launched on the spot a second invasion of that beleaguered island. Yet generally he was cool. He enjoyed the game of pleasing others, which is the actor's art.

He was also aware that vanity is perhaps the strongest of human emotions, particularly the closer one comes to the top of the slippery pole. Mrs. Kennedy once told me that the last thing Mrs. Eisenhower had done before leaving the White House was to hang a portrait of herself in the entrance hall. The first thing Mrs. Kennedy had done on moving in was to put the portrait in the basement, on aesthetic, not political grounds. Overhearing this, the President told an usher to restore the painting to its original place. "The Eisenhowers are coming to lunch tomorrow," he explained patiently to his wife, "and that's the first thing she'll look for." Mrs. Lincoln records that before the new Cabinet met, the President and Bobby were about to enter the Cabinet room when the President "said to his brother, 'Why don't you go through the other door?' The President waited until the Attorney General entered the Cabinet room from the hall door, and then he walked into the room from my office."

In its relaxed way Mr. Fay's book illuminates the actual man much better than the other books if only because he was a friend to the President, and not just an employee. He is particularly interesting on the early days when Jack could discuss openly the uses to which he was being put by his father's ambition. Early in 1945 the future President told Mr. Fay how much he envied Fay his postwar life in sunny California while "I'll be back here with Dad trying to parlay a lost PT boat and a bad back into a political advantage. I tell you, Dad is ready right now and can't understand why Johnny boy isn't 'all engines full ahead.'" Yet the exploitation of son by father had begun long before the war. In 1940 a thesis written by Jack at Harvard was published under the title *Why England Slept,* with a foreword by longtime, balding, family friend Henry Luce. The book became a best seller and (Richard J. Whalen tells us) as Joe wrote at the time in a letter to his son, "You would be surprised how a book that really makes the grade with high-class people stands you in good stead for years to come."

Joe was right of course and bookmaking is now an important part of the holy family's home industry. As Mrs. Lincoln observed, when JFK's collection of political sketches "won the Pulitzer prize for biography in 1957, the Senator's prominence as a scholar and statesman grew. As his book continued to be a best seller, he climbed higher upon public-opinion polls and moved into a leading position among Presidential possibilities for 1960." Later Bobby would "write" a book about how he almost nailed Jimmy Hoffa; and so great was the impact of this work that many people had the impression that Bobby had indeed put an end to the career of that turbulent figure.

Most interesting of all the myth making was the creation of Jack the war hero. John Hersey first described for the *New Yorker* how Jack's Navy boat was wrecked after colliding with a Japanese ship; in the course of a long swim, the young skipper saved the life of a crewman, an admirable thing to do. Later they were all rescued. Since the officer who survived was Ambassador Kennedy's son, the story was deliberately told and retold as an example of heroism unequaled in war's history. Through constant repetition the simple facts of the story merged into a blurred impression that somehow at some point a unique act of heroism had been committed by Jack Kennedy. The last telling of the story was a film starring Cliff Robertson as JFK (the President had wanted Warren Beatty for the part, but the producer thought Beatty's image was "too mixed up").

So the image was created early: the high-class book that made the grade; the much-publicized heroism at war; the election to the House of Representatives in 1946. From that point on, the publicity was constant and though the Congressman's record of service was unimpressive, he himself was photogenic and appealing. Then came the Senate, the marriage, the illnesses, the second high-class book, and the rest is history. But though it was Joe Kennedy who paid the bills and to a certain extent managed the politics, the recipient of all this attention was meanwhile developing into a shrewd psychologist. Mr. Fay quotes a letter written him by the new Senator in 1953. The tone is jocular (part of the charm of Mr. Fay's book is that it captures as no one else has the preppish side to JFK's character; he was droll, particularly about himself, in a splendid W. C. Fields way): "I gave everything a good deal of thought. I am getting married this fall. This means the end of a promising political career, as it has been based up to now almost completely on the old sex appeal." After a few more sentences in this vein the groom-to-be comes straight to the point. "Let me know the general reaction to this in the Bay area." He did indeed want to know, like a romantic film star, what effect marriage would have on his career. But then most of his life was governed, as Mrs. Lincoln wrote of the year 1959, "by the public-opinion polls. We were not unlike the people who check their horoscope each day before venturing out." And when they did venture out, it was always to create an illusion. As Mrs. Lincoln remarks in her guileless way: after Senator Kennedy returned to Washington from a four-week tour of Europe, "it was obvious that his stature as a Senator had grown, for he came back as an authority on the current situation in Poland."

It is not to denigrate the late President or the writers of his gospel that neither he nor they ever seemed at all concerned by the bland phoniness of so much of what he did and said. Of course politicians have been pretty much the same since the beginning of history, and part of the game is creating illusion. In fact, the late President himself shortly after Cuba One summed up what might very well have been not only his political philosophy but that of the age in which we live. When asked whether or not the Soviet's placement of missiles in Cuba would have actually shifted the balance of world power, he indicated that he thought not. "But it would have politically changed the balance of power. It would have appeared to, and appearances contribute to reality."

From the beginning, the holy family has tried to make itself appear to be what it thinks people want rather than what the realities of any situation might require. Since Bobby is thought by some to be ruthless, he must therefore be photographed as often as possible with children, smiling and happy and athletic, in every way a boy's ideal man. Politically, he must *seem* to be at odds with the present administration without ever actually taking any important position that President Johnson does not already hold. Bobby's Vietnamese war dance was particularly illustrative of the technique. A step to the Left (let's talk to the Viet Cong), followed by two steps to the Right, simultaneously giving "the beards"—as he calls them—the sense that he is for peace in Vietnam while maintaining his brother's war policy. Characteristically, the world at large believes that if JFK were alive there would be no war in Vietnam. The myth makers have obscured the fact that it was JFK who began our active participation in the war when, in 1961, he added to the six hundred American observers the first of a gradual buildup of American troops, which reached twenty thousand at the time of his assassination. And there is no evidence that he would not have persisted in that war, for, as he said to a friend shortly before he died, "I have to go all the way with this one." He could not suffer a second Cuba and hope to maintain the appearance of Defender of the Free World at the ballot box in 1964.

The authors of the latest Kennedy books are usually at their most interesting when they write about themselves. They are cautious, of course (except for the jaunty Mr. Fay), and most are thinking ahead to Kennedy II. Yet despite a hope of future preferment, Mr. Salinger's self-portrait is a most curious one. He veers between a coarse unawareness of what it was all about (he never, for instance, expresses an opinion of the war in Vietnam), and a solemn bogusness that is most putting off. Like an after-dinner speaker, he characterizes everyone ("Clark Clifford, the brilliant Washington lawyer"); he pays heavy tribute to his office staff; he praises Rusk and the State Department, remarking that "JFK had more effective liaison with the State Department than any President in history," which would have come as news to the late President. Firmly Mr. Salinger puts Arthur Schlesinger, Jr., in his place, saying that he himself never heard the President express a lack of confidence in Rusk. Mr. Salinger also remarks that though Schlesinger was "a strong friend" of the President (something Mr. Salinger, incidentally, was not), "JFK occasionally was impatient with their [Schlesinger's memoranda] length and frequency." Mrs. Lincoln also weighs in on the subject of the historian-in-residence. Apparently JFK's "relationship with Schlesinger was never that close. He admired Schlesinger's brilliant mind, his enormous store of information . . . but Schlesinger was never more than an ally and assistant."

It is a tribute to Kennedy's gift for compartmentalizing the people in his life that none knew to what extent he saw the others. Mr. Fay was an after-hours buddy. Mrs. Lincoln was the girl in the office. Mr. Salinger was a technician and not a part of the President's social or private or even, as Mr. Salinger himself admits, political life. Contrasting his role with that of James Hagerty, Mr. Salinger writes, "My only policy duties were in the information field. While Jim had a voice in deciding what the administration would do, I was responsible only for presenting that decision to the public in a way and at a time that would generate the best possible reception." His book is valuable only when he discusses the relations between press and government. And of course when he writes about himself. His 1964 campaign for the Senate is nicely told and it is good to know that he lost because he came out firmly for fair housing on the ground that "morally I had no choice—not after sweating out Birmingham and Oxford with John F. Kennedy." This is splendid but it might have made his present book more interesting had he told us something about that crucial period of sweating out. Although he devotes a chapter to telling how he did not take a fifty-mile hike, he never discusses Birmingham, Oxford, or the Negro revolution.

All in all, his book is pretty much what one might expect of a PR man. He papers over personalities with the reflexive and usually inaccurate phrase (Eisenhower and Kennedy "had deep respect for each other"; Mrs. Kennedy has "a keen understanding of the problems which beset mankind"). Yet for all his gift at creating images for others, Mr. Salinger seems not to have found his own. Uneasily he plays at being U.S. Senator, fat boy at court, thoughtful emissary to Khrushchev. Lately there has been a report in the press that he is contemplating writing a novel. If he does, Harold Robbins may be in the sort of danger that George Murphy never was. The evidence at hand shows that he has the gift. Describing his divorce from "Nancy, my wife of eight years," Mr. Salinger manages in a few lines to say everything. "An extremely artistic woman, she was determined to live a quieter life in which she could pursue her skills as a ceramicist. And we both knew that I could not be happy unless I was on the move. It was this difference in philosophies, not a lack of respect, that led to our decision to obtain a divorce. But a vacation in Palm Springs, as Frank Sinatra's guest, did much to revive my spirits."

Mr. Fay emerges as very much his own man, and it is apparent that he amused the President at a level which was more that of a playmate escorting the actress Angie Dickinson to the Inaugural than as serious companion to the prince. Unlike the other witnesses, Mr. Fay has no pretensions about himself. He tells how "the President then began showing us the new paintings on the wall. 'Those two are Renoirs and that's a Cézanne', he told us. Knowing next to nothing about painters or paintings, I asked, 'Who are they?' The President's response was predictable, 'My God, if you ask a question like that, do it in a whisper or wait till we get outside. We're trying to give this administration a semblance of class.' " The President saw the joke; he also saw the image which must at all times be projected. Parenthetically, a majority of the recorded anecdotes about Kennedy involve keeping up appearances; he was compulsively given to emphasizing, often with great charm, the division between how things must be made to seem, as opposed to the way they are. This division is noticeable, even in the censored version of Mr. Manchester's *The Death of a President.* The author records that when Kennedy spoke at Houston's coliseum, Jack Valenti, crouched below the lectern, was able to observe the extraordinary tremor of the President's hands, and the artful way in which he managed to conceal them from the audience. This tension between the serene appearance and that taut reality add to the poignancy of the true legend, so unlike the Parson Weems version Mrs. Kennedy would like the world to accept.

Money, image, family: the three are extraordinarily intertwined. The origin of the Kennedy sense of family is the holy land of Ireland, priest-ridden, superstitious, clannish. While most of the West in the nineteenth century was industrialized and urbanized, Ireland remained a famine-ridden agrarian country, in thrall to politicians, homegrown and British, priest and lay. In 1848, the first Kennedy set up shop in Boston, where the Irish were exploited and patronized by the Wasps; not unnaturally, the Irish grew bitter and vengeful and finally asserted themselves at the ballot box. But the old resentment remained as late as Joe Kennedy's generation and with it flourished a powerful sense that the family is the only unit that could withstand the enemy, as long as each member remained loyal to the others, "regarding life as a joint venture between one generation and the next." In *The Fruitful Bough,* a privately printed cluster of tributes to the Elder Kennedy (collected by Edward M. Kennedy) we are told, in Bobby's words, that to Joe Kennedy "the most important thing . . . was the advancement of his children . . . except for his influence and encouragement, my brother Jack might not have run for the Senate in 1952." (So much for JFK's comment that it was his own "hustling" that got him Lodge's seat.)

The father is of course a far more interesting figure than any of his sons if only because his will to impose himself upon a society which he felt had snubbed him has been in the most extraordinary way fulfilled. He drove his sons to "win, win, win." But never at any point did he pause to ask himself or them just what it was they were supposed to win. He taught them to regard life as a game of Monopoly (a family favorite): you put up as many hotels as you can on Ventnor Avenue and win. Consequently, some of the failure of his son's administration can be ascribed to the family philosophy. All his life Jack Kennedy was driven by his father and then by himself to be first in politics, which meant to be the President. But once that goal had been achieved, he had no future, no place else to go. This absence of any sense of the whole emerged in the famous exchange between him and James Reston, who asked the newly elected President what his philosophy was, what vision did he have of the good life. Mr. Reston got a blank stare for answer. Kennedy apologists are quick to use this exchange as proof of their man's essentially pragmatic nature ("pragmatic" was a favorite word of the era, even though its political meaning is opportunist). As they saw it: give the President a specific problem and he will solve it through intelligence and expertise. A "philosophy" was simply of no use to a man of action. For a time, actual philosophers were charmed by the thought of an intelligent young empiricist fashioning a New Frontier.

Not until the second year of his administration did it become plain that Kennedy was not about to do much of anything. Since his concern was so much with the appearance of things, he was at his worst when confronted with those issues where a moral commitment might have informed his political response not only with passion but with shrewdness. Had he challenged the Congress in the Truman manner on such bills as Medicare and Civil Rights, he might at least have inspired the country, if not the Congress, to follow his lead. But he was reluctant to rock the boat, and it is significant that he often quoted Hotspur on summoning spirits from the deep: any man can summon, but will the spirits come? JFK never found out; he would not take the chance. His excuse in private for his lack of force, particularly in dealing with the Congress, was the narrow electoral victory of 1960. The second term, he declared, would be the one in which all things might be accomplished. With a solid majority behind him, he could work wonders. But knowing his character, it is doubtful that the second term would have been much more useful than the first. After all, he would have been constitutionally a lame duck President, perhaps interested in holding the franchise for his brother. The family, finally, was his only commitment and it colored all his deeds and judgment.

In 1960, after listening to him denounce Eleanor Roosevelt at some length, I asked him why he thought she was so much opposed to his candidacy. The answer was quick: "She hated my father and she can't stand it that his children turned out so much better than hers." I was startled at how little he understood Mrs. Roosevelt, who, to be fair, did not at all understand him, though at the end she was won by his personal charm. Yet it was significant that he could not take seriously any of her political objections to him (e.g., his attitude to McCarthyism); he merely assumed that she, like himself, was essentially concerned with family and, envying the father, would want to thwart the son. He was, finally, very much his father's son even though, as all the witnesses are at pains to remind us, he did not share that magnate's political philosophy—which goes without saying, since anyone who did could not be elected to anything except possibly the Chamber of Commerce. But *The Founding Father's* confidence in his own wisdom ("I know more about Europe than anybody else in this country," he said in 1940, "because I've been closer to it longer") and the assumption that he alone knew the absolute inside story about everything is a trait inherited by the sons, particularly Bobby, whose principal objection to the "talking liberals" is that they never know what's really going on, as he in his privileged place does but may not tell. The Kennedy children have always observed our world from the heights.

The distinguished jurist Francis Morrissey tells in *The Fruitful Bough* a most revealing story of life upon Olympus. "During the Lodge campaign, the Ambassador told [Jack and me] clearly that the campaign . . . would be the toughest fight he could think of, but there was no question that Lodge would be beaten, and if that should come to pass Jack would be nominated and elected President. . . . In that clear and commanding voice of his he said to Jack, 'I will work out the plans to elect you President. It will not be any more difficult for you to be elected President than it will be to win the Lodge fight . . . you will need to get about twenty key men in the country to get the nomination for it is these men who will control the convention. . . .'"

One of the most fascinating aspects of politician-watching is trying to determine to what extent any politician believes what he says. Most of course never do, regarding public statements as necessary noises to soothe the electorate or deflect the wrath of the passionate, who are forever mucking things up for the man who wants decently and normally to rise. Yet there are cases of politicians who have swayed themselves by their own speeches. Take a man of conservative disposition and force him to give liberal speeches for a few years in order to be elected and he will, often as not, come to believe himself. There is evidence that JFK often spellbound himself. Bobby is something else again. Andrew Kopkind in the *New Republic* once described Bobby's career as a series of "happenings": the McCarthy friend and fellow traveler of one year emerges as an intense New York liberal in another, and between these two happenings there is no thread at all to give a clue as to what the man actually thinks or who he really is. That consistency which liberals so furiously demanded of the hapless Nixon need not apply to any Kennedy.

After all, as the recent gospels point out, JFK himself was slow to become a liberal, to the extent he ever was (in our society no working politician can be radical). As JFK said to James MacGregor Burns,

"Some people have their liberalism 'made' by the time they reach their late twenties. I didn't. I was caught in crosscurrents and eddies. It was only later that I got into the stream of things." His comment made liberalism sound rather like something run up by a tailor, a necessary garment which he regrets that he never had time in his youth to be fitted for. Elsewhere (in William Manchester's *Portrait of a President*) he explains those "currents and eddies." Of his somewhat reactionary career in the House of Representatives he said, "I'd just come out of my father's house at the time, and these were the things I knew." It is of course a truism that character is formed in one's father's house. Ideas may change but the attitude toward others does not. A father who teaches his sons that the only thing that matters is to be first, not second, not third, is obviously (should his example be followed) going to be rewarded with energetic sons. Yet it is hardly surprising that to date one cannot determine where the junior Senator from New York stands on such a straightforward issue (morally if not politically) as the American adventure in Vietnam. Differing with the President as to which cities ought to be bombed in the North does not constitute an alternative policy. His sophisticated liberal admirers, however, do not seem in the least distressed by his lack of a position; instead they delight in the *uses* to which he has put the war in Vietnam in order to embarrass the usurper in the White House.

The cold-blooded jauntiness of the Kennedys in politics has a remarkable appeal for those who also want to rise and who find annoying—to the extent they are aware of it at all—the moral sense. Also, the success of the three Kennedy brothers nicely makes hash of the old American belief that by working hard and being good one will deserve (and if fortunate, receive) promotion. A mediocre Representative, an absentee Senator, through wealth and family connections, becomes the President while his youngest brother inherits the Senate seat. Now Bobby is about to become RFK because he is Bobby. It is as if the United States had suddenly reverted to the eighteenth century, when the politics of many states were family affairs. In those days, if one wanted a political career in New York one had best be born a

Livingston, a Clinton, or a Schuyler; failing that, one must marry into the family, as Alexander Hamilton did, or go to work for them. In a way, the whole Kennedy episode is a fascinating throwback to an earlier phase of civilization. Because the Irish maintained the ancient village sense of the family longer than most places in the West and to the extent that the sons of Joe Kennedy reflect those values and prejudices, they are an anachronism in an urbanized non-family-minded society. Yet the fact that they are so plainly not of this time makes them fascinating; their family story is a glamorous continuing soap opera whose appeal few can resist, including the liberals, who, though they may suspect that the Kennedys are not with them at heart, believe that the two boys are educable. At this very moment beside the river Charles a thousand Aristotles dream of their young Alexanders, and the coming heady conquest of the earth.

Meanwhile, the source of the holy family's power is the legend of the dead brother, who did not much resemble the hero of the books under review. Yet the myth that JFK was a philosopher-king will continue as long as the Kennedys remain in politics. And much of the power they exert over the national imagination is a direct result of the ghastliness of what happened at Dallas. But though the world's grief and shock were genuine, they were not entirely for JFK himself. The death of a young leader necessarily strikes an atavistic chord. For thousands of years the man-god was sacrificed to ensure with blood the harvest, and there is always an element of ecstasy as well as awe in our collective grief. Also, Jack Kennedy was a television star, more seen by most people than their friends or relatives. His death in public was all the more stunning because he was not an abstraction called The President, but a man the people thought they knew. At the risk of *lèse-divinité*, however, the assassination of President Nixon at, let us say, Cambridge by what at first was thought to be a member of the ADA but later turned out to be a dotty Bircher would have occasioned quite as much national horror, mourning, and even hagiography. But in time the terrible deed would have been forgotten, for there are no Nixon heirs.

Beyond what one thinks of the Kennedys themselves, there remains the large question: What sort of men ought we to be governed by in the coming years? With the high cost of politics and image making, it is plain that only the very wealthy or those allied with the very wealthy can afford the top prizes. And among the rich, only those who are able to please the people on television are Presidential. With the decline of the religions, the moral sense has become confused, to say the least, and intellectual or political commitments that go beyond the merely expedient are regarded with cheerful contempt not only by the great operators themselves but also by their admirers and, perhaps, by the electorate itself. Also, to be fair, politicians working within a system like ours can never be much more than what the system will allow. Hypocrisy and self-deception are the traditional characteristics of the middle class in any place and time, and the United States today is the paradigmatic middle-class society. Therefore we can hardly blame our political gamesmen for being, literally, representative. Any public man has every right to try and trick us, not only for his own good but, if he is honorable, for ours as well. However, if he himself is not aware of what he is doing or to what end he is playing the game, then to entrust him with the first magistracy of what may be the last empire on earth is to endanger us all. One does not necessarily demand of our leaders passion (Hitler supplied the age with quite enough for this century) or reforming zeal (Mao Tse-tung is incomparable), but one does insist that they possess a sense of community larger than simply personal power for its own sake, being first because it's fun. Finally, in an age of supercommunications, one must have a clear sense of the way things are, as opposed to the way they have been made to seem. Since the politics of the Kennedys are so often the work of publicists, it is necessary to keep trying to find out just who they are and what they really mean. If only because should *they* be confused as to the realities of Cuba, say, or Vietnam, then the world's end is at hand.

At one time in the United States, the popular wisdom maintained that there was no better work for a man to do than to set in motion some idea whose time had not yet arrived, even at the risk of becoming as unpopular as those politicians JFK so much admired in print and so little emulated in life. It may well be that it is now impossible for such men to rise to the top in our present system. If so, this is a tragedy. Meanwhile, in their unimaginative fierce way, the Kennedys continue to play successfully the game as they found it. They create illusions and call them facts, and between what they are said to be and what they are falls the shadow of all the useful words not spoken, of all the actual deeds not done. But if it is true that in a rough way nations deserve the leadership they get, then a frivolous and apathetic electorate combined with a vain and greedy intellectual establishment will most certainly restore to power the illusion-making Kennedys. Holy family and bedazzled nation, in their faults at least, are well matched. In any case, the age of the commune in which we have lived since the time of Jackson is drawing to a close and if historical analogies are at all relevant, the rise of the *signori* is about to begin, and we may soon find ourselves enjoying a strange new era in which all our lives and dreams are presided over by smiling, interchangeable, initialed gods.

Esquire, April 1967

Postscript: June 6, 1968

It is curious how often one prefers his enemies to his friends. Although I certainly never wanted Bobby to be President, I had lately come to accept him as a useful figure on the scene—and now that he is gone I find that I genuinely miss him. Nevertheless, I still think "The Holy Family" worth reprinting partly for what it has to say about that doomed family, partly for what it has to say about the way in which our political system has become a game for the very rich.

Unlike most Americans I do not think that to be rich is automatically to be virtuous. More to the point, I think it tragic that the poor man has almost no chance to rise unless he is willing to put himself in thrall to moneyed interests. Unless drastic reforms are made, we must accept the fact that every four years the United States will be up for sale, and the richest man or family will buy it.

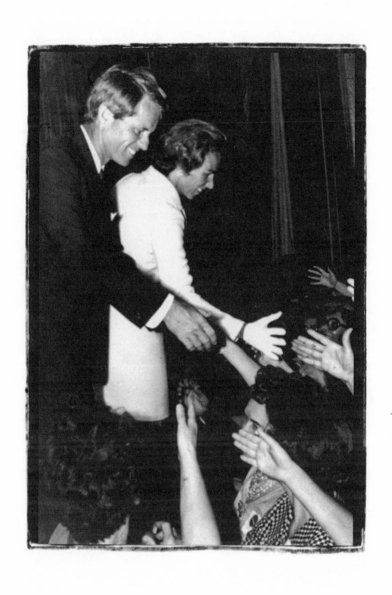

from Robert Kennedy: A Memoir
by Jack Newfield

For a former ally of Joe McCarthy, Robert Kennedy had a lot of friends on the political left. They included Jack Newfield, a respected muckraker at New York City's Village Voice *from 1964 to 1988. Newfield here makes the case for RFK as a man who with experience changed fundamentally and for the better.*

There was one obligatory paragraph that every journalist who liked Robert Kennedy felt compelled to write. It was a defensive ritual, a ransom paid to the reputation that followed Kennedy wherever he went. The shock of unrecognition when you finally got to know Kennedy was universal, and so the obligatory paragraph always managed to sound the same, no matter who wrote it.

Historian and family friend, Arthur Schlesinger, wrote in his Pulitzer Prize winning book, *A Thousand Days*:

> I do not know of any case in contemporary American politics where there seemed to me a greater discrepancy between the myth and the man. The public theory of Robert Kennedy could only appear, to those who know him, as James Wechsler later described it, a case of mistaken identity.

A few weeks before the assassination, David Halberstam wrote in a particularly perceptive piece for *Harper's Magazine*:

> His reputation was for ruthlessness, yet in 1968 there seemed no major political figure whose image so contrasted with the reality; most politicians seem attractive from a distance but under closer examination they fade; the vanities, the pettiness, the vulgarities come out. Robert Kennedy was different. Under closer inspection he was far more winning than most. . . .

Two weeks after the assassination, Jim Stevenson wrote in an unsigned reminiscence for *The New Yorker*:

> We occasionally experienced a shock when we encountered the man himself. Lindsay always turned out to be Lindsay, Rockefeller turned out to be Rockefeller, McCarthy turned out to be McCarthy, but Kennedy bore little resemblance to most of what we read or heard about him.

When I began to work on this book in the autumn of 1966, my own feeling about Kennedy was suspended midway between the static reputation and the changing man. My view of his public politics was sympathetic, since he had by then voiced opposition to the Vietnam war and the military intervention in the Dominican Republic, and he was beginning to develop his identification with all of life's losers. But my sense of his private character, even though I had already met him a few times, was uncertain, influenced by what I had read about him, and by the mistakes he had made in the past. A few days before I was scheduled to spend my first full day with Kennedy, I drew up a list of the twenty adjectives most often invoked by other writers to describe him:

Intolerant, spoiled, courageous, emotional, rude, moody, cold, simplistic, tense, pragmatic, authoritarian, competitive, tough, loyal, vindictive, honest, ambitious, restless, moralistic, and ruthless.

I still vividly recalled that the first time I saw Kennedy I was picketing him. It was in June of 1963. Medgar Evers had been assassinated in ambush a few days before, and in Birmingham the fire hose was becoming history's latest symbol of oppression. About 3,000 of us, black and white—in that nostalgic season of integrated protest—were assembled outside the granite slab of the Justice Department in Washington. We were chanting and singing our demand that the Attorney General do something to protect Martin Luther King's schoolchildren, then congesting Alabama's damp jails.

After about an hour, the slight, taut brother of the President emerged in shirt-sleeves from his fifth-floor office, stood framed in the doorway, and began to talk to us. I had, by then, been jailed twice in civil rights demonstrations, and with pure fury stared at Kennedy's crew-cut face. It was, I remember, a hard, Irish face; alert, but without much character, a little like the faces that used to follow me home from Hebrew school, taunting, "Christ killer."

"We haven't seen many Negroes come out of there," an angry voice shouted out from the crowd, referring to the well-dressed white employees entering and leaving the building during the demonstration.

Kennedy tensed up even more. His skin seemed to draw even tighter around his sharp features, and the hostility radiating from his blue eyes became even more intense.

"Individuals will be hired according to their ability, not their color," Kennedy shouted back into a hand-held bullhorn that made his voice sound both squeaky and strident. It was exactly the sort of impersonal, legalistic response, blind to the larger moral implications of our protest, that we felt made Kennedy such an inadequate Attorney General.

As civil rights activists in 1963, we liked Kennedy as little as the Southern governors did. We saw him recommend Harold Cox, James Eastland's college roommate, to be a judge in the Fifth District Court, where he was to call Negro defendants "chimpanzees" from the bench.

We saw him indict nine civil rights workers in Albany, Georgia, on conspiracy charges, while white men who burned down Negro churches,
and shot at civil rights activists, went unpunished. We saw Negroes
trying to register to vote in Greenwood, Mississippi, urinated upon by
a white farmer, while lawyers from the Justice Department calmly took
notes destined to be filed and forgotten. We agreed with James
Baldwin, who pronounced Kennedy, after their stormy confrontation,
"insensitive and unresponsive to the Negro's torment." So when he
bragged about his hiring policies, while our friends languished in
Southern jails, we booed him in a hoarse, throaty roar that ricocheted
off the white marble walls of the Department of Justice.

I was not fully prepared for the changes in Kennedy the first day I spent
traveling with him as a reporter in November of 1966. Instead of the
military crew cut, his graying, ginger hair now lapped over his earlobes
in the shaggy style of the alienated young. His blue eyes were now sad
rather than cold, haunted rather than hostile. The freshly carved lines
of sorrow in his brow, around his eyes, near his mouth, made him look
ten, not five years older. The metamorphosis seemed to prove the
wisdom of Albert Camus's comment that every man over forty is
responsible for his own face. Robert Kennedy was two days past his
thirty-eighth birthday when his brother was murdered.

Kennedy was spending the day campaigning with Frank O'Connor,
the Democratic candidate for Governor of New York against Nelson
Rockefeller. He had just stumped the country for friends like John
Gilligan in Ohio, Paul Douglas in Illinois, John Culver in Iowa, Teno
Roncalio in Wyoming, and Pat Brown in California. And now, though
tired, he was campaigning for O'Connor, who was not his kind of politician, as a duty. He felt Rockefeller would win, that O'Connor did not
understand the issues, and that he would be blamed if O'Connor lost.

The first stop was in Brooklyn, where Kennedy would also campaign
for Congressman Hugh Carey, who was Irish, and whom Kennedy
liked, just as he liked Joe McCarthy, John Burns, and Jimmy Breslin.

Kennedy began walking down the street, smiling a fixed smile, shaking hands, and waving mechanically to the crowds. He was in a human cup, flanked by police, aides and local politicians. It was a typically impersonal campaign scene. But suddenly Kennedy's eye caught the face of a ten-year-old girl with glasses. Certain faces turned him on. He often spoke of the character in Andrei Voznesensky's face. And of the faces of Negro children before they reached the ages of thirteen or fourteen. He knelt to speak to the girl.

"You know something?" he blurted out. "My little girl has glasses just like yours. And I love my little girl very much." Then he squeezed the back of the girl's neck, because he was better expressing affection through action than words. Ten seconds later he was back, moving down the line, reaching out mechanically to press the outstretched hands, campaigning.

I got in his ordinary-looking car, and we began to ride back to Manhattan. For a few minutes Kennedy was silent. He was slouched down in the front seat, his mind someplace else, his fingers drumming nervously on the dashboard, the wind blowing his hair askew. His lips moved wordlessly as he tested some private thought.

Finally he turned and asked, "Do you still like me, Jack?" I had written a friendly article about him that June for *Cavalier* magazine, but not anything since.

"Yes," I answered, "but why do you have to campaign for a guy like Carey? He's for the war, he's against the civilian review board, and he never says anything about poverty."

"I know," Kennedy replied, still half abstracted. "But he's such a decent fellow. He works very hard and he's very bright. Whenever we meet at least he's concerned about the issues. He's not like Scheuer [James Scheuer, a reform Democrat from the Bronx] who has such a great reputation, but only asks me about patronage. It's all so complicated. Also, Carey has trouble with his district. He was telling me the Church is such a problem. I wonder why the kids who come out of parochial school are so conservative." And then he turned to look out the window, that distant look on his face, to ruminate on his own question, preventing any other.

There were three rallies for O'Connor in Manhattan. Kennedy spoke briefly at each one, playfully teasing the children who always managed to position themselves closest to the platform, closest to him. He said little about O'Connor. The crowds were small.

After the last rally on the Lower East Side, O'Connor said he was tired and cold and decided to cancel the two remaining rallies back in Brooklyn. Kennedy's face showed he felt this was a sign of softness. He was not wearing any overcoat, and it was only 5 p.m. Later, he would spend election night with the Soviet poet Yevgeny Yevtushenko, rather than with the professional politicians at O'Connor's losing headquarters. And after he would pay a brief condolence visit to O'Connor on election night, an aide would ask how O'Connor looked, and he would quip, "relieved."

As Kennedy was about to leave the last rally, he saw two girls, nurses from Albany, who left work to welcome him at the airport whenever he visited the state capitol, and who had been volunteers in his 1964 campaign. They were not very political, but they idolized the Kennedy family. They were spending their vacation together in New York, watching Kennedy campaign. He invited them up to his United Nations Plaza apartment for a drink. Blushing, they accepted.

While the record player whispered syrupy music by Andy Williams and Jack Jones, Kennedy awkwardly tried to entertain me and the two girls. He would talk to them for a few minutes about their jobs, their families, about what they thought of the day's speeches. Then he would turn to me, and talk about the St. Louis Cardinals' backfield, and about how terrible most New York Democratic politicians are. "In Massachusetts they steal, in California they feud, and in New York they lie."

Then the girls, still a little bewildered, left, and Kennedy, sitting in his shirt-sleeves and sipping bourbon, suddenly asked me with some embarrassment if I liked poetry.

I said yes, and that I especially liked William Butler Yeats and Hart Crane.

"Can I read you some poetry by a poet I like very much?"

He disappeared into the bedroom for a minute. I expected him to return with Shakespeare, whom he quoted often, or perhaps, if he was doing this just as a con job, he would march out with "Howl" by Allen Ginsberg. I recalled how his brother won Norman Mailer's vote by telling him he had read *The Deer Park*, rather than the more popular *Naked and the Dead*.

But he returned with a thin, dog-eared, jacketless volume of poetry by Ralph Waldo Emerson, the poet categorized as "minor" by the academic and literary establishments, but read by the rebel young.

Kennedy stood in the center of his own living room, silhouetted at twilight against a neon Pepsi-Cola sign in Queens, and began to read, in an unmusical monotone that was at the same time very intense in its buried feelings, a poem he must have associated with his brother:

> He pays too high a price
> For knowledge and for fame
> Who sells his sinews to be wise,
> His teeth and bones to buy a name,
> And crawls through life a paralytic
> To earn the praise of bard and critic
>
> Were it not better done,
> To dine and sleep through forty years;
> Be loved by few; be feared by none;
> Laugh life away, have wine for tears;
> And take the mortal leap undaunted,
> Content that all we asked was granted?
>
> But Fate will not permit
> The seed of gods to die,
> Nor suffer sense to win from wit
> Its guerdon in the sky,
> Nor let us bide, whate'er our pleasure,
> The world's light underneath a measure

Go then, sad youth, and shine,
Go, sacrifice to Fame;
Put youth, joy, health upon the shrine,
And life to fan the flame;
Being for Seeming bravely barter,
And die to Fame a happy martyr.

The last stanza he seemed to know from memory, and his eyes were focused on the middle distance as he recited it.

When he finished, he walked to his fourteenth floor window and looked down at the tugs and barges slicing through the East River.

"Look at that!" he exclaimed. "There's a ship called *World Justice,* and it is moving away from the United Nations."

After a silence he asked, "Do you want to hear one more?" And he began to read again, in his soft, unrhythmic voice, a poem that seemed to be a metaphor for Vietnam.

Though loath to grieve
The evil time's sole patriot,
I cannot leave
My honied thought
For the priest's cant,
Or the salesman's rant.

If I refuse
My study for their politique,
Which at best is trick,
The angry Muse
Puts confusion in my brain.

But who is he that prates
Of the culture of mankind,
Of better arts and life?

Go, blind worm, go,
Behold the famous States,
Harrying Mexico
With rifle and with knife!

Because rapid, superficial adjustments of image are so common in America's personality and media-centered politics, authentic interior change is doubted when it happens. The country is too skeptical. It has seen "a new Nixon" almost as often as it has seen new models from Ford. It was told there was "a new Johnson" after the President unwrapped his expansive, earthy, style previously used only in Senate cloakrooms. Other political figures have claimed new incarnations after two-week visits to Vietnam, hiring new press secretaries, or after receiving professional speech lessons.

But serious men who inhabit the realm of ideas do change. Reverend William Sloan Coffin, who was convicted in June of 1968 for conspiring against the draft, once worked for the Central Intelligence Agency. André Malraux was once a Communist. Justice Hugo Black was once a member of the Ku Klux Klan. And Robert Kennedy was once a McCarthyite, who often acted as if error had no rights.

Attempts by his friends to minimize Kennedy's early conservatism and aggressive, abrupt personality are not persuasive. In 1952, when he was twenty-six, and had the protection of being the candidate's kid brother, he made many enemies during John Kennedy's successful Senate campaign against Henry Cabot Lodge. When he saw union leaders or local politicians twice his age standing idly around head-quarters, he would order them to lick envelopes, or get out.

In 1953, against his brother's advice, Kennedy went to work as a counsel to Senator Joseph McCarthy's investigative committee. He left after six months, mostly because of conflicts with Roy Cohn, and later went to work for the Democratic minority. In 1955 he walked out on a dinner speech by Edward R. Murrow because it was so critical of McCarthy. When McCarthy died in May of 1957, Kennedy flew to Appleton, Wisconsin, to be present for the interment.

He directed his brother's 1960 Presidential drive with a single-minded intensity. Delegates and rivals were threatened, and Kennedy seemed indifferent to substantive issues of policy. The tactics used to win the West Virginia primary were ugly and foul. At one meeting of campaign workers Kennedy said, "It doesn't matter if I hurt your feelings. It doesn't matter if you hurt mine. The important thing is to get the job done."

This seems to have been Kennedy's primitive credo, even into the early days of the New Frontier, when employees and public officials could be demoted or exiled if Kennedy doubted their loyalty or energy. There are many legends of Kennedy's rudeness and bullying during this period, and most of them are probably true.

It was during this period, from 1952 to 1961, that the classic images of Robert Kennedy were shaped, and were never to be totally erased: taunting underworld figures during the McClellan committee's investigation into labor racketeering; warning Hubert Humphrey, "We'll get you" at the 1960 Los Angeles convention, after finding out Humphrey would not support his brother; jabbing a finger into Chester Bowles' stomach, and telling him he was now in favor of the Bay of Pigs invasion, no matter what he thought privately; testifying in defense of legislation with wide provisions for wiretapping.

Later he would grow and forge a new identity. Later he would become one of the Senate's most influential critics of the Vietnam war, although not its most persistent or radical critic. Later he would create and sponsor a pioneer experiment in slum regeneration in Brooklyn's black ghetto of Bedford-Stuyvesant. Later he would make the victimization of the Mexicans and Indians not just a cause, but an obsession. Later he would be one of the two Senators to receive a 100 percent rating from the Americans for Democratic Action for his 1967 Senatorial voting record. Later he would campaign against the gun lobby, against General Motors, against the oil and cigarette industries.

But his critics always insisted there was no change or growth. Or else they would say any change was opportunistic, motivated by the fact that he just had less power to abuse, or represented a new, more liberal constituency, or just anticipated coming trends. But the changes would be authentic, just as authentic as the mean little things he could always do for his brother, but rarely for himself, just as real as the narrow conservatism he believed in, until experience began to stretch him, and tragedy transform him.

It would be simplistic and melodramatic to assert that all the changes in Robert Kennedy began with the murder of his brother: grown men do not undergo total revolutions of politics and personality at the age of thirty-eight. Yet, if the assassination of John Kennedy was a traumatic experience for the entire nation, particularly for the idealistic and innocent young, who can measure its impact on his younger brother, who had no personal goal in his adult life that was not his older brother's goal first?

The assassination punctured the center of Robert Kennedy's universe. It removed the hero-brother for whom he had submerged all of his own great competitive instincts. It took away, in one instant of insanity, all of the power they had struggled together for ten years to achieve, and gave it to another, whom they both mistrusted. It thrust a man trained for the shadows, into the sunlight. It made Robert Kennedy, a man unprepared for introspection, think for the first time in his life, what *he* wanted to do, and what *he* stood for.

It took Kennedy months to begin to recover. He would slouch for hours at his desk in the Justice Department and stare out the window. He lost weight and lacked vitality. He would stroll alone, or with his dog Brumus, aimlessly around Washington's streets, or the grounds of his home in Virginia. He frequently visited his brother's grave at Arlington. Even in crowds he seemed alone. When he spoke of his brother, on St. Patrick's Day, 1964, in Scranton and at the Democratic Convention in August, he wept openly. When crowds mobbed him in Manila, and Cracow, he would mumble to aides, "It was for him, it was for him."

Kennedy was never to recover fully from the trauma of Dallas, the way his brother Edward seemed to. The President's assassination was always like an amputation that never healed. He spent each anniversary of Dallas in prayer and brooding seclusion. "All of November is a bad time for him," said one of his friends in 1967.

The tone of every conversation with him changed when his brother was mentioned. The wound would always come back into his eyes. Even in 1968 it was too painful. He walked out of a hotel room in Indiana when the conversation turned to speculation over whether there was a conspiracy in the assassination of Martin Luther King. Sitting next to him in an airplane, I would see his eyes avoid any newspaper article about the assassination. He could only speak around the event, or in euphemisms. When I asked him when he began to read poetry, he answered, "Oh, at the very end of 1963, I think."

During the months following the death of his brother, Robert Kennedy almost certainly experienced the classic identity crisis most of us go through during adolescence. For the first time he began to try to find out who he was—an exploration that was far from completed when he was shot down. The idea that he could be a voice for all the voiceless only came to him at the end of his last campaign. So did the confidence that people liked him for himself, not for his brother.

During the post-assassination period Kennedy displayed many of the same symptoms that Professor Robert Jay Lifton perceived in the survivors of Hiroshima, and reported in his book, *Death in Life.*

Like the *hibakusha*, Kennedy also suffered "survivor guilt," a feeling that if fate were fair, he should have died, and the President should have lived. He also began to feel a sense of community with other victims, like the poor and the powerless. Litton describes several Hiroshima survivors who dedicated the rest of their lives to working among the dispossessed.

Kennedy also experienced an "immersion in death" of which Lifton wrote,

> the embrace of the identity of the dead—may, paradoxically enough, serve as the means of maintaining life. For in the face of the burden of guilt the survivor carries with him,

particularly the guilt of survival priority, his obeisance before the dead is his best means of justifying and maintaining his own existence. But it remains an existence with a large shadow cast across it, a life which, in a powerful symbolic sense, the survivor does not feel to be his own.

And when Robert Kennedy finally awoke from his long night of mourning, his collar a size too large, he began to will himself into an avatar of his martyred brother. In his public speeches he quoted his brother with an almost morbid obsession. He started employing his brother's characteristic gestures—one hand thrust in his suit pocket, the other jabbing the air, crooked index finger extended. He began smoking the small cigars his brother favored. He began consulting his brother's circle of intellectual advisers. He let his hair grow longer. He filled his office with memorabilia of his brother. In a cathartic five-day effort, he climbed 14,000-foot Mount Kennedy in the Canadian Yukon. And he began to wear, or sometimes just carry, a worn-out, oversized tweed overcoat, that was once his brother's. He often misplaced the coat, leaving it behind in one town or another, but he always sent an aide back to retrieve the symbol of the past.

The assassination was also the catalyst that accelerated other changes. Softer personal qualities, long latent and repressed, came to the surface. He began to identify himself with a romanticized notion of what his brother stood for—peace, Negroes, the next generation. His deep, moralistic rage against evil did not change; it merely discovered new outlets. Violence and suffering replaced the old devils of Communism and corruption. The pragmatic man, who thought history could be manipulated through anticipation and hard work, learned the power of fate, and became a doubter and a skeptic. He would not calculate for his own future the way he did for his brother's. "I can't plan. Living every day is like Russian roulette," he would say a few months before he was killed.

In June of 1964, in a personally written speech to 3,000 students at the Free University of West Berlin, Kennedy summed up his feelings:

> There were many who felt . . . that the torchbearer for a
> whole generation was gone; that an era was over before its
> time . . . But I have come to understand that the hope Presi-
> dent Kennedy kindled isn't dead, but alive . . . The torch still
> burns, and because it does, there remains for all of us a
> chance to light up the tomorrows and brighten the future.
> For me, this is the challenge that makes life worthwhile. . . .

Robert Kennedy's motto, like Andre Gide's, could have been, "Do not
understand me too quickly." He was not just complex, but contradictory. His most basic characteristics were simple, intense, and indirect
conflict with each other. He was constantly at war with himself.

The rational, conservative Catholic part of his nature was juxta-
posed with his brooding and rebellious Irish streak. His pragmatic,
goal-oriented intellect was in opposition to his emotional, romantic
instincts. His political streak, with its taste for polls and safe arith-
metical majorities, was in conflict with his existential streak, which
hungered for action and was trained to dare.

He was an activist who thought "people should make that extra
effort," and that "one person can make a difference." But at the same
time he was a fatalist who knew how much of life was absurd. He radi-
ated an animal intensity and was a sexual symbol to millions. But he
was introverted and strongly Puritanical himself: The two human qualities he said he most admired were "courage and sensitivity."

"The pendulum just swings wider for him than it does for other
people," Lawrence O'Brien said. Any stereotype of Robert Kennedy was
bound to be inaccurate.

Hate was the third reason Kennedy was misunderstood. It was almost
a fad to hate him. Often there was no reason, just a feeling. Politics
didn't matter. His name was the equivalent of an epithet in seedy
Southern bars, in exclusive suburban country clubs, in union offices,
and in reform Democratic clubhouses of Manhattan. Logic and reason
could not compete with passion and paranoia. After Lyndon Johnson

announced he would not seek reelection on March 31, 1968, much of the free-lance hate in the country flowed to the magnet called Robert Kennedy.

The hatred of him on the hard Left in the last few weeks of his life was a frightening symptom of irrationality. In California, followers of the radical Peace and Freedom Party interrupted one of his campaign speeches with shouts of "Fascist pig," and then pelted him with pebbles and rotten apple cores as his motorcade drove away under an overpass.

The week he died, the *Guardian,* an Old Left weekly with pro-China politics, printed a poem by Julius Lester entitled "Not in memory of Robert Kennedy." The closing lines were:

> The martyr is not he who was killed
> but he who fired the gun

One reason people hated Kennedy was that almost all his roles and jobs had a high, built-in potential for conflict and controversy: investigator for Senator McCarthy's witch-hunting committee; chief counsel to the Senate Rackets Committee; campaign manager for his brother; Attorney General; and United States Senator. While his brother was alive it was his function to be the lightning rod that deflected hostility, and to say no to all the anxious people who wanted to hear yes.

In addition Kennedy was an active participant in some of the most emotional political events of the last fifteen years: McCarthyism; wiretapping; the 1960 Presidential campaign; the Bay of Pigs; the integration of the University of Mississippi; the opposition to the Vietnam war; the 1968 campaign. Toward the end of his life, Kennedy was an easy target to attack, since his past reputation for controversy and ruthlessness made it almost impossible for him to counterattack. Thus, Representative Joseph Resnick based most of his unsuccessful campaign for the Democratic Senate nomination from New York in 1968 on baiting the silent Kennedy. Kennedy also took some vicious barbs from Eugene McCarthy without retaliating.

John F. Kennedy was a controlled and consummate politician, cool enough to personalize his political differences rarely. Very few politicians or journalists expressed any personal dislike of John Kennedy. Lyndon Johnson and Barry Goldwater liked him. So did Joseph Alsop and James Wechsler. John Kennedy told his pre-Presidential biographer, James McGregor Burns, "When I was in the House, I used to get along with Marcantonio and with Rankin. As long as they don't get in my way, I don't want to get into any personal fights."

But Robert Kennedy was more Irish and more Boston and more volatile. Kennedy's emotionalism was one of the crucial differences between him and his brothers. It was the quality that made him so vulnerable to actual experience. For example, it was Michael Harrington's book, *The Other America*, that opened the more intellectual John Kennedy's eyes to poverty. But for Robert Kennedy, it was his walks through the ghettos, his visits to the Mississippi Delta and Latin America, that made him feel the question of poverty so personally and deeply. For Robert Kennedy, the sight of one hungry black child in Greenwood, Mississippi, had a greater impact than a million words or statistics. On December 14, 1967, he lost his temper on the floor of the Senate in a way his less emotional brothers never did. A welfare reform bill Kennedy opposed as "coercive" was quietly pushed through the Senate that morning by Majority Whip Russell Long and Robert Byrd, both of whom promised there would be open debate on the bill. But Kennedy was at a subcommittee meeting on education when Long called up the measure, and was enraged when he found out it had been passed without debate. When he reached the floor of the Senate Kennedy exploded with enough emotion to violate the Senatorial code of politeness:

"A number of us wanted to speak about the conference report prior to the vote, and asked for that elementary consideration and decency that exists among men. Then not to have received it, as we did not this morning, certainly is a reflection not only on the Senate, but also on the integrity and honesty of those who participated . . . I think what went on this morning is a reflection on all those who participated, not just as United States Senators, but as individuals and as men."

Another example of the different way people looked at John and Robert Kennedy was reflected in a report pollster Samuel Lubell released in 1961, just after the Freedom Rides:

"On the whole . . the Freedom Rides do not seem to have hurt President Kennedy much in the South. The American voter has always made excuses for Presidents he likes, and it is 'brother Bobby' in the Attorney General's office, rather than President Jack, who has been blamed for how the Alabama bus violence was handled."

Lubell closed his report with a quote from an anonymous Birmingham fireman who said, "I don't blame Jack, but that Bobby is out for trouble."

Robert Kennedy's own considerable communications problem exacerbated what James Wechsler called his "case of mistaken identity." He was basically introverted and nonverbal. He did not come across well in artificial and impersonal settings like television studios. He was a Kennedy, and too proud to justify himself to every critic. A strong bias against interpretations of unconscious motives made him less prone to self-analysis.

When CBS announcer Roger Mudd asked Kennedy, on a network television special on June 20, 1967, to explain his ruthless reputation, Kennedy's usually mobile face became a blank mask as he tried one more time to explain himself without success:

ROGER MUDD: But, in the public prints, people are not surprised by a—they think there's always an ulterior motive in what you do. Is that—

SENATOR ROBERT KENNEDY: Is that what?

ROGER MUDD: Is that—is that accurate?

KENNEDY: No. What did you think I was going to say?

ROGER MUDD: Is this something now that's gotten started and you can't do anything to stop it, the public image that you have?

KENNEDY: I don't know.

ROGER MUDD: How did it get started?

KENNEDY: I don't know . . . I don't know . . . I don't know . . .
I don't know.
ROGER MUDD: The McCarthy thing, and the Hoffa thing, and
the '60 campaign.
KENNEDY: I suppose I have been in positions in which—but
I don't know exactly. I don't know.

Kennedy found it painful to verbalize anything important about himself. He was not fluent, and words were too easy to manipulate. He preferred action, and wished other people judged him by what he did, rather than asking him to justify and analyze his motives.

When he became angry with a friend he would stick out his tongue. When he had to do something he didn't like, he would make a face like a child about to swallow some medicine. If he liked you, he gave you a thumbs-up sign with his fingers. Words were not necessary. But if a reporter asked why some people hated him, or thought he was ruthless, he would freeze, and mumble like a little boy. He never learned to give a glib little speech explaining it. All he could do was show it, do it, be it.

The mass media—newspapers, television, and publishing houses— were also culpable for the failure of the nation to get any accurate sense of Robert Kennedy's character. They turned him early into a one-dimensional stereotype, and never bothered to keep up with the changes. Growth, mystery, and complexity could not be simplified and packaged for wire service copy, or two minutes of film on Huntley-Brinkley. The media never had the time to probe beneath the misleading exterior.

The textbook example of the way Kennedy's motives were distorted to fit the preexisting image took place during the Indiana primary. Dozens of reporters and columnists* came to Indiana, followed the candidate for a few days, and then wrote that he was jettisoning his liberal values in order opportunistically to appeal to the provincial and conservative Hoosier electorate.

---

*See especially Kenneth Crawford in the May 20, 1968, issue of *Newsweek*.

This had some validity up to a point. Kennedy did emphasize his commitment to law and order and his law-enforcement role as Attorney General more than he would have in New York or California. But his entire approach to the issue of decentralized democracy was misunderstood. To interpret this vanguard idea as conservative was not only the mistake of the wire service reporters, but also such influential opinion makers as Warren Weaver of *The New York Times.*

On April 28, 1968, Weaver wrote a lengthy analysis in the Sunday *Times* under the headline: "Kennedy: Meet the Conservative."

> It almost sounded as though Richard Goodwin and John Bartlow Martin, the Senator's speechwriters** had been put to work rewriting the old speeches of Gov. George Romney. . . . Mr. Kennedy is emphasizing criticism of the Federal Government as a bureaucracy, he is championing local autonomy, and endorsing the old Republican slogan: "The best government is a government closest to the people.
>
> "We can't have the Federal Government in here telling people what's good for them," he told a college audience at Fort Wayne. "I want to bring that control back to the localities so that people can decide for themselves what they think is best for themselves."

First, Kennedy had been urging decentralization for several years, and did not just discover the idea for the benefit of the Indiana electorate. And his decentralization was always accompanied by pleas for more public spending and Federal standards. Second, much of Kennedy's thinking about democratic practice derives not from Republicans, but from radicals like Thoreau, Lewis Mumford, and Thomas Jefferson, who wrote before the Republican Party was founded, "That government is best which governs least." Also, the intellectuals closest to Kennedy, speech writers Adam Walinsky and adviser Richard Goodwin,

---

**Most of Kennedy's speeches were written by thirty-year-old Adam Walinsky and by twenty-four-year-old Jeff Greenfield.

had been vocal partisans of decentralization and participatory democracy for several years before the Indiana primary. Goodwin had written in the June, 1967, issue of *Commentary:*

> . . . the most troubling fact of our age [is] that the growth in central power has been accompanied by a swift and continual diminuation in the significance of the individual citizen. . . . More important to the growth of central power . . . is the dwindling influence of local government and private associations . . . decentralization is designed to help combat the social and spiritual ills of fragmentation; it also responds to the fact that centralized bureaucracies tend to become increasingly ineffective and coercive. . . .

Kennedy himself, in his last book, *To Seek a Newer World*, published in late 1967, wrote:

> Lewis Mumford observed recently that "democracy, in any active sense, begins and ends in communities small enough for their members to meet face to face." One may argue about the ideal size, but certainly there are strong arguments to support the decentralization of some municipal functions, and some aspects of government into smaller units . . . We are far removed from Jefferson's time. Still, nearly a century and a half of history has also brought us new assets to help us toward his vision of participating democracy . . ."

Thus Kennedy in Indiana was testing the platform of a new liberalism, based on ideas from Mumford and Jefferson, not George Romney.

The one place where the growing margins of Kennedy's politics and personality might have been portrayed was in the books published about him. But none did, because they were mostly written from clippings, and conceived as commercial ventures to exploit his family's legend and the country's need for a royal family.

British magazine writer Margaret Laing wrote *The Next Kennedy* after following him around for a month in 1966. Dick Schaap wrote *R. F. K.* after observing his subject on and off for six weeks early in 1967. Ralph De Toledano never interviewed Kennedy at all while writing his right-wing hatchet job called *The Man Who Would Be President.* The misleadingly titled paperback *The Bobby Kennedy Nobody Knows* was written by Nick Thimmesch and William Johnson, and published under the collective pen name of William Nicholas. It was merely an updated (from clips) version of their earlier book, *Robert Kennedy at 40.* (When he saw the paperback Kennedy asked, "Why didn't they just call it *Robert Kennedy at 40 1/2?*")

The most perceptive pre-assassination biography of Kennedy was *The Heir Apparent* by William Shannon of the editorial board of *The New York Times.* But while discerning when analyzing Kennedy's politics, the book failed to make vivid Kennedy's contradictory character, and Kennedy claimed that Shannon had personally interviewed him "only once or twice" after his election to the Senate.

All the books written about Kennedy missed his distinctive extra dimension of myth and symbolism. Murray Kempton understood this when he exclaimed, after leaving an interview with Kennedy, "God, he's not a politician! He's a character in a novel!"

With his moralistic, gloomy nature, Kennedy might have been a character out of a novel of exile and expiation by Joseph Conrad. Conrad wrote in *Nostromo:*

> In our activity alone do we find the sustaining illusion of an independent existence, as against the whole scheme of things, of which we form a helpless part.

Any politician is much more than the computed sum of his speeches, votes, and advisers. The one authentic gesture can reveal more than a dozen carefully programmed performances on "Meet the Press."

The literary imagination can often see through the mask of synthetic issues and homogenized rhetoric, when the reportorial eye cannot. Norman Mailer, for example, in his occasional articles, struck closer, I think, to the essence of John Kennedy, than did William Manchester or Theodore Sorensen in thousands of pages of intimate biography. Largely through novelistic insight and intuition, Mark Harris, in *Mark the Glove Boy*, revealed more about Richard Nixon, than did Earl Mazo and Ralph De Toledano in their square, data-filled political biographies. And the best evocation of Lyndon Johnson does not appear in any conventional biography, but in the character of Governor Arthur Fenstermaker, in William Brammer's novel, *The Gay Place*.

So much of Kennedy demanded a literary imagination to be understood. The changes in his face after Dallas. Why he became a symbol of glamour and royalty to the poor. The symbolism of his long hair, his nickname of Bobby, his trip to South Africa in 1966, his relationships with Lyndon Johnson and his brother, his compulsive confronting of death in river rapids, mountaintops, and Amazon jungles. None of this had much to do with his position on the gold crisis, or the speeches he gave, but they were a necessary guide to his interior conflicts, and to the way others perceived him.

There was, for example, a whole side of Kennedy's personality that was converted into a contemporary cultural symbol. Teenyboppers reacted to his presence as if he were a fifth member of the Beatles. Merchants in Greenwich Village sold as many personality posters of Kennedy as they did of W. C. Fields or Che Guevara. He was a pop and folk hero like Marlon Brando or Frank Sinatra, a public repository for dreams and fantasies, a myth who made people feel better than they were.

The young especially saw in him, or projected onto him, the qualities they most easily identified with—youth, dissent, authenticity, alienation, action, even inarticulateness. They saw in him the same incongruous combination of toughness, humor, and sensitivity they saw in other generational cult figures like Belmondo, Dylan, and Bogart.

The final irony may be that the existential hero Norman Mailer glimpsed was not John Kennedy, but the younger brother who so idolized the older one. In his "Superman Comes to the Supermarket," Mailer defined the existential hero as:

> . . . central to his time, a man whose personality might suggest contradictions and mysteries which could reach into the alienated circuits of the underground, because only a hero can capture the secret imagination of a people, and so be good for the vitality of a nation. . . .
>
> . . . a hero embodies his time and is not so very much better than his time, but he is larger than life and so is capable of giving direction to the time, able to encourage a nation to discover the deepest colors of its character . . . a man who has lived with death.

from In Love with Night
by Ronald Steel

Admirers of Robert Kennedy sometimes suggest that he could have changed the course of American history if he'd lived, helping to realize dreams of peace and social justice that were thwarted during the final decades of the 20th century. Ronald Steel thinks RFK's admirers are wrong about that.

P resident Johnson arranged for Kennedy's body to be flown to New York in an official jet. There it lay in St. Patrick's Cathedral, where the great and the humble came to pay tribute. Early in the morning of June 7 the people began to arrive, and by the end of the day more than 100,000 of all ages and descriptions, waiting in a line at times a mile long for as much as eight hours in the summer heat, had filed past the bier.

Following the funeral on the morning of the eighth, nearly a thousand people—family, friends, journalists, big shots, publicity hounds, and hangers-on—went to Penn Station to board the special train to Washington for the burial at Arlington Cemetery. The journey was supposed to take four hours; it lasted eight and a half as the train wended its way for 225 miles down tracks lined on both sides by people who had come from their homes to watch and to honor.

The scene resembled the passing of a feudal chief before his assembled subjects. The other America, the people without glamour—

housewives in hair curlers, nurses in starched dresses, schoolchildren, factory workers in overalls—came to the tracks for the last journey of Robert Kennedy. "I seen people running all over!" an electrician exclaimed. "They were running toward the train. They tried to touch the train as it went by. . . . A lot of people crying. I seen *nuns* from all around with signs like REST IN PEACE, ROBERT and I'LL PRAY FOR YOU. A lot of nuns! . . . I seen one fellow there with a gun! He was like he was on guard. . . . He just stood there at attention."

Another train worker reported: "Everyone had a rose or a banner. They were throwing roses at the train. . . . People were praying. The men had their hats off. They were crossing themselves. . . . The signs read, WHO WILL BE THE NEXT ONE? and WE HAVE LOST OUR LAST HOPE. These were signs the colored had. It was mostly whites that had the signs that said, GOOD-BY BOBBY and WE STILL LOVE YOU. Further along a suburban family—a man and a woman in shorts, and two young children—stood next to their station wagon holding up a sign that said simply THE GEBHARTS ARE SAD."

Like an immense coffin on wheels the train rolled on through the long summer day and into the evening, past the sad Gebharts, and the nuns with their sunglasses and rosaries, and the Boy Scouts in uniform, and the saluting Legionnaires, and the people who put coins on the tracks to be flattened into souvenirs, and those who threw roses, and those who softly sang the "Battle Hymn of the Republic."

They were informed, if they had not realized it already, that this was the end of an era. Dick Tuck, the campaign wit, summed it up soberly: "Camelot is ended. It began in violence and ended in violence. It began with John Kennedy's death, not before, and it ended with Bob Kennedy's assassination. It will never exist again, whether Ted gets to be president or not."

Robert Kennedy's death was mourned not like that of a politician seeking his party's nomination for a run at the White House, but like that of a revered leader. Once again television, as it had four and a half years earlier, provided not only a description of the funeral, but a quasi-religious context in which the public—through endless repetition of the details of the event, and pontifical explanations by various shamans and "experts"—could be apprised of its deeper significance, while being reassured that the nation would survive this tragedy by honoring the dead man's memory.

Genuine sorrow was mixed with a media-driven pathos that inevitably descended into portentous morbidity and even banality. As they were to do in later decades with the deaths of other Kennedys, commentators vied in their efforts to sanctify the victim (while embellishing their own personal connection to him) and to deplore the moral condition of a people among whom such terrible things could happen.

Columnist James Reston set the tone for the general morbidity in interpreting the event not as the effort of a deranged young assassin to achieve his immortality, but as a demonstration of a "world morality crisis" marked by a "defiance of authority, a contagious irresponsibility, a kind of moral delinquency no longer restrained by religious or ethical faith." Kennedy's admirer, journalist Jack Newfield, declared that "from this time forward, things would get worse" now that his generation had lost its leader, and lamented in a portentous metaphor lifted from Camus, "The stone was at the bottom of the hill and we were alone."

Because much of the mourning was based upon the assumption that Kennedy would have been nominated, there was among many the sense that a future president, a redemptive president, had been lost. Yet there is reason to question such a course of events. His victory in California was another inconclusive one, much narrower than he hoped for, and not nearly big enough to finish off McCarthy. In fact, from McCarthy's point of view the results were ideal. Had McCarthy won the primary, Kennedy would have dropped out of the race and his delegates would have drifted over to Humphrey, thereby assuring the vice president's nomination. McCarthy's only hope was that a three-way deadlock in Chicago would induce party bosses to compromise on him.

One factor in their decision was the upcoming New York primary on June 18. McCarthy had a strong and dedicated following in the state and, unlike Kennedy, few political enemies. He also would have been a stronger candidate nationally among moderates, independents, and mugwump Republicans unable to swallow Nixon than either Kennedy or Humphrey. Since most of the convention delegates would be chosen not in primaries but by party officials, Kennedy put his own chances at only 50 percent. For a real chance at the nomination he had to sweep the remaining primaries and somehow conceal from party leaders how dependent he was on black voters.

Furthermore, the assumption that George Wallace's supporters were planning to vote for Kennedy but not for any other Democrat is not persuasive. Since Humphrey in the 1968 election easily carried blue-collar areas like Lake County Indiana (by 47 percent to Nixon's 36 percent and Wallace's 16 percent), "the hard evidence that Kennedy was the first choice of many Wallace voters remains thin," Brian Dooley has written in his informative study of Kennedy's final years.

But even his nomination was hardly a sure thing. He was hated by the powerful southern faction within the party, distrusted by many liberals, opposed by organized labor, and resented by Democratic loyalists for fracturing party unity. His strongest support—among blacks, the poor, and the alienated—lay outside the party's power structure. Thus they would have been relatively ineffective at the convention.

"Couldn't they see," said campaign director Lawrence O'Brien, "he didn't have a chance?" In any case it would have been a tough battle. As journalist Tom Wicker explained: "At one and the same time he wanted to have Mayor Daley's support and the support of the college students. The two are incompatible in the long run . . . it isn't a feasible alliance, and it isn't an alliance that's going to hold political power."

Even if he had been elected, what would he have done as president? What exactly was it that "might have been"? All that we can go by is what he *did* when, as his brother's deputy, he had power—and then by what he *said* when, as Johnson's enemy, he was out of power. As attorney general he was a law enforcer who cracked down on organized crime and came late and grudgingly, though ultimately decisively, to the protection of civil rights. As his brother's unofficial foreign policy adviser he was an ardent and conventional cold warrior. As a U.S. senator he was primarily a candidate for the presidency.

We are informed that he underwent a profound "transformation" following his brother's death that sensitized him to the plight of life's victims. It is difficult to know what to make of assurances of such psychological changes, if indeed they did occur. Certainly he began to speak in moving terms about the problems of the poor, and of racial and ethnic minorities. However, beyond his undoubtedly sincere empathy for such people, and his often-cited declarations that the deplorable conditions in which they lived were "not acceptable," his remedies for dealing with their problems were quite modest.

One should not confuse Kennedy's actions, or his feelings, with the changes in his rhetoric that took place after his entry into the Senate— and even less with the rhetoric of those who wrote for, and about, him. The "transformation" that journalists and admirers discerned in Robert Kennedy once he was on his own might have been real. On the other hand, it might equally have been merely evidence of different speech-writers or new political tactics inspired by the results of opinion polls. Just as JFK's speeches were geared to an Augustan era of great expectations, so Bobby's, with equally sensitive timing, reflected and played upon mid-sixties anxiety. Both men were honored, and are today remembered, more for what they said than for what they actually did.

It is impossible to know what kind of president Robert Kennedy would have been or what policies he would have pursued. Had he been elected, which is far from certain, many admirers would have been disappointed. Although he would probably have worked out some means of extrication from Vietnam earlier than Nixon did, his opposition to unilateral withdrawal and his vague formulas for a negotiated settlement hardly differed from Nixon's "peace with honor" formula.

On domestic policy, his anti-poverty plan was far less radical than McCarthy's, and was essentially designed to get private investors to gild the ghetto so that it would be more tolerable for its inhabitants, not to make it easier for them to live and work elsewhere. The Bedford-Stuyvesant laboratory to which he had devoted much attention helped stabilize the neighborhood, but failed to gain the business investment needed to provide jobs. As a national program to attack the causes of poverty, or as a means of breaking down segregation, it was insignificant.

He likely would also have disillusioned the white radicals who found him a "rebel" because he was youthful, let his hair grow longer, and expressed an interest in their music. He was at heart, and had always been, a Catholic conservative deeply suspicious of the moral license of the radical left, with its celebration of drugs, sexual anarchy, and politics as theater. He was no champion of women's rights, and would likely have been appalled by the very notion of gay liberation, had he ever been confronted with it.

He has become a hero to millions not for what he did, but because he was the ghost of his sanctified brother, and many were persuaded that he would have done things that they desperately wanted. But had he ever gained the high power he sought, he would have had to stop being a challenger and become an administrator, to shed his charisma as redeemer and become a constitutional leader within a bureaucratically confined order. Instead of being the "tribune" of the underclass, he would have had to become what every president ultimately is: a power broker. Signs of this were apparent in his 1968 campaign, for those willing to see them.

A product of troubled times and heir to a thwarted legend, he became a hero to millions who were looking for a hero. But we should be wary of such a yearning. People have a need for heroes, particularly during times of trouble. To escape situations they deem to be intolerable they are willing to suspend disbelief and even surrender their will. The yearning for heroes is deeply embedded in our culture, and perhaps in our consciousness. "Unhappy is the land that breeds no hero," says one of the characters in a play by Bertolt Brecht. "No, Andrea," replies the scientist Galileo, soon to become a martyr to fear and superstition. "Unhappy is the land that needs a hero."

The need to follow, to serve, and to worship is not a healthy thing in a people. Heroes are granted license to do things that men of less exalted reputation, or ambitions, would shrink from. Julius Caesar began, after all, as a hero, and then was deemed a tyrant, only to be transformed back into a hero again by the demagogic interpretation put on his assassination. Napoleon Bonaparte, too, was a hero acclaimed throughout Europe as a liberator until he donned an imperial mantle and began losing battles—thereby losing his vaunted charisma as well. Stalin was for many Russians a hero, as was Hitler to Germans.

Passing time and increasing disillusion with the politicians we have lead us to embellish past events as moments of glory, and to inflate certain figures—particularly dashing, youthful ones cut down in their prime—as tragic heroes. In 1968, Americans were desperately searching for a hero. Robert Kennedy offered himself and millions responded. They saw him as one who would deliver the promise aroused by the rhetoric of his brother, who by this time they had already elevated above the level of mortal men.

This is the Robert Kennedy we honor and whom we have created to fulfill our own needs. In this sense he has become "our Bobby," because of what he was, but more because of what we wanted him to be. He himself seemed not always sure of who he was. A narrow and rigid man, he came near the end of his life to have an awareness of moral complexities that both deepened and troubled him. In the end he seemed no longer the dogmatist he had been. But neither was he the moral redeemer that many saw in him.

He was a man embarked on a journey he did not fully understand. He had been driven to it by forces beyond his control, and had good reason to feel that he would never arrive at an only dimly glimpsed destination. He had done dark deeds, and there was a part of his character, reinforced by his fierce brand of Irish Catholicism, that drove him to seek atonement for them. He had become, as in Robert Frost's melancholy poem that JFK liked to quote, "one acquainted with the night." He was always driving himself to feats of endurance, to gratuitous dangers, to acts of penance toward those less privileged, and ultimately to a political quest whose deepest purpose he only half understood himself.

Ultimately he learned to go through a politician's motions during his last campaign, for he was a tireless worker in whatever task he set for himself. He did everything that had to be done, and even more. But he did not seem to enjoy it much. Watching him those last weeks, both feeding and recoiling from the impassioned crowds that seemed to want to take home a piece of him, he appeared to be carrying out an onerous but inescapable duty.

"To the fervor and adulation of his supporters," the *New York Times* reported just after his narrow victory in the California primary election, "he seemed curiously aloof, exhibiting neither pleasure nor fright. Those close to Mr. Kennedy noticed that his eyes rarely sparkled, but instead were sad and withdrawn, and that his manner, despite a grin, was unemotional."

Some have said, reading backwards from the tragic ending of his life, that disaster was inevitable. "Doom was woven in your nerves," Robert Lowell writes in a posthumous poem to him. "He felt he was doomed, and you knew that he felt that," the poet later explained. Perhaps. But such phrases seem meaningful only after an event. It is enough to say that, even during his campaign for the presidency, it seems likely that the future, whatever it held, would not bring him an easy pleasure.

There was a sense of the obligatory about his last campaign. He had dallied for months before committing himself to making the race for president, continually finding reasons the moment was inopportune, publicly anguishing over the decision. It was as though he were looking for a way to be relieved of the burden. Like a man who finally understood that there was no escape from his fate, he embraced it not with excitement but resignation.

This resignation was reflected in his compulsive risk-taking, his fatalism, his offering of his unprotected body to emotionally aroused crowds, and by his willful indifference to physical security. When asked during the 1968 campaign whether he worried about what would happen to his family if he were shot, he replied: "But they're well taken care of, and there's really nothing else I can do, is there? So I really don't care about anything happening to me. This really isn't such a happy existence, is it?"

This is not to claim that he had a conscious death wish, but rather that in this religious and often pessimistic man there was what educator Michael Novak has called a "quest for martyrdom" rooted in his puritan character. To become a martyr was in the most literal sense to become one with his brother, with whom he was bound by an iron sense of guilt and obligation. It was to compensate for his ruthless drive to win, the other side of his vaunted and often insensitive pragmatism.

Semi-legendary figures like John and Robert Kennedy "represent the hero, handsome, courageous," artist Saul Steinberg noted on the funeral train. "They look for drama; and it attracts the counterpart. Just the way the hero is in search of a dragon, the dragon is always in search of a hero." The mysteriously named Sirhan Sirhan was such a dragon. In that moment in a hotel pantry, very near where, weeks earlier, someone had written enigmatically on a wall, "The Once and Future King," he sought immortalization by slaying the immortal hero.

The mythology that has been generated around Robert Kennedy in the years since his death is simply that: a mythology. Like many legendary figures, the Bobby of legend has been created by us. There is little, beyond hope and need, to lead us to believe that he would have bridged the divisions between blacks and whites, narrowed the chasm between rich and poor, dedicated himself to the values that inspire liberals, quickly ended a divisive war, or brought about the magical restoration of a mythical golden age. Only from his early death have we, as with his brother, created a heroic figure to fill our needs.

Why, then, do so many honor him to this day? Because he generated a set of ideals that resonated deeply among Americans at a time of social crisis, and remain unfulfilled to this day. The very fact that his promise was never fully tested made it possible to believe that he would have been able to achieve the goals he espoused. Like his brother John he had the ability to inspire others, through his words more than his deeds, to hope and to acts of service.

Walter Lippmann, who had been an early supporter of John Kennedy and then had grown critical of his performance, wrote about the Kennedy "legend" at the time that Robert was deciding whether to run for president. He was impressed by the fact that millions had come to believe that the murdered president, despite an undistinguished record in office, was a herald of better things to come. This gave the columnist a new respect for the mythmaking process. "I am glad of that legend, and I think that it contains that part of the truth which is most worth having," he concluded in words that also apply to Robert Kennedy's "legend" today. "This is the conviction, for which he set the example, that a new age has begun and that men can become the masters of their fate."

The best of Robert Kennedy was not in what he did, but in what he has inspired in others. As he told a convocation of university students in South Africa two years to the day before his death, it is crucial to recognize that "idealism, high aspirations, and deep convictions are not incompatible with the most practical and efficient of programs—that there is no basic inconsistency between ideals and realistic possibilities, no separation between the deepest desires of heart and of mind and the rational application of human effort to human problems."

It was not his idealism that made him a more accessible and interesting figure than his brother John. Rather it was his efforts, near the end of his life, to compensate for his failings by identifying himself with the deprived. This gave him a romantic dimension suited to an era of powerful emotions.

More than any other politician of his time Robert Kennedy required, like the improbable scripts and personalities of grand opera, a suspension of disbelief. We have read into him what we have wanted to read. It is his very image as the renegade prince that has given him his allure. For millions he has represented not a rational political alternative, but something more powerful and attractive: an escape from politics. What people found in him was not political but emotional satisfaction. He did not inspire programs; he aroused feelings. The response he stimulated was not polite applause or mild disapproval, but love or hate. He had the compelling, and disturbing, appeal of a demagogue.

Among those who followed him, and later have yearned for him, there is the belief that he could have done miraculous things, that he would not have made the compromises of ordinary politicians, that he would not have disappointed. This belief came not from what he did or said, but from what he represented. It came from the "legend."

There is a danger with legends, and the heroes who embody them. They can paralyze as well as inspire. "The love of the hero," Emerson warned, "corrupts into worship of his statue." Robert Kennedy had no answers that are, like an ancient Egyptian's treasured objects, buried with him. Rather he raised interesting questions, and in so doing, and with the often tormented passions he displayed, influenced many to participate in public affairs. The lesson that they drew from his life, however imperfectly he may have exemplified it, is that politics can be a worthy calling, that even the humblest person can make a difference, and that the greatest satisfaction can lie not in the indulgence of private pleasures but in pursuit of the public good. That is the part of the legend most worth remembering: not what he might have done, but what we can do.

Myths can inspire or they can imprison. The important thing is that they lead us to thought and action, not to idolatry. The Bobby Myth is our creation, not his.

from American Journey
by Jean Stein,
edited by George Plimpton

After RFK's death, his body was flown to New York and then carried by train to Washington, D.C. for burial at Arlington Cemetery. Jean Stein, editor of the literary magazine Grand Street *and George Plimpton, both friends of Kennedy (Plimpton helped subdue his assassin) created this oral history of Kennedy's career, including these passages that describe the funeral train's journey.*

JUNE 8, 1968
PENN STATION, NEW YORK CITY . . . 1:03 p.m.

VINCENT EMANUEL, *electrician*
They had two locomotives on the funeral train; I was on the second one. That's procedure with the railroad when they have a heavy train; in case one goes sour, they have another one. They were both working, both pulling . . . they had couplings in between so one engineer could operate the two engines just like a subway car. I was on the second car with the Secret Service man. He introduced himself—Mr. Kellerman. He is in the William Manchester book about John F. Kennedy because he was in the fatal car in Dallas. He was going to watch from the right side of the locomotive. We began chatting about different things, like this was the first time he'd been on a locomotive and this was one trip he didn't like. Neither did I, to tell you the truth, on account of it was a funeral train.

GILLIAN WALKER, *theatrical producer*

While waiting to start, I was impressed with the kind of sterile atmosphere of the train—very aware of the steel, and the glass, and the sort of sterility of the inside of the train, the people in their little black dresses looking very tidy and almost unhuman. Their hair was done very nicely, and their faces looked very composed. Somehow it all seemed as if everyone had turned out for an Antonioni movie. There were these steel carts that went down the aisles with sandwiches, these closed steel boxes, and these seemed to be part of the unreal interior. It was very silent in the beginning; nobody talked; it was very hushed and very cool because of the air conditioning.

ANTHONY M. BOYSA, *fireman*

The train started late. We expected a slight delay. It was delayed all right. No one had the slightest idea that all those people would be along the route. We got going about one o'clock, and we came out of the tunnel on the Jersey side. The people were standing along the tracks and on the factory roofs. I didn't know what they were doing there at first.

JOHN KENNETH GALBRAITH, *economist*

If you were burying Ronald Reagan, you would obviously want to do it with an airplane; but if you are going to bury Robert Kennedy, his people live along the railway tracks.

MILTON GWIRTZMAN, *campaign aide*

There were people standing in the marshes in New Jersey, watching. I had the impression that it was almost two different worlds. When you looked outside and saw the emotions of the people standing beside the tracks, you got very drawn to the tragedy of the occasion; so you would leave that and turn back to the people in the car and almost forget the nature of the occasion.

RUSSELL BAKER, *columnist*

It was a Saturday afternoon; warm and kind of summery. Remember how warm it was? And all these people were out doing their Saturday things; it was sort of Saturday-afternoon America. But they ended up at the railroad track, and the reaction was kind of varied, as you'd expect. A lot of solemn people and a few carrying flowers and signs and what not. But it really impressed me to see America with its hair down on Saturday afternoon. It was like seeing the whole country. And what impressed me was, you know, we're not really a beautiful people. This is really quite apart from what the day was all about. The Kennedys, in a way, had this kind of grace and glamour that people loved or hated. They had beautiful people around them. And there, outside, were all the ugly people. Really, you know, all of us ugly Americans in our undershirts and our potbellies hanging over them; the women with their hair up in curlers. Everybody just looking dreadful and over-weight and pasty. And they were all out there looking at this great symbol of what they voted for and what they cared about.

MICHAEL HARRINGTON, *author*
Aside from its own tragic aspects, it evoked all the other deaths I have ever known. I think Dylan Thomas' line is very true: "After the first death, there is no other."

So I could not face squarely and candidly what my feelings were. But as I looked out of the window of the train, I could see my own grief mirrored in other people's faces. And that was the experience that would threaten my composure.

SYLVIA WRIGHT, *reporter*
I didn't talk to anybody on the train. But I thought people shouldn't be saying, "Why are all those horrible people out there along the tracks, staring? Those scavengers!" I heard Jack Paar say, "Those scavengers all come to stare, and don't give the Kennedys any privacy."

He was wrong. The people *needed* some tangible proof that it really had happened and really was true. When we rode from St. Patrick's Cathedral to Penn Station, I thought, "Isn't it incredible? Thousands of people lining Fifth Avenue in the streets of New York, ten and fifteen deep, to watch Greyhound buses roll by!" But I understood that. It made it official. There was a police car with a flashing red light; and then they got to see a hearse and black limousines in order, and buses rolling by in order. Something had indeed happened. It was their way of touching it and believing it! You know, people always have said how terrible that Jacqueline had to be there and see her husband shot, and have him in her lap. But I think how terrible if she had been in Washington, and the last she had seen was a whole, healthy man running off across the lawn to the helicopter; then she's supposed to believe that man is dead because somebody said so! But she saw it happen, step by step, and her mind was able to adjust slowly; when he fell in her lap, she saw what might be. So that by the time they got to the hospital, she already was aware of the possibilities. . . .

I think it's selfish to say that people shouldn't come to stare. I can even see why they want to go and stare at Jackie or Ethel, and snoop in their privacy by looking under their veils. They want to see, are you okay? are you a real person like me? are you okay? People don't mean to be rude. They mean to care.

CHARLES QUINN, *television correspondent*
You'd see a man standing way off in the distance, saluting; you'd see another man standing with his hand over his heart; or a fire truck on top of a knoll with four, or five firemen with their hands over their hearts, and the little light going around and around. And the girls on horseback; and the boats . . . all those bridges we passed over and those dozens of boats bobbing up and down in the water, and the people just watching. The American flags; the fireboat named the *John F. Kennedy*, with the people on it saluting. . . .

LOUIS COLLINS, *fireboat captain*
We had no permission from the powers that be. Still, we are allowed fifteen minutes away from quarters by boat without having to notify our chiefs. So we took it upon ourselves to do it. We're at the foot of Center Street on the Passaic River. We have a little house there for an

office and a bunk room. We're all Catholic, all four of us, and we thought it would be a nice gesture. The train bridge is only five minutes down the river. I'm the acting captain. The other three are firemen. The fireboat is called the *John F. Kennedy*. The city council got together and decided it would be nice to commemorate the Kennedys' name. We have thirteen and one-half miles of waterfront to cover—loose boats and barges to retrieve, and drownings and lost bodies, and we go dredging and all that. We have three turrets that we use to put fires out, and some thought we should put water out—that is, turn on the turrets—but I said no, that they'd take it for a celebration if we did that. They'd get the wrong idea. So we just stood in silence when the train went through. That's all. We saluted the train. We couldn't see very much inside, naturally. We said at the time that it must have been a very sad ride for them because there were so many of the family there. We didn't put anything in the log about it. After all, it wasn't official. We were out there a half-hour or so. It's always nice on the river. There's always a breeze.

CARTER BURDEN, *campaign aide*
I think it was Bill Walton who said, "You know, you could tell the story of Robert Kennedy by telling the story of the people on this train."

THE REVEREND RALPH ABERNATHY, *civil-rights leader*
I went back to the last car to express my condolences. When I got there, Mrs. Jacqueline Kennedy said, "Oh, Reverend. Thanks for coming in." She said, "You'll be able to help us lift this. It should be elevated so that the crowds of people watching the train might have the chance to see it." They weren't seeing anything because the casket was on a very beautiful stand that wasn't more than six or eight inches off the floor. So we got some chairs and set the casket on them. That was the experience I will not forget—lifting his body. In any funeral, the most important persons are not those who read the scriptures or pray the prayers, or even

deliver the eulogy. They are the pallbearers. When I die, the people who carry my body I want to be the dearest of friends that I have in the world. I was not an official pallbearer for Robert Kennedy, but at least I lifted the weight of his body when he could no longer lift it.

CARTER BURDEN, *campaign aide*

As I came to the glass-paneled door to enter the small sitting room where the casket lay, they were just practicing folding the flag. John Glenn was instructing them. When they finished, I went into the room. Impressions are never what you expect; I suppose I expected a very somber, solemn scene . . . and, indeed, in many ways it was. But in many ways it was just the opposite. The casket was raised up so that it could be seen through the window, and all around the ledge just beneath window level were paper cups and Coke cans and half-eaten sandwiches and overfilled ashtrays. Just like the remnants of an ordinary picnic. It was a room that people had been living in—the family had been waiting out the long afternoon like everybody else on the train—eating and drinking Cokes and talking and laughing. It jarred me at first.

When I came in, most of the family were out on the back platform; only Ethel was there, sitting beside the casket. It was the only moment, then or since, that I saw her cry. She sat there, immensely still, and hunched over in a plain straight-backed chair. She had a rosary in her hands, and her head was resting against the casket.

ART BUCHWALD, columnist

The coffin itself was on chairs. And it was not just the honor of standing vigil. You literally had to *hold* the coffin so it wouldn't fall. I was sort of embarrassed to stay in that compartment because Teddy was there, and Pat, and Jean; and they were talking. I didn't know what to do. So I went out on the platform where the children were. And that was the first time, being on the train, that I really had a feeling of what was going on outside the train. Inside the train, you couldn't hear anything. But on the platform, you could hear the cheers, and the people crying. At several places along the way, I noticed kids running out after the train would go by and picking things up off the rail. I asked one of the Kennedy kids what that was about. They said that people were laying things on the rails, and then the train ran over them, and they were souvenirs. They were medals or money, I guess, or coins.

WILLIAM RICHARDS II, journalist

I kept a notebook. Here's how it reads about Elizabeth, New Jersey, and the accident there:

An old man carrying a cane (I'm at the platform now) walked by. "Just curiosity. You only see something like this once in a lifetime." Time is about 11:45. There were maybe 300 people lining the westbound platform.

[I wrote that the platform was narrow, maybe 10–12 feet wide.] The sun was shining through blue skies. Some clouds. Men in Bermuda shorts, women in gay print dresses. Some people with movie cameras.

12:32—Crowd somber, quiet, pensive. Not much talking. Maybe 500 to 600 people.

Elizabeth Honor Guard and Mayor Dunn arrive 12:35.

Police constantly moving along, moving people back from edge of walkway.

People at every overpass. Maybe 1,500 at station, lining both sides of the tracks, 5 to 7 deep.

A breeze blew intermittently, helping to cool it off. There were three men atop Goerke's, near the water tower on the roof.

Four more men on the Elizabeth Town Gas Co. building.

A baby kept crying. Seemed like maybe 2,500 people there.

A light appeared. "Here comes something." The people started to lean, their necks craning, looking.

It came on. It was an engine, black, huge. Three cars.

Police cars began radioing the word down the line. "That was the pilot," the radio crackled.

Then another message: "Forty-five miles an hour—that's the best they can do. The remains are in the last car, the observation car."

Another broadcast: "We got a call that some kids are gonna attempt to switch the tracks. All units watch switches and tracks."

Forty minutes late.

At 1:10, another broadcast: "It's in Secaucus Flats."

Up to the north, the tracks are lined with people.

"His major contribution was that he was," a woman said.

1:16—"Train passing through Penn Station, Newark." Police radio.

Another murmur. People guessing how long it will take to get here.

Cops: concentrating on people on tracks; getting people on platform; some dangling legs over edges.

"The feeling of being here is important," a man said as he passed.

"The draw of the man, even in death, is amazing," another guy remarked.

The man with the crew cut, and the Bermudas and glasses, said, "His contribution is that he had the courage to be different."

Broadcast: "Train is moving at a high rate of speed. Keep those people off the tracks."

Seriousness impressive. Quiet, eyes fixed to the north, awaiting appearance.

Good twenty minutes pass . . . nervous, awaiting train. Light appears.

I get goose-pimples. At North Avenue at 1:20.

Bright light. People run across track north of station. A plane in air following route. Two helicopters.

Light and black mass loom larger. Noise. Crowd chattering more now. Copter overhead, roaring—U.S. Army copter.

People stepping on tracks to take pictures.

Slow, very slow. Hats being taken off. Fifteen miles an hour. Large and black. Secret Service men in engine.

Nuns and photographers on board. Sonny Fox of Channel 5.

It slows even more.

Ethel, Jackie. Coffin, a Kennedy child on rear, garlands streaming.

Jackie and Ethel together. Ethel wide-eyed. Jackie pointing at something over us.

Panic. Woman been hit. Faces turning away from train.

Rush of crowd.

A cop shouts: "Get them people the hell outa here."

The woman, blonde, blue dress.

Second train came through from other direction on north side. People never saw it coming. Many on north side didn't even see Kennedy car.

Another woman hurt, receiving oxygen. Kennedy train slowing.

A black and white shoe lying on tracks.

One woman

One man

Screams.

Cops trying to clear people on West Grand Street to get emergency vehicles through.

Train No. 50, Chicago to New York. Penn Central. Dragged from station to bridge. Put emergency brake on.

Dr. Henares, intern, looks at woman. It didn't look like a person. More like a bundle that's been pounded.

A penny, a camera case. Down a bit farther, the woman. Then some more, the man's leg on the other side of the outside track. On the bridge is his body.

Another woman got her hand hit by train.

GENEVIEVE MURPHY, *housewife, Elizabeth, New Jersey*
The first few cars had very few people in them, and Michael—poor Mike is retarded, my son, he's fourteen—well, he was looking for Sidney Poitier. He saw him in *To Sir With Love*, and since then he's admired him so. Whenever he sees him on TV, he gets excited. I think because Poitier was a schoolteacher, and the children were giving him a hard time—I think that's why. When the Senator died, and we were watching the TV—constantly, we never left the TV—Mike and I saw Sidney Poitier at the vigil in the Cathedral; he was standing at the

coffin. Mike couldn't get over that—that Sidney Poitier could know the Kennedys and feel as bad as everybody else. Then we watched it again Saturday morning, and we knew he was going to be on the train. I wanted to go down anyway; I didn't know about Mike. So I said, "Mike, maybe you'll see Sidney Poitier." He wanted to know if Sidney Poitier would cry . . . this is Michael's way of feeling. So I said I thought he might. If we cried, he would cry too. So we went to the train station. When we saw the first few cars, they had very few people in them, then I saw the more crowded cars coming. I said, "Look, Mike! Look, Mike!" I wanted him to see Sidney Poitier if he could.

I was quite far away from most of the crowd because my husband, who was with us too, was ill and he had to hold onto things to stand. So we were at the very edge of the crowd—I guess closest to the bend of the other train when it came through. I didn't see or hear the train. I did hear a horn, but I thought it was the Kennedy train. Just as I heard the train horn, it was then—you know when I try to recall I get such a headache because this is when it all happened—the train must have *bumped* me, because I feel now as if I had my left hand out—I had my back to the train—and that's all it hit, my left hand. But when it hit my left hand, it threw me back into the crowd so that I knocked people over with the force. I didn't know that I was hurt until my husband picked me up. I saw the contents of my pocketbook all over . . . and especially some letters that I treasured; so I went running after them. Then, as I went to pick up something, I felt a pain in my left hand; I looked down, and that was the first I realized that I had been hit. My hand was covered with grease; it was bleeding; it was swollen. With that, I turned around to my husband: "Look—the train hit me."

FELICIA TEDESCHI, *high school student, Elizabeth, New Jersey*

We still had our pajamas on that morning. We saw the train on television, and when they said it was delayed, Lucy and I decided to go. We just made it there on time, about thirty-five minutes before the train finally came.

We could see the helicopters flying overhead, and we were really getting excited. Lucy and I started sobbing—we were going to be emotional. We saw four cars of the Kennedy train, and there were people waving to people on the platform.

Then we saw the light of the train coming in the opposite direction, and people were standing on the tracks. It was horrible. The best way I can describe it is when you see a movie and someone's about to die—someone's falling over a cliff—and you hear this horrible scream of terror. It was heartbreaking.

That was it. After the accident, I didn't even care to look in the direction of the Kennedy train.

I think the grandmother tripped over the track. In the *Superman* comics or movies, Superman comes and stops the train just before . . . well, that didn't happen, because her legs were right over the track and the train was about two feet from her. I saw a man try to pull her up, and this man—John Curia—died also.

The baby was turning with the wheel; the baby's clothes were caught into the wheel, or maybe it was the friction or the air suction of the train, but she rolled about two or three times. She was completely still. And I was scared to death because I've never seen a dead person in my life. I've never been to a wake, and my mother says I'm afraid of a mosquito, which is true. I didn't really want to pick up the child because I thought she was dead. There were plenty of adults around, and I didn't really think it was my duty to go to her. But no one else moved. I guess people were in shock. Since no one else moved, I went to pick her up. People thought she was my baby. They were just pointing at me and saying, "Look at the lady with the dead baby!" No one would help me.

I thought the baby was dead. I ran out into the street, and I thought everyone knew what had happened; but people were just coming out of the stores. They just saw me screaming. They didn't know what was the matter with me.

There happened to be a detective out there, for security reasons. He didn't know what had happened, but he saw the baby was injured and took me to the hospital.

He was driving, and I was crying—really, I couldn't control myself—

and the detective said he was going to sock me. He said, "Control your-self, because you're going to do something to that kid." He thought it was mine. It's funny because before school, I always went for breakfast to a store across the street, and this detective goes there also. I never noticed him, but he happened to notice me. After a while, we began talking, and he realized that I was only in high school and not this baby's mother.

The little girl was unconscious, and the following day the detective told me that at the time he thought she was dead. But finally, she started crying. She had no blood on her. She just had bruises.

My mother wanted me to go and see the child afterwards, but I couldn't bring myself to do it. She was two and a half years old.

MARIAN JAVITS *(Mrs. Jacob Javits)*

All those nervous Congressmen just to do something were serving sandwiches. I guess they felt they had to get out of their seats; or per-haps they did not feel the need to sit down because it had been such a long church service. So they were serving *sandwiches,* and I remember it was about an hour and a half out of New York. I had passed one group of sandwiches by and also an offer to go into the next car. Then another Congressman came by with a bunch of sandwiches, and I took one. I started to bite into the sandwich as we were pulling in toward a station. We slowed down a little, and I remember seeing the beginnings of a huge crowd of people standing at the edge of a platform. And then, suddenly, the other train came by. I had chewed into the sandwich, and turned to look back—slightly back—and saw the body of a woman thrown up into the air. I remember that she wore a green dress, and her legs went up.

SAUL STEINBERG, *artist*

A ship is isolated by the ocean; a plane flies high up; but a train—the way a train travels is very near reality. Except the American train is air-conditioned; you can't open the windows . . . so that the whole train had this dramatic reality of a giant coffin. It's isolated; it's sealed

. . . so that this train was really a coffin on wheels, advancing, and expecting to be buried—the whole train—in Washington.

Part of the primitive system of the political funeral was that this coffin on wheels took along some sacrificial victims. It's part of this dramatic system of marking somebody of political importance; the hero cannot seem to die alone.

ANN BUCHWALD, *family friend, Rahway, New Jersey*

She looked just perfect—if it hadn't been black, which Ethel hates. Somebody said, "She's never liked black. She once told me that she wouldn't buy a dress with any black in it." You look at her house, and you see her adoration of pinks and greens and blues, and her bedroom and her pool house. I can't think of anything that has black in it. So that was a shocker. You had never seen her in black! Nobody had. Yes. Then she came through and did all this talking to people.

ROOSEVELT GRIER, *former professional football player*

She wanted to go through and thank all the people. I was sitting up a couple of cars when I saw her coming. I said, "You know, there's twenty cars on this train and it's real hot, but if you want to go, we're going to take you." She said, "We're going to go." And that was it. So we took her the rest of the way, all the way up front. Then we sat down for a little while. A couple of times I got her some water. She just talked to people and she thanked them for coming. I felt so much for her. I remember that any time I would drift off into a really down feeling, she'd say, "Now, Rosey, come on over here." She'd keep pulling me back, you know. Pulling me back.

ADALBERT de SEGONZAC, *journalist*

The rumor came through that Ethel was coming. There was a man sleeping two or three seats in front of me, and his wife rushed to wake him up. She shook him and said, "Wake up! Wake up! Mrs. Kennedy's coming. Put on your shoes! You've got to put on your shoes!"

JOSÉ TORRES, *former light heavyweight champion*

The first one who came by was Matthew, the small one, and he says—very proud—that he just took a nap, that he didn't know what was going on. He was very excited seeing all those people in the train. Then I think the second one to come was little Bobby, and then the other kids came by and I said, "Do you remember me?" Kerry, the girl, said, "Yes, I know who you are." And she went like this with her fist. "You are the fighter," she says. And then she walked away, and then Joseph came, and he saw me and he said, "Hi, José," and shook my hand, and he kept walking. Ethel came, and you know I had the crutches because I had this operation on my foot, and it was the first time I saw her since this happened. She says; "José, where have you been?" I couldn't talk, of course, and she says, "Look at that, half a day campaigning for Bobby and look what happened, you have crutches." She was just kidding around. When she got no response from me, then she took both my hands, pressing very hard.

PETE HAMILL, *columnist*

Holy Christ! She had enough problems. Everybody just sort of shrunk back and gasped. They didn't know what the hell to do. She came through trying to cheer us up, but everybody was in tears by the time she got through the car. That was the first time I broke on the train. Of all the people, she was the one that had the right to grieve and yet she was worried about our grief more than anything else. Remarkable! She's really some woman. Jacqueline was wandering around with a tray at one point, and looking sort of icy; it was an interesting contrast. I don't know how she remembered everybody's name. José Torres was with me, and he had a cast on his leg, and all she wanted to know about was the cast; what had happened and was it going to be all right. That wrecked him.

• • •

SHIRLEY MACLAINE, *actress*

The two women: Mrs. Ethel Kennedy and Mrs. Jackie Kennedy came through. Jackie first, very regal, as only she can be, with this marvelous sense of sort of anticipatory dignity. She was always able, somehow, to anticipate when the train was going to lurch or when it would bump, and queenlike, take hold of something so that when the bump came, she wasn't disturbed or dislodged. Ethel, standing right beside her, was so unaware, with a complete lack of self-consciousness about herself, that she got bumped every single time. She lurched and fell against a chair or against somebody, always recovering and doing it with humor; but it was so poignant that she allowed herself to be exposed that much.

Ethel stopped and talked with everyone, and remembered things like people's second-removed-generation cousin's names and how did that tennis match turn out.

BURT GLINN, *photographer*

It stopped your heart! In the car where I was sitting, Joe was the first of the family to come out. I was sitting with a guy from the Chicago Sun-Times, Dave Murray, who was at Harvard at the same time that I was there. All of a sudden, Dave looked over my shoulder and kind of stiffened, and he said, "My God! It's Bobby when we first knew him!" I turned around. Well, Joe was sixteen, and I guess Bobby was eighteen or nineteen when we first saw him, but a lot of it was there. The strange images that people have who knew him back at Harvard that time, like Dave and myself, Tony Lewis . . . my memory is of a strangely slight young man, standing on the Harvard football field. He looked so out of place there. But the personal gestures and characteristics carried on.

DOLORES HUERTA, *vice president, United Farm Workers Organizing Committee*

And the little Kennedy children were coming by . . . You know, they kept passing by, going back and forth, and one of the little children said to his sister, "Well, California . . . . Weren't we in California? I remember California," he said to her, as he passed by.

• • •

GILLIAN WALKER, *theatrical producer, New Brunswick, New Jersey*

I was in the ladies' room. You can't see out those windows. I just heard this noise coming from outside the train, and I couldn't imagine what it was—people singing or what it was.

KATE HADDAD *(Mrs. William Haddad)*

The bands! You couldn't hear anything from where we were—just see the bands playing. All the people along the way just were miles and miles and miles of little strings of people . . . not at the station, where there were crowds, but just all along the way . . . people who had stopped obviously in the middle of doing something else, even girls in bathing suits; but it wasn't disrespectful! All the hair curlers—Americana, you know. It was an American Saturday afternoon, and people were in hair curlers.

GEORGE KRAUSS, *bandmaster, New Brunswick, New Jersey*

Now, the question was raised why we were not in uniform. The main reason: we had collected our uniforms at the conclusion of the Memorial Day parade. We had them in storage. Due to Field Day, it was just an impossibility to get children into uniforms. So we were dressed in regular school clothes. I told them to come dressed presentable in school clothes. The most important thing was not the fact that they did not wear uniforms, but that they contributed their musical contributions in the best traditions of dedication. Our band has done many fine projects for the school, community, and the state. The group has played in the Miss America Pageant; they've been to perform for Vice-President Humphrey and Governor Hughes; we've had a variety of experiences around here. The band is highly integrated. Sometimes people say, "How do you do it?" Well, we just involve our children in activities. We have had Chinese, Negroes, Japanese this year—all types—we even had a Redskin in there—so we've had Indians and everything.

Actually, I don't do much directing in front of an orchestra. That's not my job. But this was a special occasion. I was amused that Edwin

Newman, the broadcaster—I've learned this from my wife's remarks and other remarks that have come in—said that I conducted in a "Toscanini-like" manner. Quite something. My children have been kidding me about the little bald spot I've got back here, and all the TV coverage it got.

The singers on the platform who joined in and sang along were not organized. They were strictly people singing from the platform and becoming involved. I was very pleased and, to be frank with you, I personally feel, and I think this is the reaction they have from NBC, that the singing was *fitting* . . . and appropriate, that it added dignity and a somber feeling to what could have been bedlam because that station was so overcrowded.

I was in a position in front of the band to see down the track. When I saw the train reach a certain point, I started my "Taps." I was facing away from the train; I purposely stationed myself so that I could see it coming and gear the length of the "Taps" so that the train, which must have been going three or five miles an hour, would reach me just as I had concluded "Taps." Then we'd swing into the "Battle Hymn of the Republic." In every single letter that comes through, people ask who played "Taps." Well, there's a reason why I did it. Under an emotional crisis like that, I've seen professional musicians *crack* on "Taps," and it was a hot day, and I did not want to put any boy in the band under that type of strain; it takes great control. It's not easy to do, because you can choke up. It's a situation whereby experience prepares you. I was in the Navy on the battleship *New York*, leading the band at burial services, and many times I experienced the playing of it, so I know the problems. Besides, I thought it would be wiser if I played it and gave the band a chance to get ready because we wanted to get the "Battle Hymn" in there. It worked out very satisfactorily.

WILLIAM J. SHIELDS, *Penn Central supervisor, Trenton, New Jersey*

I don't think too many people saw the accident in Trenton—it all happened so quickly. But I had the radio on, and Jerry Bruno was with me when the engineer yelled over it, "Holy smoke! Someone just touched the wire right next to me!" It was an 11,000-volt wire over a freight car on a siding.

VINCENT EMANUEL, *electrician*

The boy touched the wire just as we passed by. I didn't see it because it was on the side of the Secret Service man. He seen him when he fell to the ground. He said, "Boy, that fellow just got it! From the overhead wire!" People were doing foolish things . . . on top of boxcars, waving their arms, and that was real foolish. Oh, they were close! We always consider that wire energized . . . even if it's dead, we always consider it energized—alive. Because you never know. You only get one chance with that! That kid is lucky, recovering. See, he was on top of a boxcar, probably standing on the wooden runway on top of the boxcar and just got enough juice to knock him off.

RUSSELL BAKER, *columnist*

I was leaning out the window there, as we were coming into Trenton, and I looked ahead. Maybe several hundred yards down the track I could see a commotion, some guy getting a boy down off the top of a boxcar. And I thought, you know, they've caught a kid on a boxcar, and it's the railway police chasing him down. But he was lying on the ground and I looked down as we went by, very slowly, and he was lying out there, you know; still smoking!

ARTHUR SCHLESINGER, JR., *historian*

The accident gave a kind of terrible sense—a kind of juggernaut of violence tearing through the country.

CHARLOTTE CURTIS, *journalist, Morrisville, Pennsylvania*

More of my notes: "Then the Little Leaguers waving their caps; the nuns in sunglasses." I'd never seen a nun in sunglasses before, I guess.

"And the baseball games had stopped on the diamonds. And on the embankments: daisies, lavender, clover, wild raspberry bushes, and white blossoms." Do you remember? It was June, and it was beautiful. "And the yellow mustard blossoms and ferns all through the fields. And the children standing near a pond." In fact, I remember this. There were rushes, kind of, and then there was a pond in the background. Four little boys in T-shirts and short pants stood with their black caps held over their hearts.

GEORGE MCGOVERN, *Senator from the state of South Dakota*

I didn't even want to be interrupted. I just sat there looking out the window all the time. My wife was the same way; she was looking out one side, and I was looking out the other. I resented it when people came along and started talking politics.

JOHN KENNETH GALBRAITH, *economist*

I kept an open seat beside me. I omitted the obeisances because it seems to me the political process does go on. As the train moved along, people did drop down beside me. And, frankly, I don't see any need for apology. Life does go on. So I omitted the effort to give an immature imitation of a bad undertaker, and instead I engaged in political conversations during the course of the trip. We discussed who would represent the poor and what the effect would be on the sort of people along the tracks who no longer felt they had a champion like Bob Kennedy; and how people with such concerns could continue to be engaged politically; how much their belief in the political process would be shaken by the assassination of not only Bob Kennedy, but John F. Kennedy and Martin Luther King; we talked about the meaning of this on the more immediate political future; and about the effect it would have on the convention.

One of the people who came along and sat down at the beginning of the long ride was Stewart Udall. He told me that he was doing a book on poetry and politics. Or poets as politicians. I told him the last—almost the last—time I had seen Bob in his office in Washington, he had come in with a copy, I think, of Aeschylus and read me a verse or two, and had commented on its appropriateness to some current situation. All of which I'd forgotten. We talked a little bit about Bob Kennedy's reading and the fact that he did have a sense of words, a sense of the music of words.

Earlier a man came by with a tape recorder and said he was making an oral history of the journey for the Kennedy family, and could I tape my impressions; since we were just a few hundred yards out of Newark, I told him I hadn't formed any. He gave me the impression that I was very much in default; that certainly, having gone through the Pennsylvania tunnel and having gone across the Jersey Flats, I should have some pretty strong impressions. So he went away and never came back. Then, a little while later, a man from CBS came along and said, "Professor Galbraith, could we interview you on your impressions of the train?" And, I said—I felt so badly, having disappointed the earlier man—I said, "Yes." So he said, "That's fine. I'll be back." And then he disappeared, and I never saw him again either.

ROGER HILSMAN, *university professor*

We talked about Bob mainly . . . the things we remembered. But it always turned to the question, What the hell are we going to do now? . . . phrased that way . . . What the hell are we going to do now?

THE REVEREND WILLIAM GLENN, *Baptist minister, Philadelphia, Pennsylvania*

The pilot train came first, slowly. This brought the people up on their feet. They had been dangling their feet over the platform. The crowd seemed to be hushed—a mourning tone. A woman in back of me said in a Southern drawl, "This engine looks like death itself."

NAIDA COHN, *tourist, Philadelphia*

There were thousands of people at North Philadelphia Station . . . absolutely thousands. We were right on the platform in the front line. We must have been there about three hours. Originally no one was to be allowed on the platform, but then they finally had to . . . it was very warm. As the train began to approach, maybe three or four hundred police disgorged from I don't know how many paddy wagons. They didn't go on the station platform; they marched down and lined the tracks.

JOHN McHUGH, *patrolman, Philadelphia*

It was just a human herd of policemen standing on the tracks below the platform. We usually face the crowd. We would love to have saluted the train, but we were facing the wrong way.

NAIDA COHN

Then, as the train passed by, Ted Kennedy was standing on the back platform . . . which was the real shock! He wasn't really waving; he was nodding. The crowd reacted frightfully; they were just in complete shock. No one expected him. There were two smaller Kennedy children standing with him; and you could see the flag. You could see Ted sort of standing there with his hand slightly raised . . . and nodding. It was just very shocking and kind of frightening. The crowd gasped. He wasn't really waving; he was more acknowledging. Then the singing began again. After the train went through, people stood there transfixed for maybe five or six minutes. It was difficult to leave . . . so many people mainly stood there.

from The Kennedys: An American Drama

by Peter Collier and David Horowitz

The so-called third generation of Kennedys (children of John, Robert, Ted and their siblings) are often presented as stereotypes—spoiled or ruined or courageous offspring of a tragic dynasty. Peter Collier and David Horowitz offer a glimpse of how the cousins coped during the year that followed the death of RFK.

W hen he thought about it later on, Chris Lawford was struck by how much that Saturday afternoon resembled others he had spent at his Uncle Bobby's house—a swirl of activity, laughter and argument erupting almost volcanically from groups of guests, children and dogs battling against the mainstream of adults in endless serpentining games. A semi-ward of the Robert Kennedy family since his own parents' acrimonious divorce five years earlier, Chris had seen many parties like this one at Hickory Hill. As always, Robert McNamara, John Glenn, Lem Billings, and others of the Kennedy's favorite people were circulating through the crowd. As always there was the guest who suddenly shot out screaming into the pool, emerging soggy and spluttering in formal attire and pointing a finger at whoever had pushed him. And, as always, there was a sense that this was the way things had been and would forever be at the place Chris had come to think of as the center of the universe.

He and his cousin had been on their own all day, as they usually were at such functions, playing catch-as-catch-can, a game his Uncle Bobby said he and his brothers had played when they were young. Then a pudgy thirteen-year-old who barely managed to hold his own in the nonstop family athletics, Chris had managed to keep from being caught for quite a long time, hiding first in the stable area near the three-hundred-year-old stand of hickory trees for which the estate was named, then inside the tack room. After almost half an hour had passed without anyone looking for him, he came out into the open and noticed that the guests were beginning to leave. He came back cautiously toward the house, trying to find Bobby Junior and David, the cousins who were also his best friends. Unable to locate them, he finally saw Ina, the family's Costa Rican maid, and asked where they were. She gave him a strange look, and when she answered the music in her voice was sharper than usual. "Don't you understand? They bury their father today. They are feeling sad and have gone on up to their beds."

At that moment Chris understood how successful his Aunt Ethel had been in maintaining her illusion since *it* had happened: that nothing had really changed; that Bobby was in heaven, happy to be with Jack and awaiting an eventual reunion with them all. He sat down on the grass, physically sickened by the feelings of loss and abandonment he hadn't had time to feel on first hearing that his uncle had been shot.

Like others in the family, Chris had been galvanized by Bobby's vision. Something like a moment of epiphany had occurred just before the California primary, when he accompanied his mother to the Park Avenue church they always attended. Standing on the front steps and about to go in, he had suddenly stopped, feeling that it was wrong for them to worship with the rich instead of devoting their lives to the poor and helpless as Bobby was urging. His mother had argued with him, her voice straining to a crescendo that caused others to stare, but he had refused to compromise. He would never, he said, set foot inside this church again.

Sitting on the lawn at Hickory Hill, he tried to piece together the events of the past few days, understanding that he could never make a coherent story out of it, and that it would always remain a mosaic of rumors and impressions.

His cousin Bobby Junior had told him during the funeral about how he had gone to bed soon after the announcement that his father had won California and then gotten up eagerly the next morning to read about the details of the victory in the *Washington Post*, only to see headlines about the shooting; he had sat on the living-room hearth for an hour, feeding the newspaper page by page into the fire. Sixteen-year-old Joe, oldest male of the generation, had been at boarding school when his Uncle Teddy called to say there had been a shooting but not to worry because it wasn't as serious as it sounded. When Joe arrived in Los Angeles and saw his father inside the oxygen tent, the familiar face so black and distorted from the bullet that had smashed into the back of his head, he had known immediately that it was more serious than he had been told. And when death finally came, the operating room at the Good Samaritan Hospital had become what Joe, trying to describe the scene to Chris and others who hadn't been there, called a "hellish environment," with doctors and nurses crying and screaming and the adults so incapacitated that he had been the one who had to tell his younger brothers and sisters that their father hadn't made it.

When the body was brought home, those Chris was closest to in the family—his Uncle Bobby's oldest boys, Joe, Bobby Junior, and David—had served at the requiem mass at St. Patrick's. Then the whole family had boarded the funeral train winding slowly down to Arlington. John-John, as they sometimes still called the eight-year-old son of the dead President, had been bewildered by the possible relationship of this new tragedy to the other one he remembered; at one point he asked Christopher Kennedy, Bobby's five-year-old son, if his father would still be going to his office at the Senate "Oh yes," Christopher Kennedy answered. "He's in heaven in the morning and he goes to his office in the afternoon."

David, thirteen, who had been alone in a Los Angeles hotel room watching his father's victory statement on television when the shooting occurred, had also been in a daze. For much of the trip to Arlington, he had his head out of the window of the train, letting the wind batter his face. Once, as they were entering a tunnel, Phil Kirby, David's close friend from Hyannis whom Ethel had asked along to keep him company, noticed that David didn't see the protruding arm of a steel girder and yanked him back into the compartment to keep him from being decapitated. Both boys had their heads out the window again when a train running on a parallel track to theirs struck a group of bystanders at a crossing; two were killed, one of them cut in half under the wheels. David had been mesmerized by the bloody scene, unable to tear himself away until a Secret Service man got him back down into his seat.

The climax of the train ride, at least for Chris and the others of his generation, had come when Joe, accompanied by Ethel, walked up and down the aisles of some of the passenger cars wearing one of his father's pinstriped suits, shaking hands and saying, "I'm Joe Kennedy, thank you for coming," with such composure that Ethel later said excitedly, "He's got *it*! He's got *it*!" The pronoun needed no antecedent; it meant the touch, the destiny, the political genes all the Kennedy grandchildren were already talking and wondering about.

As the last guests departed from Hickory hill and shadows began to creep across the grass. Chris Lawford thought about all these events of the past few days, trying to make sense of them; feeling alone and, even worse, unprotected. When Uncle Bobby was alive, he thought to himself, we knew who we were. But now he's gone. What will happen to us? What comes next?

These questions were on the minds of many of the others as well. There were twenty-seven of them, soon to be twenty-eight. as Ethel's swelling pregnancy attested. When they were all together they looked like a remarkable experiment in eugenics—several strains of one particularly attractive species. There were the darkly handsome Shrivers, five children with their father's sensitive eyes and their mother's aggressive jaw; Stevie and Willie Smith, whose round-faced impassivity emulated the masks that had allowed their father to prosper in the family; Peter Lawford's striking good looks in the faces of Chris and his three sisters, as well as a hint of the actor's troubled vulnerability. Among those bearing the family name, Bobby's children had the Skakels' big bones and imposing size, while Teddy's—Kara, Edward Junior, and Patrick—were blond and surprisingly frail. Caroline and John-John had a regal poise all the others lacked.

The country had seen these wind-swept, photogenic faces at different stages of development and watched their growth and change as if by time-lapse photography. They were, as one journalist had remarked, "America's children." Yet while they had been in the spotlight all their lives, they had a curious innocence. The importance outsiders attached to being a Kennedy amused them. They gawked back at the tourists who peeked through the hedges at Hyannis. They scooped up sand from the public beach and sold it as "Kennedy sand" for a dollar a bag. They stood at the fence and answered "Kennedy questions" (What does Jackie eat for breakfast? Where do the Kennedys shop?) for a quarter apiece. Asked what it "meant" to be a Kennedy, Bobby's son David had once replied, "It means that we're exactly the same as everybody else, except better."

But as in their parents' generation, it was the opinion of family members that really mattered to them. They competed with other children in swim meets and sailing contests, succeeding so well that Hyannis Port officials barred them from a certain number of these competitions every season so that other residents could win some ribbons. The competition within their own group was far more intense, far more metaphoric of what they saw as the challenge of their lives. Each of them was always looking for an opening to outperform some rival in the family, always searching for an opportunity to improve his or her standing, always wondering if someone in an age or ability group just above them would slip, always aware above all else that their parents were watching and assessing their performance to see which of them had *it*. If the Beals Street house where some of the prior Kennedy generation were born had been an enigma of latency, the Compound where this generation gathered every summer was a training ground to recapture the achieved greatness that had once belonged to the family. As Chris Lawford said later, "We were all, every one of us, raised to be President."

Some of the older ones remembered what their parents referred to as ``that brief shining moment": trips to the White House; Friday afternoons when the presidential helicopter would swoop down, their Uncle Jack would get out and, after disposing of his aides, drive them all downtown and give them each a dollar to spend at the candy store. Some had the treasured memory of a more intimate contact. For Joe, it was the time he was invited to a special showing of the film version of *PT 109*. ("Thank you for inviting me to the movie," he wrote his uncle the President afterward. "I had lots of fun. I think you were very brave. When I grow up, I hope I can be as brave as you are.") For Chris, like all the others a victim of Joe's bullying, it was the time he was being chased through the Compound and came up to the President studying a briefcase full of papers on the porch of his house. "Joe's after me," he'd panted. "Can I hide?" Jack had answered without looking up: "Sure, go hide in the attic." He didn't tell Joe where Chris was: neither did he stop Joe from punching Chris in the stomach when he finally came out of hiding.

But if Jack represented what the family had been—"the President," they all grew up calling him, as if there had been no other—Bobby had represented what they would become. It was he who would come through a room where one of them was lounging on a sofa reading a comic book and say, "Put that junk down right now and get outside and *do* something." It was he who attended christenings and confirmations, graduations and commencements. When their grandmother Rose repeated her favorite saying from St. Luke; "To whom much is given, much will be required," it seemed just another of the religious homilies she left strewn through her conversation. Bobby translated the admonition into terms they could understand: "America has been very good to the Kennedys. We all owe the country a debt of gratitude and of public service." He was the energetic, embracing figure who demanded that they be better than they thought they were; who brought them into the family games and the family destiny as well; who kept them from being nothing more than an exotic collection of celebrities' children. Because of their grandfather's sickness, Bobby was the only head of the family they had ever known. Whether Lawfords, Shrivers, Smiths, or Kennedys, they had thought about their future in terms of him: working at his office, on his campaigns, perhaps even in his administration. He was the one who had defined their Kennedy-ness, and now that he was dead, the definitions were all called into question.

Sarge Shriver and Steve Smith didn't have the moral authority to fill Bobby's shoes. Teddy was too wrapped up in the political ramifications of the death to be available to them. Rose walked on the beach alone, wearing a tight smile and saying, "God gives us no more than we can bear." Only Joseph Kennedy seemed aware of their dilemma. "Sometimes Grandpa would look at us as if he wanted to say something," Chris Lawford remembers. "His mouth would move sort of convulsively as if some words were trying to get out. Then this cloudy look would come over his eyes and he'd slouch down into his wheelchair and the attendant would wheel him off."

And so 1968 became their first summer of discontent. Before, they had been individuals who drew their respective families closer together by their special relationships (Chris and David, Bobby's son Michael and Stevie Smith, Teddy's Kara and Vicki Lawford). Now they felt as though they were being dealt with as groups, each with demeaning names: The Little Kids, the Girls, the Big Boys. The Girls spent much of that summer going to mass with servants and praying fervently for Bobby's soul. The Little Kids went about the usual summer-camp-style activities with the recreation director Bobby had always hired for them—swimming lessons; then tennis, then horseback riding—but with none of the old spirit. The Big Boys played football games degraded by undercurrents of "Win one for the Gipper" sentimentality. They all had a sense of contraction, of shrinking back inside themselves. "It was so different from Jack's death," Eunice's oldest son,

Bobby, said. "Then there had been a coming together. Uncle Bobby had seen to that. In a strange way we'd felt even more like Kennedys than ever—proud at what Jack had been, determined that our time would come again. But once Uncle Bobby died, there was just this sense of splitting apart."

The impact was greatest on Bobby's own children, whom his magnetism had made the center of the clan. By the time of David's birthday on June 15, marked by a spiritless party at Hickory Hill whose high point was Bobby Junior's decision to put a laxative in everybody's milk, the heroic denial Ethel had been practicing since the funeral had begun to crack. Tension was thick in the house. The Little Kids and the Girls were immune from Ethel's dark moods. But the Big Boys were not; on the threshold of manhood themselves, they seemed to pose painful questions about the fate of Kennedy males. Their mother punished them constantly and capriciously, almost as if she blamed them for reminding her of her dead husband. She told Joe he must be the man of the house now and allowed him to sit in his dead father's chair at the dinner table. But when he hit his younger sister Kerry for making noise, she gave him the infantile punishment of having to walk up and down the stairs a hundred times. (Later, Joe went into the yard and, in a moment of tenderness, took the hands of his younger brothers and sisters and began to sing the "Battle Hymn of the Republic," their father's favorite song.) Meanwhile, Ethel kept saying to Bobby Junior and David, "Get out of here!" as if the house itself, with all the pictures of family triumphs, were a sanctuary they defiled by their presence.

A few days after David's birthday, Ethel and the kids flew with Teddy to Connecticut and chartered a boat from Mystic to Hyannis Port. Ethel careened between gloom and febrile gaiety all during the trip. Once she took Bobby Junior and David below and hit them repeatedly with a hairbrush, the first such punishment they could remember, and one that made them cry in spite of their teenager resolutions to be stronger than their mother. "I can't stand it anymore," she said when they reached home port. "You guys have got to get away from here." Thus began a diaspora that would continue for years to come, a process of leaving and returning that symbolized the next generation's ambiguous tie to the Kennedy Legacy.

Joe and his friend Chuck McDermott were sent to Spain, where they stayed with the Guardiolas, a large family recommended to Teddy by the American Embassy. For the first few days Joe walked around like a displaced person. He had the Kennedy smile, which had been so striking on his father's funeral train. But it was tenuous and suspicious and usually accompanied by a knot of perplexity at his forehead. Barrel-chested and slow (a lineman, Chuck McDermott felt, in a family that valued quarterbacks and receivers), he had experienced another bad year at Milton Academy. Scholastically behind to begin with, he had lost further ground. Being a Kennedy had also resulted in being constantly tested: girls solicited mash notes not because they wanted a date but because they thought the signature might someday be valuable; boys short-sheeted his bed and even came into his room to vomit on his pillow. Joe had been looking forward to the presidential campaign to release him from his troubles. His father had already been trying to groom him—taking time out from the last raft trip to take him alone to the Navajo reservation, explaining the special plight of Indians in America, introducing him to key aides and letting him sit in on low-level briefings. He had promised Joe that after school was out he could join him full time. "That had been the big thing in his life," says McDermott. "It had allowed him to forget his troubles. Now that future was gone and he was stuck with who he was."

The Guardiolas raised bulls for bull rings throughout Spain. Joe and McDermott watched matadors test the bulls in the practice ring. Joe decided to fight a cow and was slightly gored. They went to see El Cordobes in Seville and were accorded the honor of being invited into his quarters to watch him dress in his "suit of lights" for the ring. As they left, Joe, who was so quiet that he seemed almost to have taken a vow of silence, said to McDermott, "He'll probably get killed out there." El Cordobes fought well and was awarded an ear for his bravery, which he brought to the Guardiolas' box and handed to the Kennedy heir. Joe threw it into a garbage can as they were leaving the stadium. He and McDermott spent the rest of the summer riding motorcycles. Once they found a house which was temporarily uninhabited. Joe ran his motorcycle up the stairs to the second floor, saying that it was something he'd always wanted to do.

Occasionally Joe wrote home, always asking about Bobby Junior. His brother was dark, wiry, and enigmatic, a loner by choice rather than necessity since unlike Joe he had no trouble making friends. The family regarded him as somewhat like the falcons he kept—hooded in intent and conveying a suggestion of danger. Even the practical joking he had inherited from the Skakels had an eccentric and sometimes dangerous bite. When Hyannis neighbor Philip Kirby was invited to join Bobby Junior and his brothers in serving at a memorial mass for their father, for instance, he had told the priest that he was unfamiliar with the liturgy and wasn't sure when to ring the bell. The priest replied that he would signal him by a touch on the shoulder. At the beginning of the service, Philip felt the touch and rang the bell, then immediately realized it was the wrong time. Deeply chagrined and almost in tears at having made a mistake during such a solemn ceremony for his friends' dead father, Kirby had turned to discover who had touched him and seen Bobby Junior smiling triumphantly.

As a youngster Bobby Junior had become interested in animals— first lizards and snakes and later falcons. His father had commissioned naturalists from the Bronx Zoo to make him a walk-in terrarium for his thirteenth birthday. He had encouraged the interest in falconry, although admitting to his son that he was disturbed by the implications of feeding pigeons to the predators. The two of them worked out a compromise with a distinctive Kennedy twist: if a pigeon managed to avoid a hawk on two successive flights, it was "retired" and never forced to face death again.

Struck by the boy's range of interests, Bobby Senior had once remarked that Bobby Junior was "just like the President." Lem Billings had thought so too and had taken him on as a protégé. When Ethel became increasingly difficult in the weeks after the assassination, Lem had volunteered to take Bobby Junior to Africa on an animal-watching expedition, fulfilling a promise his father had made shortly before his death. And so, while Joe was watching bullfights in Spain, Lem and Bobby were touring the Serengeti Plain. Bobby crouched in the veldt grass and stalked animals with a camera, telling Africans that he planned to become a veterinarian. He and Lem kept a journal, which Lem said they would be able to sell to a magazine for a lot of money.

David was very conscious of the coup his brother had scored in having an adult who was fully devoted to him and ready to help him deal with the tragedy. "Lem could have chosen any of us," he said. "I remember the day it happened. Lem appeared and they just sort of walked off together. I thought to myself: Bobby's lucky. I wish I had someone." If his father's death hit David harder than the others, it was because there had been a special bond between them—both were the runts of the litter, sandwiched into the middle of a large family—and because he had always been a sort of golden boy for the family, with his open, freckled face and the wispy blond hair both parents had always tousled when passing by, almost as if fingering some talisman. ("If we ever go broke," Ethel had once told an interviewer, "we'll make a movie star of David and live off his earnings.") He was the only one in the family who hadn't been enthusiastic about the run for the presidency. For weeks after his father's announcement David had been plagued by recurring nightmares about Bobby's death. Distraught over episodes that seemed premonitory, and missing the special attention his father had given him, David had gotten in trouble for throwing rocks at cars passing by Hickory Hill. His father had taken time on the campaign plane to write a note that seemed directed to David as much as the members of the press to whom it was delivered: "He feels very badly about what has happened and has apologized to all concerned. And I want tp add that he is a good boy and has always been a source of great joy and pride to the family."

The day of the California primary, he had joined his father in Los Angeles. The two of them had been swimming in the Malibu surf and his feet had been cut from under him by a riptide; he had felt himself being carried out, by the undertow when his father grabbed him, scraping his own head on the ocean floor as he reached for David's slippery arm. With a teenager's melodrama, David had decided that he owed his father a life and would look for an opportunity to pay him back in the years ahead. That night as he sat in front of the television set in his room in the Ambassador Hotel and watched the images from the hand-held cameras jostling to get a better view of the new Kennedy martyr bleeding on the floor downstairs in the Ambassador's kitchen, one of the thoughts he had was that the debt would be forever undischarged.

Once Joe and Bobby Junior were taken care of for the summer, Ethel hustled David off to Austria with Chris Lawford as a companion. They went to Meyerhoff, a tennis and ski camp run by the former tennis star Bill Talbert. They skied on a glacier in the morning and practiced volleys in the afternoon. After-hours, David was introduced to The Grateful Dead and to sex: "Some seventeen-year-old girl at the camp realized who I was and picked me up. I was hardly into puberty. Chris told me to take her out and try to feel her tits. I did it. All of a sudden she was unzipping my pants and pulling them down and sort of moaning about how bad she felt that my father had died."

For the rest of their time in Austria, he and Chris sneaked out of their rooms at night with sleeping bags which they took into the girls' dorms, propositioning girls there who they discovered felt guilt and morbid fascination over Bobby's death. They knew it was wrong, but they also knew it was part of a great change in their attitude toward everything having to do with being a Kennedy. "It was like watching a huge balloon lose its air," Chris said later. "Things just didn't have meaning any more." An outstanding tennis player, Chris now found himself not caring whether he won or lost. "I'd be out on the court and I'd just say 'the hell with it' in the middle of the match and walk off. Before Uncle Bobby's death I wouldn't have dared do that. It just wouldn't have been possible: you never gave up, never stopped trying to win. But those kinds of emotions didn't have much meaning anymore. David and I sort of decided together that there really wasn't any reason to try to be good any more, so we might as well try to be bad."

When David returned home, things were in a state of ongoing disorder. It had been difficult for Ethel to keep domestic help in the best of times; during the summer there had been several resignations and his ten-year-old brother Michael, most resilient of the children, had taken to answering the phone with the words: "Confusion here." Although the Hyannis Compound was insulated by several acres, Ethel had played music so loudly that the neighbors had been forced to call the police. Seven months pregnant, she bounded around the tennis court every day, even though she was worried about the baby, which she had come to see as an obscure symbol of Kennedy will. In a doubles match pitting her and Jim Whittaker against Andy Williams and Art Buchwald, she had become so furious with frustration that she knelt down to bang her head on the court surface.

As summer ended with a stream of friends visiting the family—Dave Hackett, Rosey Grier, Rafer Johnson, and John Glenn were the regulars—David kept waiting for someone to talk to him about his father's death. During a rare lull in his mother's almost nonstop activity, he cornered her in the kitchen and asked her about it. "It's not a subject I want to discuss," she snapped, elbowing her way by him.

His brothers were back but leading separate lives—Joe driving around Hyannis with older friends in their cars, and Bobby Junior spending most of his time by himself in the woods with Morgan Le Fay, a red-tailed hawk he had captured and tamed a few years earlier. They all met on the football field, but the games had turned into desperate Freudian struggles, with Joe looking for opportunities to smash them into the ground while they waited for the inevitable moment when his trick knee went out. When this happened, Joe would writhe on the ground as Bobby stood above him sneering, "Oh, has our sister hurt his knee?" These were such ugly scenes that Mary Schreiner, one of their sister Kathleen's friends, once yelled at Bobby: "How can you ever expect to be President if you talk like that to your brother?"

David spent time with his friend Philip Kirby, while Bobby hung out with some older boys, notably another neighbor, John Kelley. One afternoon when they were all together, Kelley happened to ask Bobby what he'd done with the LSD he'd sold him. Bobby tried to change the subject; when Kelley persisted he said that he'd fed the drug to his parakeet. Later, in the Kelleys' garage, a favorite meeting place, after David had chided Bobby for keeping secrets from him, Bobby laid out some mescaline on a piece of wood and dared him to take it. Kirby, who had watched David try to prove himself time and again by taking dares, begged him not to take the drug: "Don't do that, David. Please don't do it." But Bobby egged him on, and after hesitating a moment, David swallowed the mescaline. Later on, when he was hallucinating, it seemed to him that the hedge Bobby was leaning against had sharp leaves. He asked Bobby to move away so he wouldn't get hurt. But Bobby laughed and backed deeper into the hedge, whose spines seemed to David to penetrate his brother's body. "You're dying," he cried out, "just like Daddy." Bobby smiled and sagged to the ground with his eyes staring and his tongue lolling out of his mouth in a mime of death.

Although they were not able to articulate it, the boys were aware that they were stepping over lines they had never expected to cross, lines between good and evil that Robert Kennedy himself had drawn. Now they found themselves standing on an opposite shore from the one he had occupied, as if to better see his memory. No matter how old they became, he would always be "Daddy," as if his meaning had been set in amber at the time of his death, a time which would come to represent antique virtue and morality for them. Not long after the death, when the family was out sailing, the dog Freckles slipped overboard, and each of the four oldest boys dove into the water to save him. "Daddy would have done it," they told an aunt who asked them why they had jeopardized their lives for an animal. "Daddy believed competition brought out the best in us," Joe would often reply when asked about the ferocious gamesmanship in the family. And years later, when Bobby Junior was nearly thirty, he described his father's code in these terms: "Daddy got in fights, but he would never hit anybody smaller.

He was absolutely moral. He was never with another woman before he married or afterward. He was completely moral."

Daddy: the personification of a love they would never again feel and moral order they would never again experience.

As the worst year of their young lives came to a close, they decided to surprise their mother at Christmas with a book comprised of letters about their father. David's said: "Daddy was very funny in church because he would embarrass all of us by singing very loud. Daddy did not have a good voice. There will be no more football with Daddy, no more swimming with him, no more riding and no more camping with him. But he was the best father their [sic] ever was and I would rather have him for a father the length of time I did than any other father for a million years."

The Thousand Days of
Edward M. Kennedy
by Burton Hersh

What happened at Chappaquiddick? This 1972 Esquire article by Burton Hersh (born 1933) offers a context, if not an explanation, for the accident.

In mid-April of 1969, conceding "reluctantly" to Senator Ralph W. Yarborough's request that he himself take over Bob Kennedy's Special Subcommittee on Indian Education, Edward Kennedy directed a bipartisan group of Senators through a three-day, tundra-hopping investigation of the shacks and deer-hide hogans of Alaska's 55,500 Indians, Eskimos and Aleuts. Like so many attempts to muddle among the effects of Bobby before and afterward, the trip proved emotionally perilous. The touring was rugged, 3600 miles punctuated wherever the party's three little C-130's bounced down onto northern rivers to let its caravan of legislators and staffers and newsmen wade thigh-high Arctic snow after diseased villagers and forgotten stone-age corners of the North like Tuluksak and Nunapitchuk. The expedition simply could not help looking, to White House strategists, like an ice-cap version of Bobby's travels in darkest Delta Mississippi—the squalor sought out, the cameras, the Heir Apparent discovering the inevitable pathetic aboriginal child wasting away bravely, wordlessly,

in a corner (this time of pneumonia, not pellagra), the furious estab-
lishmentarian charges of opportunism . . . . Exciting perhaps, satisfying
for sure to the ham in Kennedy, but *hard,* harder minute by minute,
because as the tour became so intensely politicized the chance to
accomplish anything substantial receded and the opportunity for
hurtful blunders was everywhere. Every question had to be read as gesture, every gesture was threatening. As the strain tightened, writer
Brock Brower—listening to Kennedy patch into his thoughts during
one of the plane rides, produce some justification to himself for being
there, doing this—watched him withdraw, "an inch at a time," in anticipation and with a heavy telltale sigh of concession, the silver hip flask
that had been Bobby's. Taste. "First time I've used it," Kennedy told
Brower, needing badly to make *that* clear.

Returning hop by hop to civilization, the atmosphere bore down
more heavily on Kennedy hour by hour. Still loosened up enough to
search himself, he talked about his father, his dead brother Joe, examined himself against Joe, dead, and Bobby, dead. "They're going to
shoot my ass off the way they shot off Bobby's," he kept insisting.

He was exhausted, dead-eyed by the time his entourage of staffers
and media people filed aboard a commercial jet in Fairbanks. Except for
one small family, the Kennedy group—which had held the flight up for
more than an hour—was alone in a large compartment. Most newsmen
drink, and many are devoted to drinking, but that night Kennedy
shocked the most case-hardened. "He started whackin' the bottle in
Fairbanks," one of them remembers. "He'd had nothing to eat, and it
was drink drink drink drink *drink,* no sleep at all. He was all over the
place, weavin' up the aisle, chanting Es-ki-mow Pow-er, pelting one of
his guys with pillows, y'know, 'C'mon, wake up, you're not supposed to
sleep on these goddamned trips!' There was this poor hapless family, I
remember, in the seats in front of where he wound up standing, the
baby was trying to sleep on the plane seat, and one of the aides brought
Kennedy some very hot coffee, and he took it, and it just hung there in
his hand, scalding hot, wavering, over the sleeping kid's face, until a
couple of us got up and went over and eased him back down into his

seat. His staff guys—Drayne—did what they could, but what the hell—
" "Ted was celebrating the fact that he had escaped for a few days from
[his longtime administrative assistant] David Burke," another observer
says simply. "Burke is, after all, a cop's son, but Dick Drayne simply
couldn't control Teddy when trouble was coming."

Kennedy kept at it on the last leg of the flight, from Portland,
Oregon, to Dulles Airport in Washington. A sizable crowd, fronted by
Joan and the three Kennedy children, was waiting for him. "We started
to get ourselves together," a newsman remembers. "I looked out and
everybody was there all right, the TV cameras, the whole world. I left
behind Kennedy and he did look awful, his eyes were like oysters on
the half shell. Joan saw him and her jaw dropped four feet. I remember
thinking, *That's all for you, buddy.* Then little Patrick rushed over to him,
and Kennedy picked the little boy up and kissed him, and Patrick's
head blocked off the cameras, and Kennedy was home free. The kid
stole the show."

It was a revealing incident, although the pre-Chappaquiddick press, as
usual, buried it. Ted Kennedy had never been particularly guarded
during his most discreet moments, but there had been about his performance on that long plane ride home an intensity of desperation, of
abandon, that bothered everyone there: limited-distribution memos
circulated, especially inside the editorial offices of the magazines. The
most celebrated of these became the one John Lindsay of *Newsweek's*
Washington office pulled together. Lindsay had personally been very
devoted to Robert Kennedy, and he had seen enough of Edward
Kennedy over the winter to pick up constant signals of deep-seated
emotional disruption: a tendency to stop in mid-sentence, shift moods
inexplicably, break into unexpected tears, turn up boisterous with a few
early "pops" at public events. Kennedy, Lindsay concluded, was slipping out of control, careening toward some unavoidable crack-up.
Kennedy's driving, always wild (as the President's had notoriously
been), was frightening even among his closest staffers, who fended the
subject off in tight, half-humorous asides. He had a tendency at times

to lose himself in conversation, look back laughing over his shoulder while at the wheel, pay little attention to where he was going, so that he was forever threading back onto main routes. The tendency in April among senior editorial people was to brush aside such reportorial observations, dismiss them as exaggerated, all out of proportion. But they lay ticking in files throughout the late spring and early summer. By the middle of the session a number of Kennedy's colleagues too were well aware of all this, concerned about it: Ed Muskie, speaking with typical frankness off the record, conceded the '72 nomination to Kennedy, except that—shaking his head gravely—the way Ted had recently been drinking at times, and driving at times . . . .

Inside the circuit of Kennedy intimates, that magnetic grid of associates and accumulated trustees of the compiled Kennedy legacy, the general discouragement with Ted Kennedy's off-hour antics was quickly becoming, if anything, more prevalent and heavily emphasized than among the following press. Few among the advisers had much occasion to pay attention, against the buzz and stress of their own chivying for position in New York or Washington, to the slow accession to influence and cumulative legislative effect Kennedy had managed, shunning publicity as he worked, inside the Senate.

What many among the palace guard, the retainers, *did* see, toward midnight around the big Stephen Smith apartment across from the Metropolitan Museum, or at the Cape, or after the outsiders left in McLean, was the same hulking hilarious buffoon, the inimitable lifetime kid brother still playing it for laughs, full of Irish drinking songs and blue-eyed pratfall charms, who had tickled his brother the President with his rendition of *Hooray for Hollywood* twenty years earlier. It was a role Ted Kennedy still cherished in a way, and detested in a way, but—especially when walled in by the Bobby and J.F.K. people—could not seem to help continuing to play. Habitually, like most lifetime pluggers, Kennedy arranged to get to bed by ten-thirty or eleven; when he stayed up later, put-on artist that he was still, he avoided showing how much the lower back hurt him; the old sense of competitive tension toward his brothers' legatees, as toward his brothers, was likely to tighten in him enough to start the drinking. Several drinks normally did it; Kennedy is congenitally receptive to people, buoyed simply by feeling them around himself, so that it actually took very little to tempt him into hilarity. To Kennedy insiders—many of whom were not Catholic, not Irish, and evidenced the skepticism toward the uses of alcohol bred into serious Calvinists and Jews—to them heavy drinking was not so much a good man's weakness, as the Irish adage had it, as a weak man's goodness. Neither Robert nor John Kennedy, faithful to the old financier's dread of liquor, normally drank very much. And so it was especially horrifying to the loyalists to see the surviving Kennedy brother, in whom a good many, in their own ambivalent questing hearts, were already starting to reside some hope of a belated restoration, easing into what a number regarded as a psychological dependency on drink. "A com*put*ah?" one intimate of John and Bobby replied on being told about Kennedy's knack for absorbing and interrelating information. "Well, maybe that's what we need now in the Presidency. A computah, a computah with alcohol in all its circuits."

As acutely, the insiders were alarmed that Joan Kennedy should show every sign—while still sweet, frank, considerate and unworldly as ever—of problems of her own. Uncertainty, loneliness, the omnipresence of hardened security men in the resented blue suits that seemed to infiltrate their very pastel dreams now—it all seemed to be trapping them both.

Joan developed an intermittent tic in her cheek. "People criticize Jackie for going her own way where the Kennedys are concerned," she told a reporter a year later, "but this family can be overwhelming. For years I went along with everything they said because I didn't dare to do otherwise, but now I speak up and say what I think and it seems to work out better for everyone." Joan had developed in 1964 into too effective a campaigner to waste—she had worked hard for Bob in Indiana in 1968, gone back to tour for Birch Bayh that fall, accommodated herself to the separations, the private trips to Paris, the refreshments and polite evasions wealth permits to anxiety. Nothing helped enough.

Nothing was dependable, the children felt it—the susceptible little Teddy was obsessed all day with the idea that he would never see his father again, so that his father broke off whatever he was doing to call him up and calm him down, reassure him toward nightfall.

Throughout all of which serious Kennedy advisers watched. "If you get drunk regularly in public with various important personalities," one of them ventured privately, thoughtfully, of Ted, "there has to be an element of self-humiliation present, doesn't there?" It was a question worth asking about a man who was generally regarded that spring as very probably the oncoming next President of the United States.

Yet who among the intimates could claim, the Saturday morning the calamity at the Chappaquiddick bridge shattered the political news, to have anticipated something like *that?* Who started with any inkling, from the office-clambake/bugs-biting/Gasoline-Alley *frame* of the thing, that overnight it was going to turn into something close to epochal, halfway Wagnerian, The Fall of the House of Kennedy? Out of a . . . a gesture, something so . . . so desultory, so mundane. Out of this unpromising several hours of Kennedy's sailing weekend devoted to making worthwhile for the help their memories of the efforts so far, evoking whatever was sentimentally of use.

It started, most people involved agree, with Joey Gargan, willing, eager, hapless Joey busy playing out his role, his "lot in life," as he liked to refer to it sometimes after enough drinks, in hopes that you would *really* understand what almost-Kennedy-hood meant. If anybody was the prod that weekend it was—he was himself the first to make the point—Gargan. Joe envisioned the traditional long regatta weekend at Edgartown as the perfect format within which to combine a soupçon of Kennedy sociability toward longtime advancing sidekicks during the grueling Massachusetts campaigns of the Sixties—Ray LaRosa, Charlie Tretter, Paul Markham—with an effort to show some gratitude to the boiler-room girls Gargan had gotten to know in the Spring of 1968 bouncing in and out of the 20th and L Street D.C. headquarters between advancing sessions around the primary circuit. Among the brusque driving aides who slammed Bobby's late hard effort together, Gargan's talents had not been taken very seriously compared with, say, the assertive genius of the advancing showman Jerry Bruno; around the boiler room, however, the overworked girls—pressed constantly to keep straight the massive influx of information, examine it and feed it back to the "road show" of the peripatetic Robert Kennedy—appreciated Gargan's unvarying solicitude for them, his reliable good-humored concern. Needing it badly, he basted himself in their unlooked-for fondness and their touchingly clear common regard. Joe Gargan himself was reluctant when the time came—in the judgment of the directive people in the Kennedy intelligence setup—to phase out the pattern of gesture to this assortment of able if overall rather homely young women.

Fixated as the press remained on the "six married men-six secretaries-inaccessible cottage-slept overnight" formula the pulps immediately started to feed their readers, almost nobody in the alerted and suspicious public seems then or afterward to have caught on very clearly to who was who that uncomfortable night on Chappaquiddick Island. "If the Kennedys had intended to stage an orgy I'm sure they would have gone after a higher standard of excellence," one insider remarks; this struck the girls themselves: "If *that's* what people thought, they should have circulated pictures of ourselves with our clothes off," one girl laughed afterward to her lawyer. In fact, within the Kennedy operations, many of the girls were formidable. "People brought *them* coffee," a Kennedy staffer says simply, epitomizing the boiler-room girls' status. Cautiously picked for discretion, brains, loyalty, humor under strain and the ability to stay ahead of a fluctuating set of intelligence estimates, the girls were accorded wide freedom to act, negotiate, close deals in the name of the candidate, even, at times, to share judgment in situations of which they themselves in many ways had the sharpest operative knowledge. Mary Jo Kopechne was among the most highly regarded. She herself worked exhaustively with Bob's staff, spent one whole night typing his decisive breakaway Vietnam speech at Hickory Hill, traveled in his behalf—they knew each other well enough to share Kennedy-style "in" jokes, banked, like so many Kennedy jokes, off such drolleries as those of a prominent Louisiana politico whose silk suits and shirts and alligator shoes left both of them giggling.

Overall, among the boiler-room girls, Mary Jo Kopechne was pretty much of type: she, like the Lyons sisters Mary Ellen and Nance, was an alert, discreet, crisis-tested girl of middle-class origins, self-assured, frankly ambitious. Most were already beyond their early succulent marriageable mid-twenties. Mary Ellen would shortly go after a law degree; Esther Newberg soon stepped into key organizing-level jobs in the Goldberg and Muskie campaigns. None of the girls were later willing to comment on what they collectively made of the unlikely mixture of escorts Joe Gargan had lured onto the Vineyard for them for the weekend—all well-settled-in married men except for Kennedy's sour sixty-three-year-old driver Jack Crimmins, Ray LaRosa, a terse ex-fireman of forty-one, the Senator himself only around for a couple of hours . . . . There is a . . . a class difference here, to put a finger on it frankly; perhaps the only appropriate opposite number provided was malleable Charlie Tretter, constitutionally full of smiles, a Boston lawyer now but willing for the weekend, as ever, to double up as part-time driver and errand boy if that's what the Senator wants—

Among up-to-the-minute Boston-based statehouse tipsters, the shocker on the guest list of Joey Gargan's breathlessly organized beach party was Gargan's onetime Georgetown Prep schoolmate, Paul F. Markham. By July of 1969 Paul Markham might have seemed well beyond office-party filler-duty for the weekending Kennedys. Unlike the rest of the Gargan collection, Markham had already reached a mid-career checkpoint from which he could now begin to think of himself as really *arriving*. Knowing Gargan had certainly helped; still, any professional rise that depended as his did on a gently nurtured association with so powerful a group as the Kennedy family *must* owe a lot to a combination of real ability and assured tact—why else would the Kennedys, after all, for whom there is really so little anybody outside can do, go out of their way? In 1967 Lyndon Johnson, on Ted Kennedy's strong recommendation, appointed Paul to the top Federal prosecutor's job in the Commonwealth, U.S. Attorney. With the party change in January, Markham had resigned his job the May before the cookout at Chappaquiddick.

Among politicians in Massachusetts, payoff-prone and favor-seeking as so many always were and continue to be, Markham's kind of rung-by-rung ascension takes savvy. Good family man, no-nonsense wife, seven kids, moderate—he kept himself available nonetheless when Joey wanted somebody to josh and go baleful with. Approached with the usual jocularity by Gargan a few weeks before the Edgartown regatta weekend, Paul had readily agreed: surely, he'd come along and fill the party out if that was what Joey wanted.

By cookout night, Paul Markham had already banged his leg up severely sailing over in the *Victura* with Gargan and a kid, Howie Hall, in a preliminary race, lost his chance to share in the glamour of crewing for Ted, even had to give up his bed at the Shiretown Motor Inn when Ted came. He now looked forward to two nights of listening to Jack Crimmins, the Senator's chauffeur, grumble nonstop about the unappealing Lawrence cottage. He was to find himself drifting through two more aimless uncomfortable days, offend Esther Newberg by inadvertently brushing her leg, sleep in the back of Gargan's rented car, and finally watch helplessly while a shocked Kennedy gave senseless orders that he, Markham, would later be vilified for obeying. He started that weekend fair-haired, at thirty-eight a personage; three miserable days later he was all but busted, utterly reduced, singled out nationally beneath the klieg light of the scandal as Joey Gargan's Gargan—

On Friday, July 18, at one-thirty in the afternoon, Kennedy's charter from Boston set down on the Martha's Vineyard inland airstrip. "I *knew*," Kennedy acknowledged wearily afterward, "that the girls were up there, that we were going to get together, that there was a cottage someplace. I hadn't troubled myself as to the details . . . ." Congressman Tip O'Neill, Kennedy's seatmate on the shuttle to Boston, remembers his Massachusetts colleague as "tired as hell." Self-driven and overworked, Kennedy was now, in the view of one reporter who saw him in mid-July, "utterly uptight, wholly preoccupied," pushing, worried, tense. Kennedy had been lackluster at best about this idea of

Joey's, about once more hosting a "time" for the half-dozen or so girls who worked so hard for Bobby. Certainly he'd made a considerable effort earlier: in January, when Dun Gifford and Dave Hackett had gotten together and given a party for the boiler-room group, Teddy had made a special effort to come by and liven up the proceedings for as long as he could arrange to stay. In late spring the girls had given a party of their own at Andy Vitali's apartment for everybody who worked with Bob; Ted hadn't been able to look in, the party went flat, and Nance Lyons, who worked in his Senate office, had chided him because he had never made it over. Kennedy regretted that; when Gargan broached his idea for the Edgartown regatta get-together it seemed a reasonable idea on the telephone; by Friday afternoon a long evening of making an effort with the boiler-room girls had started to look like work. Arriving on the island an hour before the race started, Ted reportedly took Gargan aside and claimed unusual fatigue, wondered in his oblique way whether—Then, seeing how much having him around meant to Joey, he agreed finally to stay and pitch in as co-host for at least a couple of mid-evening hours.

Before the afternoon's race started, Jack Crimmins had hurried his employer to the Edgartown wharf, across the car ferry, over Chappaquiddick's Main Street, out to the Lawrence cottage, to put a suit on and then to bounce down the five-inch margin of the macadam onto the gravel-spitting Dyke Road, over the Chappaquiddick bridge and out to the lonely deserted East Beach for a quick plunge into the midday breakers. It was Kennedy's first look at the setup Joey had organized; by two-thirty he was back in Edgartown Harbor wading out to the mooring of the *Victura* with Joe Gargan and Howie Hall in time for the delayed start of the regatta competition.

By seven or so Kennedy was back in the Lawrence cottage. He had already raced, done disappointingly—ninth—enjoyed the first sip or two of beer for the day on board, plus perhaps half a can with Ross Richards, winner of the first leg of the race. Then Kennedy directed Crimmins to take him back across in time to savor a badly needed hot tub in peace before the others arrived. Soaking his torn back, Kennedy asked Crim-

mins to please prepare him a rum and Coca-Cola, the first of two high-
balls he worked on throughout the remainder of the evening.

All afternoon Paul Markham had been drifting back and forth
between the cottage, the Yacht Club, the Edgartown Wharf, East Beach;
by seven-thirty, when he and Tretter and Gargan returned to the cottage
for the evening, Kennedy was up and dressed in fresh wash pants, a
polo shirt and the back brace, red and revived-looking after his tub,
and intent on giving Jack Crimmins mock hell because it appeared to
Kennedy that Jack had, during the two nights he had been solacing
himself with the rum supply, reduced it immoderately. "Gee, Jack, who
has been drinking all the rum?" the Senator repeatedly wanted to
know. "There is hardly any left, you didn't leave me any rum." Crimmins, a veteran of Kennedy's pinprick ragging, went stolidly about getting himself neatly dressed. Everybody was relaxed; after a couple of
minutes of piling on Kennedy and Gargan about their unimpressive
performance over the race course that afternoon, Paul Markham and
Kennedy started to talk seriously about the political utility of
Kennedy's new whip situation.

At eight-fifteen precisely—Gargan had worked the logistics out
meticulously—Joey picked up the girls and Ray LaRosa in the white
rented Valiant on the Chappaquiddick side of the cut and brought
them along to the cottage. Most of the girls had been swimming late in
the morning and, throughout the late afternoon, watched the Kennedy
group race from a boat Joe had chartered for them: they arrived now in
an easygoing cluster, just up from naps and out of showers, several of
them dazed a little after their unaccustomed hours in the sun.

Gargan, already legendary for his ultra-thin buttermilk pancakes,
was sweating away out there beyond the little low pass-over divider on
which the informal bar, three huge vodka gallon bottles and Scotch
and a bowl of chips or whatever those are were available to everybody,
and Ted was making the newcomers their first round of drinks, and
outside it was getting dusky. Inside it was getting hot; Charlie Tretter,
who was in and out all evening and accordingly remembers the
evening in slices, in alternately deepening moods, remembers the

preprandial segment as if it were clipped in without the sound from vintage Our Gang Comedy: Joey, his back to everybody, at the oven working "like a Trojan," the girls and their drinks, conversation, trouble with conversation, single ticklish beads of perspiration sliding down the furrows of backs just under where light summer bras hooked . . . . Tretter had run over to Edgartown once for cigarettes and ice and Coke; when Joey discovered that, grilling the two-inch steaks in shifts, it was going to be a while before everybody was fed, Tretter and little Cricket Keough—a pal from Bob's campaign, and with a goofy subaltern's knack for observation like Tretter's, inclined to stomach trouble—Tretter borrowed the keys to Kennedy's Oldsmobile from Crimmins and went after a radio at the Shiretown. When they got back Cricket left her flowered purse in the Oldsmobile; the cottage was really hot, full of sultry seaside air the descending night had trapped; it was better outside but the saltwater mosquitoes swarmed beneath the pine trees; a slice of moon was out for an hour or so.

Tretter, accommodating instinctively but as spunky as ever with his soft held-in pageboy frivolities, walked in on a rich, even a melancholy scene. "The mood was kind of mixed," as he later recalled. "I don't think Teddy was really—I don't know, being together like that . . . . I remember listening to the girls, the long string of reminiscences I myself wasn't really privy to, anecdotes, stories that came out of the Bobby campaign. What I'm getting at is, I worked for the Senator for a long time, and I think I know him pretty well, well enough to realize that he was—he was not exuberant. He was not having a helluva good time." They ate steak, slowly, in shifts. "There were getting to be long lapses in the evening, people were standing up and Kennedy was working hard at being a good host," Tretter noted. "If there was a girl not saying much he would try and draw her out. It was just that the conversation, what was said—*Bobby*. He was a presence."

By shortly after eleven Crimmins, tiring fast and starting to worry about what kind of a night's sleep he was supposed to get *there*, was already suggesting with perhaps a little bit of pepper in his tone that everybody who was going to go back had better think about going back. Joe Gargan reassured the girls that it wasn't that late yet, he had discussed the matter personally with the ferryboat operator and there was a strong possibility of the boat remaining in service until one a.m., although that would entail an extra charge. Crimmins, not mollified, suggested that somebody drive over and give the ferryman twenty bucks to make sure that he would stick around.

At that point, despairing inside, Kennedy attempted to move the reveries away from the Sixty-Eight campaign and announced that "Charlie Tretter is now going to give one of his great Boston-pol speeches." Tretter tried, stood on a chair and went through one of his Jim Curley/Honey Fitz routines; the utterly grounded mood of the moment wouldn't tolerate that. "People kept shouting, 'Siddown, siddown.' I remember behind me seeing Joey, still working away like a one-armed paperhanger."

"As parties go," Kennedy himself commented later on, "it was dull." They sang; a few couples danced a little. "It was just . . . just something to give one the chance to talk with those people. As I remember," Kennedy continues, haltingly, "I looked at my watch. I said it was late, eleven-fifteen, eleven-thirty. I'd been talking with her. She said she was ready to go." Kennedy, from out on the patchy little cottage lawn, summoned Jack Crimmins, and informed Crimmins he would be driving himself back, that he would be taking Miss Kopechne, that she wasn't feeling very well, was bothered a little by the sun on the beach that day. The two disappeared in the humid dark and a moment later the Oldsmobile started, pulled away; the rest of the party, inside or out, stood talking, laughing there a while, desultorily. The moon was down already; it was a little cooler outside; inside, everybody was still too hot actually to notice much.

Poucha Pond, the eternally surging tidal estuary into which Kennedy's Oldsmobile pitched head over just before the hump of the Dike Bridge threw up its off-kilter back—the pond was itself a contrivance, a dead-ended man-made catchwater formed by the coming back and around of a thin long ocean-nibbled pike hook of dunes and Atlantic littoral. By his own admission Kennedy had been traveling approximately twenty miles an hour at the moment he realized that the bridge itself was about to dogleg to the left and stamped the brakes with whatever reflex startled: he remembered the vehicle lifting into air; the next thing he remembered Mary Jo was pummeling him; his eyes opening he remembers gulping air, the awareness of being upside down with water pouring in in the darkness on the two of them, the unsuccessful struggle to get the door open and feeling for the window and then a sense of blacking out. The emotion he later reported to friends was aghastness, incredulity that such a thing could be happening to him *again*; with that there was a premonition of release as seawater flooded his lungs, of composure: he would die now. ". . . then, somehow I remember coming up to the last energy of just pushing, pressing, and coming up to the surface."

Kennedy's memory of everything after the Oldsmobile's front tire left the bridge's shallow rub rail and started to bounce out over the fall-away was broken, incomplete, and was to remain incomplete and confused for the next few days. The report of Kennedy's Hyannis Port doctor, Robert D. Watt, details the medical findings: thrown against the inside of the car Kennedy had suffered "a half-inch abrasion and hematoma over the right mastoid, a contusion of the vertex, spasm of the posterior cervical musculature and . . . tenderness . . . of the lumbar area . . . ." He had "a big spongy swelling" at the top of his head: X-ray studies confirmed the cervical strain. Watt notes, "a temporary loss of consciousness and retrograde amnesia," and continues, "impairment of judgment and confused behavior are symptoms consistent with an injury of the character sustained by the patient."

Swept out and away by the very intense trapped tide, Kennedy found some kind of muddy footing and sloughed back toward the Oldsmobile's submerged weak headlights. Belching, wheezing, coughing, he was tiring fast; he claims to have surface-dived seven or eight times in hopes of pulling the girl out too; head throbbing, neck aching, he exhausted himself, and floated and crawled out to the strand, spent, and lay resting on the grass. By then, Kennedy estimates, a half hour to forty-five minutes had passed. He had enough breath back to begin to stumble up Dyke Road, unaware of lights to the extent that in the moonless blackness he strained to make out the foliage along the margins of the road itself as he stumbled toward the hard-top.

Approximately fifteen minutes later he arrived at the Lawrence cottage. It was after midnight by now; Kennedy spotted Ray LaRosa catching a breather on the cottage steps, told him, "Get me Joe." Gargan appeared; Kennedy told him, "You had better get Paul too." Gargan walked back and told LaRosa to summon Paul Markham. Orders and responses moved reliably up and down the lifetime pecking order.

Markham appeared. " 'There has been a terrible accident,' " Kennedy testified having told Markham. " 'We have got to go,' and we took off down the road, the Main Street there." Markham's memory of the exchange is slightly—but meaningfully—different. " 'There has been an accident,' " he was to claim Kennedy said to him. " 'Mary Jo was with me down at the bridge, and let's go.' " They went, Gargan driving, fast. Nobody asked which bridge.

If there was one hope of a moment during which the situation might still be salvaged, it had to be precisely this one, when Edward Kennedy, half off his hinges with shock already, settled into the back seat of Gargan's rented Valiant, and started issuing rescue orders. But among the three of them, whatever the crisis, who was about to violate the drill of a lifetime?

What survived in neither the police report nor the twelve depleting hours afterward was the terrible fatigue-poisoned over-exhilarated stress all three felt. Flooring it up Main Street, spitting back pebbles along the corrugated Dyke Road, the crazy certainty dawned that unbelievable luck *had* to reward unbelievable nerve. A lot of this trembles back into Gargan's syntax as he later recalls how he maneuvered to park and angled the Valiant so as to shine its lights at the barely submerged tires-up Oldsmobile. "Well," Gargan says, "I looked down and I saw this car. The car was completely underwater . . . . Paul Markham at that time started down toward the water. I said, Paul, don't go in that way, Paul, without taking your clothes off, and so Paul came back." The command levels held: Gargan instructed Markham. "At that time I was at the right front fender by the right front wheel. I took my clothes off, including my underwear. I was stark naked. Paul Markham took his clothes off." The precision of Gargan's recollection seems uncanny, indelible; at one point he was actually able to force himself back into the submerged Oldsmobile and ". . . then began to lose naturally my breath at one point and I tried to get out. I couldn't get out. I was stuck, and I was stuck because I was sideways, which is, to tell you the truth, stupid, and I finally realized what the problem was and I turned myself this way (indicating) and pushed myself out and came to the top of the water." When this had failed, leaving Gargan all scraped and the wavering Markham dripping in his underwear, it was a little after one in the morning. All three tottered back into the Valiant and proceeded, wearily now, in the direction of the ferry slip.

Barely one a.m. at the latest by this time, but second thoughts and a palpable uncertainty about what actually *did* happen were beginning to batter both Markham and Gargan like an eruption of Mayflies. Both accomplices that night were later to testify that Kennedy told *them* he had simply missed the turn with Mary Jo and jounced at twenty-miles an hour up the gravel and off the bridge; Kennedy himself, respectfully cornered several times by District Attorney Edmund Dinis and more openly by a dubious Judge Boyle on this question exactly, kept picking it up each time wherever it looked most harmless. "At what point, Mister Kennedy," District Attorney Dinis would later ask him, "did you realize that you were driving on a dirt road?" Kennedy: "Just some time when I was—I don't remember any specific time. . . ." Dinis: "Did you realize you were not heading for the ferry?" Kennedy: "At the moment I went off the bridge, I certainly did." Even Kennedy's morning-after police report, while indicating that the Senator was headed ultimately toward the ferry landing, was unfamiliar with the road and turned left where he might normally have been expected to turn right, never in fact states explicitly that he had left the macadamized road *unintentionally.* It was a point that was later to annoy and bother the people in Bobby's brain trust who wanted the truth, goddammit, so they could make up their own minds about what the whole affair meant. "The unsatisfactory thing was the continued suggestion that he was heading for the ferry landing," one of them complains privately. "I gather he was heading for the beach." Then, hopefully, "That doesn't seem to me the most sinister thing in the world . . . ."

A matter of weeks after the incident itself, submitting to a private interview on the details—eyes tormented, wringing an invisible hand-kerchief until his knuckles whitened—Kennedy again ducked a query as to this matter exactly, insisting only that there was a "reasonable expla-nation" why the two took that wrong turn at eleven-thirty or so. Certainly, as a lifelong intimate of Kennedy's, Joe Gargan knew, immediately, without anything direct ever having to be said, what sort of "reasonable explanation" Kennedy might have elaborated if he could have summoned the spiritual energy and believed anybody would understand. Even out there, at Joey's remote little cookout, the walls had started to close in on Teddy, even there there had been "too many blue suits," as he tended to murmur, too many secret-service men, friends, self-consciously security-watchful friends, aides, choking memories of Bobby. That summer the yearning for solitude was coming over him prodigiously at times, like a spell. His breakaway mood, ushered in very often by a display of his exhilarated leprechaun humor, that momentary mock roguishness: the road turned; one envisions him swinging the wheel right, hard. Mary Jo, who knew him slightly, would presumably have known Bobby well enough to sense Kennedy's mood. Two bumpy minutes later the daughter of the closemouthed Mrs. Malm, reading herself to sleep under-neath an open window, looked up and heard a car, "going fairly fast," headed in the direction of the nearby Dike.

"I knew Mary Jo, yes," Kennedy later said, slowly. "She was very bright, lively, personable, loyal. Intelligent, highly intelligent. I'd gone to the party the Hacketts gave for the girls in January, and I think . . . I think that was the only other time other than during the campaign I'd talked really with Mary Jo." He had seen her innumerable times, of course, taking dictation from Ethel, job hunting around Gifford's desk in his own office, working with Wendell Pigman at Bobby's, yet she had—as a newsman later commented, not unkindly meant—"the face nobody remembered." The First-Communion-style picture of Mary Jo that went over the wires in time for the Sunday edition was a kind of reverse shocker to everybody, with the mascara airbrushed in and even a soft inviting gleam to the eyes. In truth she had been, as her twenty-eighth year ended, pastier and tougher, intimidating in a quiet way, certainly not at all a girl of the sort Ted Kennedy, with his reported availability to pushovers woo-able on the telephone with his Mister Moo-ah routines, was likely to think he had much hope of dragging behind a dune and out in time for the midnight ferry.

"Senator Kennedy," Gargan later related freely, "was very emotional, very upset, very disturbed, and he was using this expression which I have heard before, but he was using it particularly that night. 'Can you believe it, Joe, can you believe it, I don't believe it, I don't believe this could happen, I just don't believe it . . . .' " Calming for the moment, Kennedy had told Gargan that "he was going down the road, the dirt road headed toward I don't know what. He suddenly saw the bridge in front of him and that was it."

Gargan and Markham were later to persist in claiming that they had, indeed, pointed out to Kennedy that somebody *must* report the accident, and immediately. But nobody moved. The two were seized by the predicament, in essence, that paralyzed not only Joey and Paul at Poucha Pond and at the approach of the ferry slip, but also the lead figures who gathered throughout the following week in Hyannis Port, men who had damped down an incipient civil war and intercontinental missile exchange: certainly everybody saw where the dangers were and grasped, in large, what needed to be done, but *nobody* was prepared to act instead of, without express permission from, the principal, Edward Kennedy, and risk his own reputation on the success of the consequences. That got to be too much responsibility.

The decision hung: Kennedy again broke down, nearly sobbing, insisting, "This couldn't have happened. I don't know how it happened." More critical minutes passed. "Okay," Kennedy demanded finally, "take me back to the ferry." But back at the ferry slip no course of action emerged of itself either. Gargan again insisted that the accident be reported and recommended to Kennedy that he call Dave Burke, his administrative assistant, who could alert the family at Hyannis Port, and Burke Marshall, "the best lawyer I know," who could frame advice, before reporting the accident to the Edgartown police. Sitting in the Valiant, looking out over the lights of the harbor five hundred feet away, the three were steps away from a telephone pay station, one of the few in Edgartown, the same phone to which Gargan led Kennedy back to call and finally reach David Burke seven hours later.

But nobody used the telephone then, and Gargan's testimony makes evident enough why. Competent lawyers in open daylight, the three were functioning now in response to tribal loyalties. Kennedy, although upset and confused, remained Kennedy, chief by accession, grantee to power. As Joe Gargan himself broke down the requirements, his cousin's first accountability was to his family, to prepare them as well as he was able, then to himself, by securing the advice of Burke Marshall, whom they had all obviously, largely by osmotic agreement, designated as the operative Shaman, the human being in whom, by unconscious consensus, Robert Kennedy's soul might be said to abide. Insofar as Bob, who all their lives had been the central wizard in any familial crisis, had singled Marshall out of all men as having the "best judgment of anybody I know." Then, all primary obligations met, Kennedy must report the accident.

Driving to the ferry slip, Kennedy remembers, "A lot of different thoughts came into my mind at that time about how I was really going to be able to call Mrs. Kopechne at some time in the middle of the night to tell her her daughter was drowned, to be able to call my own mother and my own father, relate to them, my wife, and I even—even though I knew that Mary Jo was dead and believed firmly that she was in the back of that car, I willed that she remain alive.

"As we drove down that road, I was almost looking out the front window and windows trying to see her walking down that road. I related this to Gargan and Markham and they said they understood this feeling, but it was necessary to report it."

It is as if, blown over by the shock and dementia of this unimaginable crisis, there has here upended into view the entire tangle of Kennedy's far-flung preconscious root system: his distaste for large and abrupt decisions, his paralysis at the onset of deadly violence, his uncomprehending defeat at having again been instrumental, again been present and incapable of saving somebody who had given willingly and meaningfully to *them*, served the higher purposes of the Kennedys and so had come under the seignorial protection and concern that he, as leader of the Kennedys now, took it as obligation to offer. His sanity worn thinner and thinner by overwork, by worry, by too much unwanted responsibility, what little he had drunk that evening sure to have tipped into his worn-out system a perilous toxicity; the heavy concussion Kennedy absorbed that night, with its unavoidable hemorrhaging and lesions, was, clearly enough, too much. While he was himself, subsequently, to refer to shock and panic, whatever was left of his family's over-rich communally mythologized self-esteem worked to prevent him from admitting to himself that he too, pushed brutally enough, could in fact lose control. Better guilty than crazy, better demonic than helpless. Almost from the moment the scandal broke publicly the Kennedys were accused of everything from buying judges to suborning witnesses in order to avoid disastrous legal charges: in fact, one of the most vexing struggles his friends and relatives and lawyers had with Ted was to keep him from attempting to present himself as guilty of a great deal more than the facts and the law allowed. A man whose primary fixation, after having involved himself in the death of an associate, is how he will be able to bring himself to face the *parents* of the victim has been knocked out of touch for the moment with the mind of contemporaneity: feudal emotions are in control.

The exchange continued, directionless, as the three parked just short of the ferry slip; with that, as Gargan states, "The Senator said to me, to both of us basically, 'All right, all right, I will take care of it, you go back, don't upset the girls, don't get them involved; I will take care of it,' " climbed out of his back seat, took three steps, dove off the pier and started to swim across the cut. The two retainers stood there, watching Kennedy until he was halfway across, then resettled themselves into their shared front seat and drove slowly back to the cottage, had second thoughts, swung around and drove back to the ferry slip just in case . . . . By then Kennedy was invisible out there someplace upon the water.

"Bail out, pretend you weren't there, don't disturb the girls, I'll take care of this, it's my scene," a close friend of Markham's reports Paul as having quoted Kennedy at the ferry slip. Any excuse served. After all, as Kennedy's confidants in the matter, Paul Markham and Gargan were not merely old friends vacationing together; now, functionally speaking, they were Kennedy's lawyers: as responsible officers of the court, whatever he told them they could only reveal after having been granted his express permission. As late as midmorning Saturday, when the shocked and disheveled pair were able finally to nudge Kennedy into alerting his Washington office and nerve himself up enough to file a police report, Kennedy was to persist in his confused chari- tability. "I don't want you people put in the middle of this thing," he reiterated to Markham. "I'm not going to involve you. As far as you know, you don't know anything about the incident that night." So Kennedy's accident report left out that unhidable second round. Unexplained time lapses appeared in the rendition of events; press doubts poured through like bacteria.

With Gargan and Markham snaked away by LaRosa, what party was left inside and around the Lawrence cottage seemed to drift even more irrecoverably into doldrums. Crimmins had gone to bed in disgust and the remaining girls and LaRosa, having gradually given up the expecta- tion of getting across to Edgartown now that both cars were nowhere around, started to kill time by taking aimless walks up and down Main Street in hopes of running into Joey somewhere. Not long before two a.m. Nance Lyons, greeting a car that slowed down with *Shove off, buddy, we're not pickups,* was surprised to discover that it wasn't Joey Gargan at all but—as she was to learn much much later—that most agreeable sharp-eyed Deputy Sheriff Christopher Look. Look had a few minutes earlier surprised a stopped dark Massachusetts car with three forms in it and a license plate that began with an L and had a 7 at the beginning and at the end like Kennedy's, which, when Look climbed out of his own vehicle and hailed it, backed off and rumbled down unlit Dyke Road.

Charlie Tretter and Cricket Keough tried another direction, came back after a while to look in on what appeared to be an empty cottage, both cars still gone. To the suggestible Tretter this looked like a possible joke by LaRosa on him, since he himself, a habitual latecomer, had been delayed and snarled LaRosa up when LaRosa met them all Thursday coming off the ferry from Woods Hole. Tretter and Cricket wandered hopefully toward the ferry slip; when they got back the group was already settled in at Gargan's suggestion on what beds and studio couches there were. Tretter and the long-suffering little Cricket lay out for the night on the floor near the screen door, beside the nervous, tossing Joe Gargan.

Speculation among the girls about the disappearance of Joe and Paul centered on the notion that the Senator's car had gotten stuck in sand, something that had recently bedeviled somebody several of them knew; neither Gargan nor Markham, after they returned close to two in the morning, disabused them of that idea. The two were unmistakably bushed and tense with their knowledge of *something*. Markham, slumping with fatigue against Esther Newberg's leg, was told sharply to remove his weight, at once: Markham explained that he was tired, exhausted, and that even if he were at liberty to tell her, she really would not believe what happened. Nobody followed that up. Gargan himself claimed afterward that he himself never did try to explain away their absence to anybody at the cottage that night, but Mary Ellen Lyons later testified that he *had* told her that the Senator swam across to Edgartown, that he and Paul jumped after him, and that Mary Jo had herself taken Kennedy's car over on the last ferry. Nobody pursued it: by then everybody was tired, fractious, wishing grumpily that he or she had made it back to a comfortable bed at the Katama Shores Motor Inn or the Shiretown, envying Mary Jo.

Joseph Gargan slept fitfully, moaning and rolling again and again against the uncomfortable Tretter in his sleep. Paul Markham moved around all night, relocating successively from the daybed to a chair to an attempted sleep just before morning in the back seat of the Valiant. Edward Kennedy slept very little either. Traumatized by the accident, Kennedy had very nearly been drowned again swimming across the five-hundred-foot cut; halfway over the tide grabbed him and dragged him toward the Edgartown light and the undertow began to suck him down irresistibly when the tide apparently turned; there was the momentary smooth equalization of forces through which he churned in slow empty mechanical exhaustion to pull himself up the piers of the wharf and shamble, shoeless, his pants and polo shirt plucked half off his body so that his brace was exposed, into the dying chaos of the first regatta night in Edgartown. Legs gone, Kennedy stumbled up a side street, half collapsed against a tree for strength, and finally made it into the Shiretown Inn and up the stairs. Shaking with chill, he stripped, his headache throbbing, neck torn, back half out, desolated, confused. An enormous noise was around him, in him; hand over hand and dizzy he pulled on dry pants and a shirt, descended the stairs outside, and, after mentioning the noise, asked the person hovering just beyond the balcony floodlight whether he had an idea what time it was: Kennedy remembered being told: two-thirty. He climbed the steps another time. Tossing, pacing around the room, he was unable to budge his shattered emotions from their fixated need to believe that Joe and Paul were going to come and pick him up in the morning, the sun would be up and it would be a new morning and they would tell him that Mary Jo was still alive, that the thing had not really happened and that he would be spared the terrifying responsibility of tele-phoning Mrs. Kopechne to tell her that he had acted so unwisely as to somehow have destroyed one of his own, his charges. " . . . I just couldn't gain the strength within me, the moral strength to call Mrs. Kopechne at two o'clock in the morning and tell her her daughter was dead," Kennedy said later.

Five hours after he had haltingly addressed the Shiretown innkeeper Russell E. Peachey, Senator Edward M. Kennedy, groomed neatly and freshly dressed in slacks and a pair of immaculate Top-

Siders, encountered Ross Richards on Water Street adjacent to the Shiretown; the two sailors repaired to the exposed courtyard landing their rooms in the Mayberry House. Annex shared, and fell into a quarter hour or so of small talk about the Friday racing. Saturday looked promising. Stanley Moore cropped by, Mrs. Richards came out of their entry to join the conversation at ten minutes before eight. To Richards and his wife, at least, Kennedy seemed as ever—in fact, he had met Richards after unsuccessfully attempting to telephone Steve Smith's office at seven-thirty to try to reach Burke Marshall. Ted looked cheery, was not evidencing at all the gritted amiability of the politician, but—selecting from among the refractions of his splintered consciousness—was putting on a manner even to himself that ignored completely the experience of the night. At eight Paul Markham and Joe Gargan, visibly damp-looking and woe-bedraggled, ascended the outside staircase. Kennedy had inadvertently locked himself out of his room; Gargan fetched the key. Kennedy regretted good-humoredly that he wasn't free to have breakfast with the Richards, but suggested that he might just possibly be able to join their party a little later on.

There are circumstances under which nobody lucid is serene, and the moment Paul Markham started to mount the Shiretown courtyard steps, and glimpsed that picture of equanimity—Kennedy sitting there quietly, making empty conversation, "It was obvious to me at that time that nothing had been done . . . .

"There was no commotion. There was no—he was just seated there at the table." Markham and Gargan moved Kennedy into his room like a pair of bouncers and closed the door.

"I didn't report it," Kennedy said.

Aghast, Markham pulled out of Kennedy his tumbled memories of swimming across, of his night just sitting on the hotel-room bed. " 'It just was a nightmare,' " Markham reports Kennedy as having said. " 'I was not even sure it happened.' " And again he described the car, the rolling off the bridge, the lungs full of seawater. Part of Kennedy's mental process had obviously snagged there, then.

Steered now by Markham and Gargan (who subsequently, with his advance man's smugness about the logistics of things, was to insist to the district attorney, "You have to remember that I have been coming here and racing for thirty years and one thing you can't get on an Edgartown weekend, Mr. Dinis, is a telephone. I know all the telephones on this island well and . . . I wanted a place where the Senator could talk privately . . ."), Kennedy was ferried back to the Chappaquiddick side to "that little thing that looks like an M.T.A. station with a phone in it just beside the drive-off." Steve Ewing, the ferryboat chore boy who helped dock and undock the raft-like *On Time*, remembers Kennedy's manner as easygoing still, untroubled. While Markham and Gargan waited, tensely, Kennedy slipped into the pay station and was able this time to put himself in touch with David Burke in Arlington, Virginia. Kennedy roughed in the situation for Burke, told him to try to notify Marshall, to go to the Old Senate Office Building office, and to prepare himself for a deluge of telephone calls. Perhaps more than anything that happened to him that epic morning after, the sound of David Burke's urgent, even feverish basso, with its home inflections of reverberant ethical force, started truly to ground Kennedy, began to awaken in the inoperative part of Kennedy's mind a tickle of cognizance that this thing had indeed happened, was there forever now. Burke recognized at once the extent of the dislocation his employer now suffered. Throughout the rest of that Saturday, Burke telephoned the people he himself felt they would need, groped cautiously for some kind of grip they could establish on things. By early evening, leaving Dick Drayne to kibitz and hold down the Washington press as well as he could, Burke caught the shuttle to Boston. A newsman knowledgeable enough to know who David was slid into the adjoining seat.

"All I saw was a couple of things that were moving on the wire," the reporter opened gingerly. "It wasn't working, hanging together at all. Don't you think you should make some kind of . . . of full disclosure soon?"

"No," Burke said. "I don't think we're going to do that. The Senator is not in very good shape, I'm going to go up there, and maybe sit under a tree with him, and then we'll have to see."

With Burke, as ever, reality began: Kennedy emerged from the pay station badly shaken up, undisguisedly stricken.

By that time the Edgartown fire department scuba diver, John Farrar, had slid the corpse of Mary Jo Kopechne out of Kennedy's upside-down Oldsmobile. She was in almost perfect physical condition, "as if she had just come from a party," dressed in a white blouse and blue slacks, sandals, and her come-open chain belt. Rigor mortis had set in and her hands were rigidly clawed, purportedly from holding herself so as to keep her face as long as she could in the trapped air of the rear footwell. Farrar recovered Cricket Keough's purse, too. Word of the accident had worked its way back to the Chappaquiddick ferry slip by that time. Dick Hewitt, the *On Time*'s skipper for the Saturday-morning shift, was back before Kennedy got off the phone to Washington. He told Markham that the car that had come off Dike Bridge had been identified as Senator Kennedy's. "I asked him if he was aware of the accident and he said, yes, we just heard about it." Then Hewitt took all three of them back to the wharf at Edgartown.

When Kennedy hurried up the Edgartown cobblestones to turn himself in to Chief Arena, Markham went along; Gargan, on Kennedy's suggestion, drove out to the Katama Shores to break the news to the others. The episode as Gargan appears to have edited it for the girls featured a distraught Edward Kennedy appearing outside the Lawrence cottage, summoning Markham and himself, and demanding, without another word, that the two of them "get me to Edgartown." The moment the three reached the ferry slip the Senator allegedly dove off: Gargan and Markham jumped in after him (a heroic they both were to disavow before Judge Boyle), but couldn't overtake Kennedy and returned, disconsolate and worried, to the shoreline. Gargan also informed this group that Mary Jo was now, it would appear, dead; this caused "tremendous emotional breakdown" among the affected girls.

Once Edgartown Police Chief Dominick Arena had radio-telephoned the registration number of the Oldsmobile his men were starting to winch up out of Poucha Pond to headquarters and received the news that the car belonged to Senator Edward M. Kennedy, he radioed the station house back with the intention of telling the desk officer to go find Kennedy himself. It was approaching ten o'clock; Kennedy was there already. The two played a cagey little round of Twenty Questions over the cruiser radio:

Arena: "I am sorry, I have some bad news, your car was in an accident over here and the young lady is dead."

Kennedy: "I know."

Arena: "Can you tell me was there somebody else in the car?"

Kennedy: "Yes."

Arena: "Are they in the water?"

Kennedy: "No."

Arena: "Can I talk to you?"

Kennedy: "Yes."

Arena: "Would you like to talk to me?"

But Kennedy distinctly preferred to explain things at the Edgartown station house. When Arena got back he told Kennedy he was sorry about what happened; Kennedy was direct: "Yes, I know, I was the driver." Arena accepted the information, glumly: "What would you like for me to do?" Kennedy reportedly said, "We must both do what is right or we will both be criticized for it."

Reminded of that, Arena requested a statement; Kennedy preferred to write that out, so Arena conducted him to the Selectman's office down the hall, where he and Markham—Markham block printing it out—produced Kennedy's original version of what had happened. Before he attempted that, though, Kennedy telephoned the Kopechne parents and, sobbing heavily, finally made clear to them that their daughter Mary Jo had died in an accident.

There were police details enough to keep Kennedy around Edgartown for the next five hours: he telephoned his Washington office repeatedly, attempting to be sure of background information, to try to get David Burke to locate his driver's license, which was reportedly discovered in the glove compartment of his McLean car, mostly to try to surmise and get ready for whatever in God's name was going to happen *now*. At a quarter to three, two policemen transported Kennedy, Gargan and Markham to the Martha's Vineyard Airport to catch a charter to Hyannis Port. Kennedy was in the front seat. *Oh, my God, what has happened?*, one of them reports him as having mumbled, over and over. *What's happened?* "There was," the inspector remembers, "no direct conversation."

The moment his charter set down at Barnstable Airport that Saturday, Edward Kennedy was quietly and inconspicuously driven home. Kennedy circuits had been alive for six hours now with this unaccountable but galvanizing news. "The Boss drove off a bridge on Martha's Vineyard and one of Bobby's secretaries got killed," Dave Burke called the D.C. office to inform Dick Drayne, Kennedy's press man, who was granting a magazine reporter one of his shrugged-through hinting-around interviews behind his balustrade of piled yellow clips.

"Anything happen?" the reporter asked; Drayne looked perplexed.

"No—no, nothing, really," Drayne assured the interviewer. "I sat there all through that morning waiting for the roof to fall in," Drayne later admitted. "The story was on the wires, about a former Kennedy secretary getting drowned. I knew what they didn't, that he was driving the car. It was unbelievable. People poured in here, and I could only give them what was already public." Burke got to the office; Kennedy kept calling in from the Edgartown police station, four or five times. "I could tell he was very upset, very depressed, but he could still come up with answers," Drayne says.

Burke reached Dun Gifford at his vacation house on Nantucket Island at half-past ten: Burke, then Kennedy (whom Gifford called back to corroborate his instructions) told Gifford to island-hop as soon as he could to Edgartown and help identify Mary Jo's corpse, and see to it that the remains were removed to whatever funeral home the Kopechnes selected.

By the time Gifford arrived the County Associate Medical Examiner, Dr. Donald R. Mills, had gone over the body quickly at pondside, diagnosed death by drowning—the characteristic bloody foam brought up by drowning victims had stained Mary Jo's collar and the back of her blouse—determined to his own satisfaction that there had been no indication of any kind of foul play, no bruises or fractures, nothing to suggest the need for an autopsy. Mills so informed the office of District Attorney Dinis, who had left that decision to Mills, and turned the body over routinely to Eugene Frieh, the area mortician. Frieh and an assistant washed away the brine, drew off a blood sample which, when tested, indicated the equivalency of .09 percent alcohol in her system, perhaps three drinks' worth, examined the corpse closely enough themselves to be sure that there was no noticeable bruise on it except a slight abrasion of a knuckle of the left hand, and went ahead and embalmed it. Even before Gifford had arrived, the mortician had received a telephone call from John Kielty of the Kielty Funeral Home in Plymouth, Pennsylvania, who claimed to have been authorized by Mrs. Kopechne to see that the body was returned to Plymouth as soon as possible for burial. By that time the newspaper editorialists, hungry for detail and increasingly doubting, were wondering in print why no autopsy had been performed so far; two parish priests materialized almost immediately at the Kopechnes' door to advise the family: "Mary Jo is with God. She is at rest. Don't disturb her." The Kopechnes agreed. By then the Kennedy women, Ethel and Joan in particular, had telephoned condolences and were moving in to help however they could.

Later in the morning that skullbreaking Saturday after, David Burke had finally located the legendary Burke Marshall, in Waltham, Massachusetts, working on the records at the Kennedy archives. Edward Kennedy was subsequently to refer to Marshall as "one of the oldest and dearest friends I have." If, in his way, Marshall was, the emotion arrived secondhand through Bobby. There are certain unmistakable rare faces and unforgettable voices one takes in, almost immediately, as much too worldly sad to corrupt: Marshall has one of each, his look gone honorably at forty-seven to chiseled corners and leathery pouches; a compassionate, almost tear-threatened voice within which every word is patient, solemn, carefully measured first, then bitten one final time before release. "I told him I'd come down there and help wherever I could as his friend and attorney," Marshall remembers; he arrived at the Compound between one and two, preceding the returned Kennedy.

With Marshall's arrival, control slipped irrecoverably out of Kennedy's tremulous hands. Importing Burke Marshall to deal with a motor-vehicle-code violation was tantamount to whipping frosting with the great screw propeller of the *Queen Elizabeth*. Burke Marshall was heavy legal equipment. He had made his name originally as a standout antitrust lawyer in Washington, accepted Bobby's offer to come into the Justice Department as the Assistant U. S. Attorney General in charge of Civil Rights, and—turning down the deanship of the Yale Law School for the time—had taken employment as the General Counsel and Vice-President of IBM; with him in his attaché case he brought along a note from Lyndon Johnson that maintained that "in thirty-three years of service with the Federal Government, the President had never known a person who rendered a better quality of public service." Very few of Bob Kennedy's favorites gleaned recommendations like that from J.F.K.'s volcanic successor.

"When I talked at first to Ted after he was back in Hyannis Port he was so upset he didn't . . . the question really was where to begin," Marshall remembers. "I advised him to have a medical examination. He truly did not know whether he might have had a medical problem. He was obviously disoriented, but he appeared coherent. Then, after I was with him for a while I came to the conclusion he had a blockage, that a lot of his mind wasn't accepting yet what was happening to him. He told me he had been convinced, somehow, that Mary Jo Kopechne got out, got away. I don't think he shook that idea for a while. The Kennedys have a way of seeming fine, going forward without interruption under stress—I remember them all at the time of Bobby's funeral—but inside a great deal is blocked off. That night, in that situation, I think Ted Kennedy might very well have functioned so that the people with him, particularly if they weren't strong-minded people, would think that he knew exactly what he was doing."

Marshall's corner-turning earliest decision was to try and keep

Kennedy from risking any further kind of public explanation until, at the very earliest, he had stood trial on whatever charges Chief Arena decided to press. Leaving the scene of an accident was the probable offense, but there were much more serious possibilities: driving to endanger, or even, quite possibly, manslaughter. Kennedy's condition varied hour by hour: at times throughout that week he talked of abandoning everything, leaving politics; the people closest to him found him inconsolable one moment, virtually normal an hour afterward; the danger was great of his breaking down badly at a press conference, presenting himself as hopeless. "The reason I thought he should not make a statement to the press," Marshall admits now, "was that I did not know enough about his legal situation. A lawyer's instinct with his friends and clients is to shut up. Politically," Marshall now muses, "it was a bad thing, I suppose . . . ."

Largely innocent of the gritty workings of either the Massachusetts Criminal Code or the bathos and backstabbing of Commonwealth politics, Marshall started to telephone some of the Kennedys' more workaday lawyerly contacts to confirm the details. Personal feelings were inevitably bruised. "I don't think I should have slashed my wrists or anything," says one Boston retainer who had put in his years for Ted and found himself left out of this cataclysmic turn of things. Marshall had refused to believe the man's intensely offered version of the relevant ordinance. "I told him, 'Just so you know. The statute's been changed.' He wasn't taking it in: I had already checked the whole island out; within twenty minutes, I knew that X who was involved had a drinking problem, the judge was likely to react *this* way . . . . We had the whole book on the guy. And I wasn't . . . couldn't. . . . Here they had a guy at the controls who just did not know the factual situation."

Nit pickers from the press were already arriving by the hundreds: they were already out there by nightfall, already sore in the arches and angry, pacing the elm-lined residential streets, beyond the police rope-off, peeping over Hyannis Port picket fences. Another avatar of the desperately missed Bobby, Richard Goodwin, the man Bob had respected the most, if grudgingly at times, for his reliable apprehension of the oncoming public mood, had already been buckled into the crisis in case a statement had to be readied quickly. Perhaps earlier than anybody there, Goodwin was attentive to the thunder of newsmen outside shifting from foot to foot, waiting, calling their city desks and raging editors, again, with nothing, again, no report. The delay was insupportable; still, as the very largest decisions hovered, Kennedy was "obviously panicky still," Goodwin says flatly. "Obviously really shaken up, and yet nobody else was really willing to make the kind of serious decisions a situation of this sort required. We had there a great, headless, talented monster. Nobody could decide what to do. So, finally, by the middle of the week they transformed it into a political problem, which they could deal with. I left after the third day; by then they were trying to say something and still avoid the connotation of immorality—the old Irish-Catholic fear of ever suggesting that you were screwing anybody outside of marriage. Drink and sex acquired a disproportionate size." Goodwin had already prepared a comprehensive description, low-keyed, based on the facts he had been told, with as many loopholes covered as possible, which he recommended affixing to the police report and so making available to the ravening press indirectly.

Kennedy remained paralyzed. "Never would have happened if Bobby was there," Lyndon Johnson had snorted in Johnson City on viewing the first reports of the incident; Ted Kennedy, in his heart, was fully aware of that. A piece of his mind knocked flat, he was being looked at, waited for, playing a numb Bobby himself throughout that unending personal missile crisis. Old Kennedy hands like McNamara, angry for the legacy, were demanding, pique showing, to hear the entire truth. As he came to himself slowly Ted was being reduced, more the baby brother again hour by hour, the confidence he needed shaken by the dubious Camelotians who were catechizing him unremittingly, and discovering him short.

"The week afterward I remember as a time of great and searching speculation over the incidents surrounding the whole tragedy," Kennedy says now. "I didn't want to set up any kind of discussion with the funeral coming up, the grief of the family . . . many cross streams, people coming up and saying you ought to go to press conferences, my own feeling about the circumstances. It was just a very . . . I don't know how you'd describe the period other than as a great . . . great—What seemed important one hour seemed unimportant a second hour, enormously difficult and complex. . . ."

As frequently, Kennedy's own later assessment of the predicament is likely to stand up as the most reasoned, the most sensitive and yet, uncannily, the most de-emotionalized around. "By the time I got back to the Cape and saw Ted—it was Sunday night or Monday, I can't remember which—he was in a state of mind I'd never quite seen him in before—down but determined," Dun Gifford says. "He wanted to make a statement, go to court and get the whole goddamned thing settled right then." Yet, as Kennedy himself says, hours later he would be wracked, indecisive, sobbing on the telephone again to the Kopechnes or shrugging off all friendship to walk by the wasted beach alone. His hellzapoppin' college friend Claude Hooten flew in from Paris to buck him up; it helped, slightly. By Tuesday, when the regulars—Ethel, Lem Billings, Dave Hackett, Joan, Dun and Bill vanden Heuvel—rallied with Kennedy himself to the Kopechne funeral at St. Vincent's in Plymouth, Pennsylvania, the terrible dread again descended; leaving through the gamut of newsmen, all pulp above his neck brace, Kennedy mumbled a promise to make a full statement as soon as possible.

By the time the charter dropped them all off at Hyannis Port, Steve Smith was back from Majorca and installed; Marshall, who had a sick father and a vacationing family of his own to resettle, had waited until Smith was back before dropping out for the rest of the week. With Steve Smith's appearance, Ted Kennedy's primary impulse in the situation, which was to go to the public directly and risk whatever legal upshots developed, was stifled, immediately and powerfully. Smith is an extraordinary personality—he has the capacity to move into almost any situation with an abbreviated quick deadliness, like a kind of high-strung faceted scorpion, so fast that it would take a Bobby resuscitated to have any hope of standing up to his murderous gifts of decision and execution. The direct heir to the money-managing side of the old financier's double-winged operations, the Apparat—Joseph P. Kennedy, Inc., become Park Avenue, Inc., become Park Agency, Inc.— Smith had about himself and his operatives out of 200 Park Avenue the hauteur, the invincible New York self-assurance of back-room specialists responsible for articulating, whoever the front figure was supposed to be, discretionary monies and media control that won the election of the moment. The Kennedys' Massachusetts handlers stayed bitter over the arrogance, during the campaign months, of the New York bookkeepers from the Agency who flew in and out to wring dry—critically, outspokenly—the Boston people during each of Ted Kennedy's two Senatorial efforts; one of the few family matters Ted Kennedy's Washington staff ever heard him mutter about was his brother-in-law's tightfistedness. There was something confusing about being billed universally as the Leader of All the Kennedys and *still* having to be as careful as a truant schoolboy about overspending one's pocket money.

Now, well into what was perhaps the prickliest crisis in the history of the Family, Steve was taking over without asking, just as he had taken over, calmed the crowds, helped cut through most of the immediate chaos while Bobby was dying in Los Angeles. Moving at once, he decided which lawyers should supplement attorney Richard McCarron up to and beyond handling the leaving-the-scene charge for which Ted was already scheduled to appear in court a week later, on Monday. Goodwin left; McNamara arrived and was greeted with the high humor typical of the advisers behind closed doors: *Well, here comes the genius who put together the Bay of Pigs and the war in Vietnam. Let's see what he can accomplish with this one.* Sorensen appeared, full already of brooding reproach for what Ted Kennedy's mischief was going to do to the legacy.

They were all vulnerable, and Smith was overstimulated. "Our prime concern was whether or not the guy survived the thing," he exploded later on, "whether he rode out the still-possible charge of manslaughter. You've got to remember that half the press of the world was standing outside in the street. Those guys acted like it was the five p.m. express, Christ, there were telephones all over the goddamn place. If this weren't a public man, in fact if this had been anybody but Edward Kennedy, we wouldn't have gotten the attention. Then when Dinis decided on an inquest, an imprecise process devoted primarily to train accidents that hadn't been used in Massachusetts since, I don't know, never, that was the toughest decision, not to go to the inquest under Judge Boyle's general ground rules, according to which it would have been treated on a small country island, a local judge hearing the burden of those rather serious questions. . . . Under those ground rules, in a circus atmosphere—" By midweek *Newsweek* roared to press with the cover story that uncorked Edward Kennedy's euphoric publicity once and for all, inserting early in the piece the claim that Kennedy's "closest associates" had been "powerfully concerned over his indulgent drinking habits, his daredevil driving and his ever-ready eye for a pretty face." John Lindsay had not himself written the piece, but the information came immediately from his spring memorandum, laughed off at the time but now the buried mine that the resettling of Edward Kennedy's reputation had detonated beneath the entire Duchy of rocking Hyannis Port. The family—Steve Smith and Ethel Kennedy in particular—started furious and remained furious. Ted was being crucified.

Perhaps the least upset about the publicity as such, with its unavoidable political damages, was Edward Kennedy himself. Shock had given way to remorse by then, and remorse to a realism and stoic resolve about the whole thing that was making it more and more possible, as each hour passed, for Kennedy to take his own crisis over for himself. He asked that his trial date be moved up, held as soon as possible, and he decided, against the advice of Judge Clark of Brockton (a lawyer widely regarded as the best motor-vehicle-accident man in Massachusetts), to plead, simply, guilty to leaving the scene. In fact, by contacting Gargan and Markham and appraising them of the situation, he had discharged his essential legal obligation; the shrewd and inventive lawyers and advisers, Edward Hanify especially, felt they could successfully plead nolo contendere; Kennedy, hating the idea of dragging the affair out further, wanted to plead guilty and take whatever punishment Judge Boyle decided on then. Boyle, fatherly for the moment, noted that Kennedy had already "suffered beyond any sentence this court can impose," and sentenced him to two months in jail—suspended.

Kennedy also felt, deeply, the need to make some sort of public statement before much longer. After securing the agreement of the newly returned Burke Marshall, he called Dick Drayne the morning of Friday, the 26th of July, and told him to set up some kind of format within which he could make a short statement to the people of Massachusetts; both men were well aware that the substance, at least, of whatever he said would be carried nationwide.

Kennedy himself determined the tones of the statement; the flesh— a lot of the richest, least digestible of the flesh, with its taint of an abandoned grandeur—owed its phrasing to Theodore Sorensen. *Who am I to question the judgment of somebody my brother relied on so closely as he did on Sorensen?* one participant remembers Kennedy having consoled himself when the strong opinion of Sorensen prevailed; Ted Kennedy's judgment, at its most hopeful, was selling at quite a discount that week. Dave Burke contributed; the solicitation of support from Massachusetts voters—joked away afterward as the Jim Curley or send-in-your-box-tops touch—was requested by Kennedy himself and crafted by Milton Gwirtzman.

Kennedy bombed. "Almost anything he could have said would have been better than what did happen," the outspoken Goodwin later remarked. "He did the worst thing he could have, he Nixonized the situation." I was myself at the Yachtsman, the press headquarters in Hyannis Port, when Kennedy's fifteen-minute address was aired live; a minute or two into the speech the mood of the room—especially among people who admired the Kennedys—curdled utterly. As a document, the statement covered the major facts adequately; the problem was tonal, the ever-ready rolling references to the Kennedy curse, to the greats of Massachusetts history, the suggestion of his "moral" guilt—as opposed (implicit nobility) to his legal guilt—for leaving the accident, his "indefensible" conduct that night, the stentorian gobbledygook about courage, what one must do, what past courage cannot provide, the soul-searching about whether he would stay in public life: the whole thing was a collage of phony-noble rags, a throat-catching tuba serenade of poseur rhetoric. As a device it worked all right; as a device it turned the stomachs of alert people all over the country. "He was like a baby, he was just like a baby, kicking his feet and holding his breath until people will say they've forgiven him," hectic little Sylvia Wright of *Life*, still crushed at breakfast the next morning, mourned again and again.

Kennedy realized all this himself only soon enough; Sorensen withdrew; still saddened and dismayed, he deleted most of the references to Ted Kennedy's bright promise from his *The Kennedy Legacy*, already in bound galleys, and made it clear enough during several subsequent television interviews that, to his mind, this kid brother just . . . didn't . . . have it. On *The David Frost Show* later on, the strenuous Sorensen blurted on about "how hard [it was] for me to suspend my own moral judgments," and pointedly recalled having been "insistent that whatever he [Kennedy] said to the public it not contain misstatements of fact," and characterized Kennedy's actions as "indefensible," and "so clear an indication of his action under pressure at this stage of his life." Kennedy, on his side, had found something out about battening on leftover reputations. Several of the same associates who had felt betrayed for almost a year because Kennedy moved away from the Democratic nomination were retroactively incensed now that he should ever have entertained the notion. He himself emerged from the crisis saddened, shaken terribly at times, but shorn of obligations to the past, of an intimidated baby brother's obeisance before other men, other moods and eras. Lighter, identified much more fully to himself, he returned grimly to the Senate early in August, prepared to rebuild. The present started.

Kennedy underwent the bends on surfacing in Washington. "Come here, right back where you belong," boomed the paternal Mansfield on spotting Ted in the cloakroom, there, kind of waiting around for somebody, timid for once about pushing through that padded cloakroom door all by himself, needing to hear Mansfield's often-reiterated litany about how he was a "better Senator than anybody else in the family"; Humphrey had already pleaded with this "remarkable public servant" not to step down; Senator Fred Harris, the Democratic National Chairman, rang with his conviction that Kennedy's decision to return and defend his seat in 1970 was "good for the country, for Massachusetts, for the Senate and the Democratic Party."

Generous intentions; dying falls; Kennedy himself knew better. "Can you imagine how it feels, walking down these corridors, and the tourists are staring at me? And I know what they're thinking," he confided, weeks after his return. "I know what they're thinking. Can you imagine that, if I had in fact done what they think, done what they think . . . that I could hurt the Senate, that I would be here?" No fornication; not drunk; Kennedy would *swear* to it, raise his right hand without realizing it like a witness in the box, over and over, to individuals who mattered. "It hurt him," one aide admitted. "These guys are all traders of power, legal prestige, moxie, and when it becomes obvious that you are no longer a Presidential candidate you lose a lot. I don't think they liked him any less. They just needed him less."

The senior Senator from Massachusetts Edward Kennedy who had returned to his front-row seat in the well of the Senate in September and sat through the pumped-up over-hearty welcomes and decent Republican silences was a phenomenon skeletonized; this Kennedy recognized sooner than anybody. He appeared reduced literally, the heft of a grieving power-intoxicated year and a half metabolized off his bones those weeks of groping around the Cape. He laughed as much as he could about the little old lady who waddled up to him on the street in Boston and, pulling his sad head down to her own, whispered, "You know you can trust me Teddy. I voted for your brother. Now, what *really* happened that night on Chappaquiddick Island?"

"The anxiety, the sadness—it comes on in waves still," Burke remarked in November. "His defenses keep breaking down. Work, that's the only real defense for him, he's working terribly hard again, too hard maybe. But it seems to help." "I'm trying not to think about it," he said, straightforwardly, to one friend. "I really think I did all I could have, given the situation, my condition . . . all anybody else could have done."

Regulars on his staff, hoping not to watch too closely, were impressed and surprised. "He was the best I've ever seen him in cross-examination," Jim Flug said of his boss's performance during the September Administrative Practice and Procedure hearings into the Federal Trade Commission. One of Kennedy's witnesses, F.T.C. Chairman Paul Dixon, presuming, evidently, that Kennedy had been too badly vitiated to worry about, felt Kennedy's well-wrought and relentless questions pinning him into unwelcome corners throughout his testimony. Dixon, stunned, suggested that other subcommittee members were laughing at Kennedy's persistence. "Now to whom are you referring?" Kennedy demanded, annoyed enough by then at a Dixon slur of Ralph Nader. "I don't see anybody here laughing. I don't think anybody here would do that. Is it all right if they smile? Can we smile? Would that just be okay?"

Scorched among the colleagues much of the time, scorched around the Massachusetts court system for nearly a year, scorched fiercely and repeatedly in the press—as winter and spring came Kennedy could tell a lot about what and who he was *now* from where the blisters were forming. It may have been too, as Joey Gargran had long expected, that when the Ambassador gave up and died finally something essential in Edward Kennedy was free to proceed, at last, into the public domain. Kennedy seemed to be slipping—one saw it happen virtually week by week now—into his belated identity, into his adult alignment.

He began to neglect, more and more, that sweetly-tutored niceness he had nurtured around the colleagues; newspeople began to look at each other when the Senator came back in public to questions in a language bereft of those empty, circuitous phrasings that sounded more like transliterations out of industrial Latin than spoken American.

"Wouldn't it be possible to produce a Democratic Agnew?" I remember hearing one eager college girl, disturbed by the widely heralded impact of the slasher Vice-President, ask Kennedy at a university forum that Spring of 1970.

"I certainly hope not," Kennedy replied.

Then, cornered by another question, he waltzed professionally around it by telling a story, full of the sound effects he loves to include in his stories, of the day a lively looking little girl with a fifty-dollar-a-day heroin habit appeared before the Senate's Juvenile Delinquency Subcommittee and confessed—"and the cameras are going whirr whirr whirr—" that she supported her addiction by selling herself.

" 'What, you sell yourself!' her aging senatorial inquisitor asked. 'When did you do it last?'

" 'Oh, last night.'

" 'And you take the money and buy *drugs* with it!'

Whirr whirr whirr whirr.

" 'Senator,' the girl says, 'you shouldn't knock something you haven't tried.' The questioning then passed to me. I don't think I've ever said 'No questions' so quickly."

The hitherto-private Edward Kennedy was attempting to float its first genuine public offering.

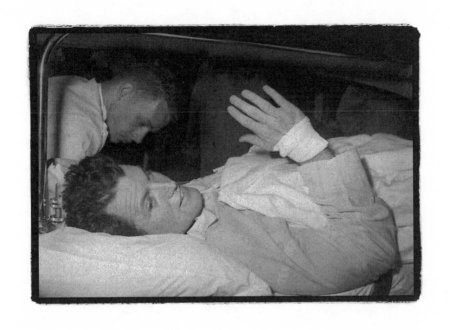

from The Last Brother: The Rise and
Fall of Teddy Kennedy
by Joe McGinniss

Joe McGinniss is at once an admirer and a critic of Ted Kennedy. That ambivalence adds tension to his 1993 book on the senator. Critics of the book attacked McGinniss for fabricating material—as when he imagines Teddy's thoughts—but the book stands as a useful investigation of the youngest Kennedy brother's motives and career.

Teddy Kennedy was riding a train the first time I met him. It was June 8, 1968. The train was carrying the body of his brother Bobby from New York to Washington. At some point during that long, doleful journey, Teddy walked through each of the crowded cars, shaking hands, thanking the mourners for being there. Stunned and somber, he softly exchanged a word or two or a silent nod with those he knew, then moved on.

Impressions linger: the sense that what might have been the last heroic era our nation would know in my lifetime had just ended; the awareness that for millions of the most luckless and helpless among us the single spark that might have ignited hope and sustained faith had been extinguished; the recognition that for the hundreds aboard that train who'd known Bobby Kennedy far better than I had, the pain, grief and despair would not fade for many years—the feeling of loss, perhaps never.

But there seemed also almost an unspoken understanding—as each of us aboard that creaking, swaying funeral train shook Teddy's hand and offered grim condolences—that he would now, in his turn, pick up the torch; would somehow, as Bobby had tried to do, breathe new life into the myth, would now become a legendary figure, like his brothers.

That, at the very least, he'd become President. Which is not how it turned out, not at all.

We must start with Jack, however briefly, because without Jack there would have been no myth. Without Jack, the lives of many, but of Teddy in particular, would have taken a different course.

One night in New Haven, in the fall of 1960, I caught a fleeting glimpse of Jack. I was a freshman at Holy Cross College in Worcester, Massachusetts, and had gone to New Haven to visit a friend at Yale. A crowd of thousands lined the streets in bitter cold on the last Saturday night before the election as Jack sped by in the backseat of an open convertible, waving and grinning, en route to an outdoor speech on the town green.

I didn't hear the speech and I never saw Jack again, except on television.

In the spring of 1962, more than a year into Jack's term, after the Bay of Pigs but before the Cuban missile crisis, it was announced that his youngest brother, Teddy, would run for Jack's former United States Senate seat from Massachusetts. I recall some distant grumbling about the Kennedys trying to establish an American royal family, but at overwhelmingly Irish Catholic Holy Cross this sentiment was muted.

No one I knew seemed to care much what happened to Teddy. Jack was the glamorous figure. Jack was the first Catholic President. Jack was the man with the wit, the charm, the beautiful wife; the public figure who first defined for so many of us who'd passed through adolescence under the Eisenhower administration the concept of style. Teddy was just the kid brother.

I was still at Holy Cross on Friday afternoon, November 22, 1963, when a friend came into my dormitory room to say he'd just heard on his car radio that President Kennedy had been shot. Then and for the next seventy-two hours, I felt the same shock, disbelief, horror, sadness and admiration for the magnificent Kennedy family experienced by almost everyone in America.

Teddy seemed a very small part of the terrible, beautiful, wrenching pageant that unfolded during those days. My only recollection of him was from the morning of the funeral when he marched, hatless, up Pennsylvania Avenue next to Jacqueline and Bobby.

Four years later, in the fall of 1967, I met Bobby. I was then a columnist for the *Philadelphia Inquirer*, soon to travel to Vietnam, and he, who had begun to speak out so fervently against the war there, had agreed to talk to me before I left.

I remember the following: The afternoon was bright and cold. He wore a blue shirt with the sleeves rolled up. He had big teeth. Behind his desk, there were cartons containing copies of his new book, *To Seek a Newer World*.

I remember how small he seemed physically: hard but small. And how ill at ease he was, talking privately to someone he did not know. In time, I recognized this for what it was—shyness—because it was a trait that I myself possessed, perhaps the only thing I can say I had in common with Bobby Kennedy.

We talked—he talked, mostly—for forty-five minutes. He spoke haltingly, his voice often trailing off, his sentences often grammatically incomplete. To be honest, I was so overwhelmed to be in his presence that I recall little that he told me about Vietnam. Soon enough, I would see for myself.

But I remember his asking me to have my office send him copies of the columns I wrote from Vietnam. I thought this was a nice gesture, a courtesy he did not have to bother to extend me, and I was pleased. It never occurred to me that he would actually read anything I wrote from Vietnam, for I was by no means an influential journalist and the *Inquirer*, in those days, was not a paper widely respected or read outside Philadelphia.

As I left, he wished me luck and, thinking briefly perhaps of what he knew of guns and bullets, said, "If you get up near, ah, areas where there's trouble, ah, be careful." I told him I would. He said, "I wouldn't want to hear that anything had happened."

There was an awkward moment of silence. I knew I should thank him and leave but I wanted to linger for just another minute.

Finally, he reached behind his desk and took one of the books out of a carton. "Here," he said, "why don't I give you this." And he inscribed it: "For Joe McGinniss—with best wishes for the future—and if you find the answer, please let me know."

I saw him again in April. By then he was running for President. It was the day after Lyndon Johnson had announced that he would not run for reelection. Bobby was scheduled to campaign in Philadelphia and some of its blue-collar suburbs that night. I'd flown to New York in the afternoon, having arranged with his office to fly back to Philadelphia with him that evening.

We spoke briefly in a private lounge before boarding the flight. He said, "That sounded like quite a trip you had through the Delta." I was surprised. Upon my return from Vietnam I'd received a short note thanking me for having sent him what I'd written, but it had seemed almost a form letter, of the sort that was mailed out daily to thousands of constituents and well-wishers. Now it appeared he'd actually read the columns. I was twenty-four. He was Bobby Kennedy, running for President, just like Jack. After that, it would have been hard for me to dislike him.

That night, I found myself standing amid a mob of people on a street corner in lower Delaware County, outside Philadelphia, a heavily Republican area where in 1968 there was also considerable support for the segregationist George Wallace.

The open limousine in which Bobby and his wife, Ethel, were riding turned the corner. Suddenly, there were the sirens of fire engines, the glare of spotlights, and thousands of young people, hysterical and mindless, screaming ecstatically, as if he were one of the Beatles. These were hero-hungry kids. They cared nothing for issues. They wanted only to touch and see and scream, and to feel close to something they knew was special.

They poured into the street, past police lines. His car was forced to a halt. The kids swarmed everywhere, mobbing the car, reaching toward him, bumping, tugging, screaming.

He was standing on the trunk of the car, swaying as it inched forward through the crowd. A bodyguard named Bill Barry—who, many years later, would answer the door in Palm Beach and tell local police that Teddy was not at home—had an arm clamped around Bobby's waist, a safety belt to prevent the crowd from seizing and devouring him.

I was up close to the car and I guess I was taller than most of the kids. At least, Bobby spotted me and gestured.

"Come up here," he said. "Come up in the car." And he reached out and pulled me with his hand, and the police and Secret Service, once they were convinced he was pulling and not being pulled, parted briefly to let the new passenger aboard.

Bobby was grinning and shaking his head to show that he thought it was crazy, but a mob like that puts an edge on the man who leads it: an artificial, temporary edge, like two martinis, but while it is there it lifts you beyond yourself and feeds you, and, fed by it, Bobby leaned again into the crowd as his wife leaned out the other way, and the mad clutching and grasping went on. The kids flung themselves at him and he rode them as a surfer rides a wave.

Later, as the car sped up and finally outdistanced them, Bobby sat down in the backseat. His face seemed alive and bright with both delight and disbelief.

The night was cold and he slipped into an overcoat. He shook his head again and grinned. "They tell me, 'Talk about the issues,' " he said. " 'Talk about the issues.' Those kids really care about the issues." And Bobby did an imitation of a frenzied crowd cheering, to show that the issues could get nowhere in that atmosphere. There would be other crowds, other occasions on which he could and would talk about the very real and significant issues that had impelled him to enter this race.

But this mindless hysteria was a part of it too, and I was grateful to him for letting me have a sense of what it was like to be the object of all its uncontrolled emotion.

A few minutes later, the car got to a shopping center where he was scheduled to make a speech. I had to go back to the paper and write my column for the morning. I never saw him again.

In early June, the phone rang. I don't know what time it was. Three-thirty, quarter to four in the morning. It was my mother.

"Bobby Kennedy's been shot."

I was sleepy. I had just gone to bed after watching him make jokes with Roger Mudd after winning the California primary. I think the first thing I asked her was where.

I thought she said in the leg.

"In the leg?"

"In the head."

I was on the next flight from Philadelphia to Los Angeles.

A large and somber crowd was keeping vigil outside the hospital. Now that I was there, I didn't know what to do next. Then I saw Jimmy Breslin, the New York columnist who had been extraordinarily generous and helpful to me all my professional life. Breslin knew everybody, of course, while I knew no one there except Bobby himself.

Bobby was on the fifth floor of the Good Samaritan Hospital. The corridor outside the intensive care room was filled with staff and friends, all those people who had tied their lives to his.

They waited with enormous self-control and dignity. Nobody argued or cursed. Nobody cried. They knew he was going to die but they waited with sorrow and composure. It was 5:00 p.m. and already people were whispering about only a couple of hours more, and in various rooms up and down the hall members of the famous, efficient Kennedy staff went to work, planning their second funeral in five years.

"He was so happy last night," a man who'd been with him was saying. "He heard early that he was going to do all right and he kept walking up to people and saying, 'Later, we'll go over to the Factory for a drink. And tell so-and-so. I want him there. Tell him to be sure he comes with us. I'll chase that Humphrey all over the country,' he kept saying. 'He won't be able to get away. I'll make him take a stand.'"

There was a television set in room 533, where I was. The news came on at 6:00 p.m. and a Los Angeles announcer said, "In case you may not have seen it Tuesday night, we are now going to show you exactly what happened at the Ambassador Hotel." Then Bobby walked into the picture with Ethel at his side, and he was grinning.

One by one, without saying anything, the Kennedy people got up and left room 533. But nobody turned off the television, and Bobby's jubilant voice followed them down the hall.

"Probably another couple of hours" was all anyone would say. But it was almost midnight before Bobby's three oldest children came down the hall and went into the intensive care ward. Half an hour later, Jacqueline, who had been in the ward, at Bobby's bedside with Ethel, came out and asked softly, "Where is room five-four-three?"

It was at the far end of the hall—the room that had been set aside for her—and two staff men took her to it. Then everyone started to sag a bit and people began drifting into the hospital rooms with empty beds. In the hall, Robert Kennedy, Jr., who was fourteen, walked by, crying.

At ten minutes before two, I was sitting in a chair in room 533, fighting off sleep, when Pierre Salinger stepped in. George Plimpton lay on one of the beds, his wife sitting in a chair beside him.

Salinger tapped Plimpton on the leg and simply nodded. Then he looked at the other bed.

"Who's over there?"

"Jerry."

Jerry Bruno, the advance man, was sleeping with his face toward the wall. He also had been advance man for Jack's trip to Dallas in November of 1963.

Salinger walked over and shook Jerry Bruno gently by the shoulder.

"It's over," he said.

Then someone turned on the television. Downstairs, outside the hospital, Bobby's press secretary, Frank Mankiewicz, was making the announcement that Robert Francis Kennedy had died at 1:44 a.m., on June 6, 1968, at the age of forty-two.

A week after shaking his hand on the train, I saw Teddy on television. He was sitting on a lawn chair in front of the Hyannis Port house where he'd spent so many of the summers of his youth, and thanking the American people for the tremendous outpouring of sympathy that had helped the family—or what was left of it—through the dark and tragic time of Bobby's death.

He was flanked by his aged but defiant mother and by his mute and paralyzed father, who'd suffered a stroke in 1961, and in the service of whose dreams his three older brothers had died.

Looking directly into the camera, Teddy said, "Each of us will have to decide in a private way, in our own hearts, in our own consciences, what we will do in the course of this summer and future summers."

That summer, he could barely lead his own life. Any thought of his leading the country was out of the question.

Yet the demands were already being made. Even before he left the Los Angeles hospital where Bobby had died, Teddy had been confronted by Allard Lowenstein, the antiwar and civil rights activist who'd tried so hard, the year before, to persuade Bobby to mount a campaign against Lyndon Johnson and the Vietnam War.

Lowenstein, who himself would later fall victim to an assassin's bullet, had shouted, somewhat gracelessly, "You've got to take the leadership! Now that Bobby's gone, you're all we've got!"

That was what it had come down to for Teddy and that was the way it would always be, not just for that summer but for as many years into the future as he could see. Joe junior was gone, Jack was gone, now Bobby was, too, and Teddy, however inadequate he might be, however unqualified he secretly knew himself to be, was the only Kennedy we had left.

It was Teddy's turn now. Only he could fulfill his father's dream, the dream that had created the mythic landscape that came to be known as Camelot, even as it had destroyed, one by one, those Kennedys who'd sought to rule it.

"You're all we've got." At thirty-six, Teddy faced the prospect of confronting those words and that sentiment for the rest of his life.

It would not be enough, by any means, to be merely "a" Kennedy anymore; to live out his own life, whatever that might have become. He was being told that he was now "the" Kennedy. The nation which had first been seduced by the myth had since grown addicted, and now demanded that Teddy live not only his own life but also, simultaneously, the unlived portions of the lives of his three older brothers.

Where one Kennedy stopped, the next began. This message had been indelibly imprinted on the sons years before. Each must, in his turn, do his father's bidding. But Teddy, that summer, could not. When the supporters of Bobby and of Eugene McCarthy were pummeled by mobs of enraged policemen in the streets of Chicago, Teddy was not to be found. He was gone. Out of the picture. Off the train.

At Christmas, I received a large picture of Bobby, signed "With Christmas wishes" by Ethel. The only time I'd met her had been in the backseat of the car during the motorcade outside Philadelphia. I put the picture in a silver frame.

The following summer, the body of a young woman was found in Teddy's car, at the bottom of a pond. He said he'd accidentally driven off a bridge.

Until the young woman's body was found, it had been widely assumed—and knowing nothing about him except what I read in the popular press, I certainly shared in the assumption—that Teddy would run for the Presidency, and undoubtedly win, in 1972. He did not run. For some time afterwards, all talk of a Kennedy Restoration stopped. Richard Nixon, whom Jack had beaten in 1960—and whom, many felt, Teddy could have beaten in 1968—won reelection.

Early in 1974, as part of a broader book project, I found myself needing to talk to Teddy. I did not yet know how difficult it was for him to talk about abstract concepts, or about himself. I did not realize the degree to which he shunned introspection.

After considerable wrangling with his press secretary, and only through the intervention of mutual friends, it was agreed that I could travel with (or near) Teddy as he made two separate three-day swings through Massachusetts, something he did every year during the Senate recess. The days and nights would be filled with public appearances. No assurance was given that I'd have the chance—or that he'd have the inclination—to talk about the subject that most interested me: how he managed to go on being Teddy when he had to be Jack and Bobby as well.

He had just turned forty-one. He was younger than Jack had been when elected President, younger than Bobby had been when he was killed. But there was about Teddy that winter the unmistakable air of someone already past his prime. He seemed jittery and guarded, moving forward—at an impossibly frenetic pace—only because he so greatly feared what truths he might have to contemplate if he stopped.

He made at least a dozen speeches a day. He would start at break-fast, sometimes before, and continue late into the night—being seen, heard, touched, being experienced. Renewing the legend at its roots. Despite the discovery, in 1969, of the young woman's body in his car at the bottom of the pond, he remained, in Massachusetts at least, a figure who created ripples of excitement wherever he went. Four years later, he was, however flawed, the last link we had to our idealized, glo-rified images of Jack and Bobby. He was the last Kennedy.

He kept moving, always moving: Quincy, Weymouth, Hingham, New Bedford, Fall River, Framingham, Worcester, Palmer, Springfield, Holyoke, Lowell, Lawrence, Everett, Tewksbury, Peabody, Malden, Waltham. For six days, he caromed around the state like a pinball.

It was a campaign atmosphere without a campaign. Before and after each appearance there was a great milling and rushing of aides. Instruc-tions were shouted, doors were slammed, cars were shifted frantically into reverse, U-turns were made on busy streets, speed limits were exceeded, traffic lights, bad weather, hunger pangs were ignored.

It did not seem to matter that there was no opponent, no genuine purpose to it all. This was the way Jack had done it and this was the way Bobby had done it and this was the way Teddy was going to do it. There would not be any slippage. The torch had to be carried and the torch had to be carried fast.

On four of the six days he was accompanied by his nephew Joe, Robert Kennedy's oldest son. On the sixth day, he was accompanied also by Caroline, daughter of Jack, and by Courtney, daughter of Robert. For one day he was joined by a son of brother-in-law Sargent Shriver, and, on the final evening, by Kathleen, daughter of Robert, and her husband.

And, each day, he also seemed to be accompanied by members of his family who were not present.

He went to the cafeteria of the Sacred Heart School in North Quincy. It was a low-ceilinged building, smoky and hot, and jammed with the adoring women of the parish. He talked about his older son, who'd just lost a leg to cancer. After the amputation, he said, his son had received a football from the New England Patriots, a basketball from the Celtics, a baseball from the Red Sox and a hockey stick from the Boston Bruins. And he'd said, "I know I have to learn sports again, Daddy, but do I have to learn them all at once?" Teddy told this anecdote at least six times every day.

He went to Holyoke High School. The band played. Female students jumped and shrieked. He was given a Holyoke High School varsity letter sweater for his son who'd lost the leg to cancer. He told the anecdote about the sports equipment, in response.

Outside, snow was falling heavily. Other schools, and many offices, were shutting down. The roads were becoming impassable. It did not matter. The show must go on.

He went to the Springfield Young Democrats Club that night. The hall was crowded, smoky and hot. He arrived at 8:30, an hour late. There was frenzied cheering and loud Irish music. Consumption of alcohol on the premises was not forbidden.

Teddy said to the crowd, "This is the biggest gathering of young Democrats I've been to since last Saturday, when I had dinner at Ethel's house." A huge picture of Bobby hung overhead. The mayor of Springfield gave a speech about Bobby. "None of us will ever forget . . . seems like only yesterday . . . touch football on the lawn . . . dedicated himself to youthful ideals . . . man of deep compassion . . . none of us can ever forget . . . wished to seek a newer world . . . dreamed things that never were and said, why not. . . . "

Then the mayor spoke about the spirit of the Kennedy brothers: "The spirit of the Kennedy brothers emanates . . . The spirit of the Kennedy brothers is a source of inspiration . . . "

Teddy was presented with a painting of Bobby. It had been done by a local artist who was almost totally paralyzed; who had, the mayor said, "only the use of a couple of fingers on one hand." He'd labored for months on the painting because Bobby had been such an inspiration to him.

Teddy took the picture, looked at it, expressionless, and passed it to an aide, who would later put it in the trunk of a car.

He went to Saint Mary's High School in Westfield. The introduction was made by a Father O'Connor, who spoke of "two beautiful women, Mrs. Rose Kennedy and Mrs. Joan Kennedy." Then Father O'Connor told a story about how once he had sat on a dais with Joan Kennedy at a time when "that beautiful woman was very, very, very much expecting." He recalled having been "very impressed by the very beautiful and radiant Mrs. Joan Kennedy." Then, taking note of the fact that Teddy had arrived an hour late, Father O'Connor concluded: "I don't know what Senator Kennedy has going for him except a very wonderful mother and a very beautiful wife."

He went to the New Bedford High School auditorium. A song was sung in his honor. It was "Abraham, Martin and John," which had to do with the assassinations of Abraham Lincoln, Martin Luther King and John and Robert Kennedy.

He went to the office of a newspaper publisher. On the wall was a copy of the front page from November 22, 1963: "PRES. KENNEDY IS DEAD..."

He went into a reception office at a high school. There was one book on a table. *John F. Kennedy: Words to Remember. With an Introductory Note by Robert F. Kennedy.*

He went to Fall River for ceremonies marking the induction into a nautical museum of the destroyer *Joseph P. Kennedy,* named for the first of his brothers to die.

He went to a New Bedford supermarket to discuss high prices with shoppers. He was approached by an old man. "Now don't you do like your brother and—like your two brothers did. We need you alive."

I approached him one night after dinner. I said, "Senator, I know you've been busy for these three days and we haven't had much chance to talk, but I hope that when you come back next week we will."

"It's hard to tell," he said. "I keep a pretty full schedule up here."

"Well, I'll see you next week, anyway."

"You think you can stand another three days?" he asked.

"Oh, sure. This is interesting."

There seemed a sudden flash of curiosity. "It is?" he said.

"Well, at least as much for me as it is for you."

He just laughed.

The second week was an almost exact replica of the first. He kept a full schedule. We did not get a chance to talk. It was obvious he did not want to talk. But I kept after his press secretary and finally it was arranged for me to see him for half an hour in his Senate office in Washington, as, some years before, I had seen Bobby.

But the press secretary warned me: "It makes him uncomfortable as hell to have people come in and want to talk about the Kennedy mystique or the myth of the Kennedys or the Kennedys as heroes, that sort of thing. That's just something he doesn't like to deal with. I've seen it happen so many times in the past: Things are going fine, he's very loose and relaxed, and then somebody brings up the Kennedy legend stuff, or asks him something about Camelot or carrying the torch, and he freezes. He absolutely freezes. His eyes glaze over and that muscle on the right side of his face starts to twitch and then it's all over, buddy. He pulls back into his shell and you've had it."

I saw him at noon. He looked heavy and tired. His wife, the beautiful and radiant Joan, had been hospitalized for alcoholism. His son had a leg cut off because of cancer. Mary Jo Kopechne had died at Chappaquiddick. His three brothers were dead, two of them murdered. His own back had been broken in a plane crash. And now he was expected to run for President.

He said he still did not understand what I wanted. I said I was writing a book and that I wanted to put him in the book. I said I wanted to spend some time with him and get to know him.

He nodded. Everybody wanted something. I was perspiring. I wished that we were having this conversation over a drink instead of on little chairs in the corner of his office. I wished that it were 1967 and that I was talking to Bobby instead of to him. Probably almost everyone he dealt with every day wished that they were talking to Jack or to Bobby instead of to him. That was a big part of what I wanted to write about.

"Tell me about the book," he said.

"Well, it's sort of a book about the hero in America and what's happened to him and why we don't seem to have heroes anymore the way we used to."

He looked at me intently and said nothing.

"I mean, well, you know, it's sort of going to be like a book about my search for the vanished American hero."

He continued to stare silently at me. His face looked awfully puffy. It occurred to me that he might be badly hung over.

"Of course," I said, "I realize that this isn't a subject we can really talk about at great length, because I know how . . . well, how it's just, ah, kind of hard to talk about." I smiled. He did not.

"But you see, it seems to me that this kind of book—and now I'm not trying to make you uncomfortable—but that there really would have to be something about the Kennedys and, I mean, about yourself in particular in this kind of book."

He was still staring. Waiting. His eyes seemed hooded. His face was absolutely expressionless.

"You know," I went on, perspiring even more heavily now, "everybody says we don't have heroes anymore, but, on the other hand, there is this special sort of feeling about the Kennedys. About, you know, the whole Kennedy thing. That's why I'd like to spend a little time with you."

There seemed so much of him that had been buried for the sake of the legend. What was it costing him, and how aware was he of the cost? Which of his illusions had survived? How tightly did he cling to them? What would happen if he let go? I wanted to know what it was like down there where he lived his inner life. "The thing itself and not the myth."

"Look," I said, somewhat desperately now, "five years ago, everybody thought your brother Bobby was a hero. Including me. I spent a little time with him that spring. I wrote about him. In fact, I was up in the hospital when he died. And now, see, there's all that feeling floating around out there loose and you seem to be the only one it can focus on."

He was still staring. But not, it seemed, quite so intently. In fact, his eyes now seemed glazed. He remained silent. And then a muscle on the right side of his face began to twitch.

The meeting ended. I did not see him again for almost fifteen years.

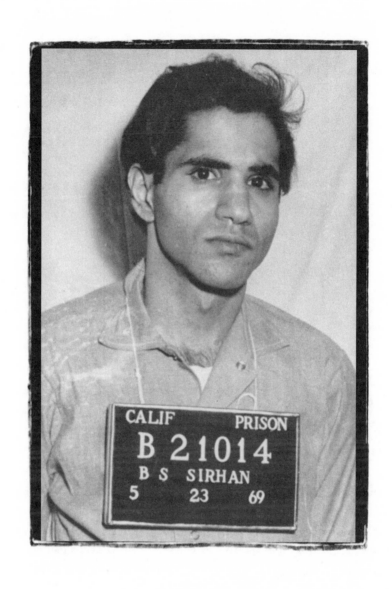

from Shadow Play

by William Klaber and Philip Melanson

Assassinations are public events involving—and creating—public figures who also inhabit private lives. Those lives play out day by day, long after the headlines fade. William Klaber interviewed Sirhan Sirhan twice in the fall of 1993, and composed this portrait of the assassin. It ran as an epilogue to his book with Philip Melanson.

A n hour north of Bakersfield, amid endless acres of cotton, Corcoran State Prison rises from the dusty plains like a fortress from the future. Dozens of one-hundred-foot steel poles housing high-powered lights protrude from the facility like spines of a sea urchin, and on the perimeter, two fourteen-foot-high cyclone fences topped with tightly coiled, stainless-steel razor wire straddle a twenty-foot alleyway, which, in turn, is guarded by gun towers at regular intervals. This is where California keeps its high profile security risks. Juan Corona and Charles Manson are here. So is Sirhan Bishara Sirhan.

Upon entering the prison one must surrender all portable possessions—wallet, keys, coins, belt—but once you are scanned and frisked, the walk to the visiting room is undramatic. There are no echoing footsteps, no reverberations from closing steel doors. The visiting room itself, with painted cement block walls and asphalt tiles underfoot, resembles an immaculately kept truck-stop cafeteria, complete with microwave for heating single-serving cans of what is normally thought of as children's lunch food. In one corner a thin man in blue prison fatigues lightly strokes the head of an overweight woman with a tired look on her face. In another, a Hispanic prisoner with tattoos on his biceps sits with his wife and three children.

Dressed in jeans, sneakers, and a light blue work shirt Sirhan Sirhan enters the room. An awkward smile betrays his initial discomfort. He greets his visitors, and then embraces his brother Adel.

Sirhan asks about the fires that have been raging in the hills near the family's home in Pasadena. Adel replies that there has been heavy damage in nearby Altadena, but only drifting smoke in their neighborhood, except that the strong winds that preceded the fires brought down the large eucalyptus tree near the house.

"Really," Sirhan says, "the whole thing?"

"No, about half. But it landed right on the fence in the side yard."

Sirhan shakes his head in dismay, but, despite the sad nature of the story, news of a tree that he has not seen for twenty-six years seems to give him fresh energy.

Corcoran has been Sirhan's home since 1992. He says it is more pleasant than Soledad or San Quentin, where he had spent the majority of his years without freedom. To the uninitiated, however, the prison's galvanized perimeter would seem to fence a bleak emotional landscape.

"The worst part is the monotony," says Sirhan, trying to describe life at Corcoran. "A bell rings, you get up. Another rings, you eat. And every day is exactly the same."

While extended imprisonment can smother a man's soul, it can also, in a perverse way, be kind to his body. In some manner this may be true of Sirhan. Though he is over fifty, Sirhan has no age lines on his face. There are just the slightest traces of gray in his hair. If he were wearing it differently, were his hair standing up on his head, then he would look remarkably like the Sirhan who was on the front page of every daily newspaper in the country the day after Robert Kennedy was shot.

But despite this resemblance to a known villain, it is difficult to escape the feeling that, as the most enigmatic man behind bars in America today, Sirhan Sirhan has been miscast. He is bright-eyed, considerate, well-spoken, and has the sly little smile of everybody's kid brother. His manners and conversation appear to lack calculation, and there is a charming boyishness about him, though he is intellectually inclined and conversant in world affairs. Yet dark mysteries, undiminished by the passage of time, still cling to this man, the most immediate being that he has been in jail for almost his entire adult life for a crime he claims he has no memory of committing.

To visit Sirhan as a journalist is difficult. One needs the prisoner's cooperation, his family's cooperation, and the often complicated approval of the prison authorities, who are strict, perhaps obstructionist, when it comes to granting access to high-profile prisoners. Over the last twenty-five years, only a handful of people have been able for see Sirhan in this manner.

To gain access to Sirhan as a visitor, as we were doing, is less complicated.* Sirhan's cooperation and that of his family are still needed, but the prison requirements are merely generic. In addition, a visitor can spend the whole day with the prisoner while a journalist is usually restricted to a one-hour interview.

A visitor, however, can bring nothing into the prison, including any kind of recording device. No video cameras, no tape recorders, no pens, pencils, or writing pads. Once inside, pencils, about two inches in length, are available as well as scraps of paper. But the pencils, dull to begin with, quickly become unusable. Employing the lip of an opened soda can, Adel does his best to sharpen them as the conversations proceed.

A handsome man at age fifty-seven, Adel Sirhan is the third oldest of the five Sirhan brothers. Living in the same house that the family owned when Robert Kennedy was murdered, Adel takes care of his mother, Mary, and manages what there is of Sirhan's affairs. In years gone by, Adel sang and played the *oud* at the Ali Baba and other Arabic

*During this visit I was accompanied by Adel Sirhan, case researcher and family friend, Rose Lynn Mangan, and journalist Dan Moldea.

night clubs, and around his eyes are the crinkled vestiges of good times and late nights. These days, however, Adel works evenings in a bookstore, and there is little in the way of time or money to devote to pursuits beyond the necessary. He survives, he tells me, "with a faith in God and a sense of the absurd."

Over the next six hours there is, of course, mixed in with the serious talk, a great deal of casual conversation—sports, gossip, current events. The other opportunity for needed breaks is provided by the vending machines in the corner. Snack food wrappers soon litter our table. Sirhan pays particular attention to a Mounds Bar he had purchased, eating it slowly, one small piece at a time. "It's a delicacy," he says in subtle mockery of his living situation, explaining that inside at the commissary, which he can visit twice a month, there is available without variation only Snickers and Pay Day.

On a normal day Sirhan is awakened at 5:30, and after breakfast he begins his duties cleaning in the prison for which he is paid $18 a month. Sirhan's cell, which he occupies by himself, is about 8 × 10 feet in dimension, with floors, walls, and ceilings of unpainted cement, and a five-inch slit for a window. This cell is part of what is called a Protective Housing Unit, which Sirhan shares with just thirty-seven other inmates, who are presumed to require special security either because of the nature of the crime they committed, or, more usually, because they have something to fear from other prisoners.

During our conversations Sirhan describes the staff at Corcoran as "professional," and their relationship with the inmates as "symbiotic." How many other prisoners in his block would make that observation is unclear, but Sirhan is the only prisoner in the unit to opt for a radio instead of a television in his cell. "TV is pretty boring," he says. "It's just the same stupid jokes and phony laughter." Sirhan mostly tunes his radio to KVPR, the National Public Radio affiliate out of Fresno. He enjoys listening to ethnic music and the evening news program "All Things Considered." The news of the Palestinian/Israeli peace accord he regards as stunning. "Really, I never thought I'd live to see this," he says. It's his brightest and most animated comment of the day.

In his off hours Sirhan likes to jog and lift weights. Though he stands five foot four and weighs 140, he claims he can bench press three hundred pounds, though he is at first reluctant to tell me this for fear people will think he is a brute. Sirhan says he gets along "well enough" with the other prisoners, but he has no friends. Sirhan must keep his distance. Because of who he is, some prisoner is always willing to sell stories or make deals with authorities based on new information they say Sirhan has told them in confidence.

Even though the event is decades old, when the conversation turns to his trial, Sirhan's emotions begin to surface.

"All this talk about killing my father and marrying my mother," he says, "it was ridiculous. It was insulting. I protested."

During his trial Sirhan did frequently object to Grant Cooper's handling of his defense. In response, Sirhan claims that Cooper would remind him how much per hour his time was worth on the open market. "I had the best criminal lawyer in California," Sirhan says ironically. "He knew all the tricks of the trade. Unfortunately, he used them all on me."

This view on Sirhan's part is, perhaps, a bit self-serving. As is documented, Grant Cooper and Sirhan Sirhan did not relate well to each other. Cooper openly admitted that he didn't understand Sirhan. Sirhan tried several times to have Cooper dismissed. But Sirhan could hardly be said to have offered Cooper constructive assistance. At the time of the trial Sirhan's dissatisfactions had little to do with his attorney's failure to explore the physical facts of the case. Sirhan was as blind in this direction as Cooper. Nevertheless, as Sirhan sits in prison several decades later, his resentment, justified or not, is still apparent.

As we begin a reconstruction of his movements on the day of the assassination, Sirhan offers his own version of unkind fate. "If the horses had been running that night," he says, "I would have been down at the track." In place of playing the horses, Sirhan claims he went downtown to observe a parade celebrating the one-year anniversary of the Israeli victory in the Six Day War.

"I'm not sure if I was just going to watch or heckle or what, but I wasn't going down there to shoot anybody, I know that."

But Sirhan had misread the advertisement and the parade was to be held the following night, so, as the story goes, he found his way to the Ambassador Hotel where several election night parties were underway. While there he consumed four Tom Collinses which, he says, "I drank like lemonade." The drinks made him sleepy, so Sirhan says he left the Ambassador and went to his two-tone De Soto parked on New Hampshire Street. Sirhan has stated in the past that he must have picked up his gun during this visit to his car.

"Do you have a memory of actually getting your gun?" I ask.

"Well, no. I must have. Pollack [the prosecution psychiatrist] told me that."

"Do you remember being in your car?"

Sirhan scrunches his face, trying. "Well, I remember walking up a hill."

Sirhan says he was too drunk to drive home, so he returned to the Ambassador where he became intrigued by a teletype machine. "It didn't seem real, a typewriter that was typing with nobody there."**

After that Sirhan remembers having coffee with a pretty girl, bright lights, mirrors and then . . . nothing . . . until he is being beaten and choked by an enraged mob.

"Do you have any vague recollections at all of the event?" I ask. "Anything, even dreamlike?"

"I'm sorry," Sirhan says. "I just don't have any mental images of shooting Robert Kennedy. Clearly, I was there. I just can't remember."

A major purpose of the prison interview was to come to some judgment as to Sirhan's sincerity. A tour of duty in the Bronx criminal courts had taught me never to confuse mild manners or good elocution with innocence. I had reviewed the audiotapes of Sirhan's police interviews and the recorded conversations with his attorneys and psychiatrists. I had found nothing to indicate that Sirhan's lack of memory

---

**Mary Grohs, a teletype operator that night, confirms this part of his story. "He came over to my machine and started staring at it," she told defense investigator Robert Blair Kaiser, for his book *"RFK Must Die!,"* "just staring. I'll never forget his eyes. I asked him what he wanted. He didn't answer. He just kept staring. No answer. . . . He just kept staring."

had been fabricated, but I now was looking for anything that might indicate deception. During our time together I found nothing false in Sirhan's words, mannerisms, or demeanor.

But the things Sirhan does recall are open to question. His recollections are a little like an old family story, remembered more from its retelling than from the actual event. In attempting to recall things that took place twenty-six years ago, Sirhan is covering ground that has been walked on so many times that no original footprints remain.

Nevertheless, it was hard to resist the temptation to probe further.

"What about the girl?"

"She was very pretty," Sirhan says, "with brown hair."

"What was she wearing?"

"Forget about polka dots," he says smiling, aware of the controversy, but unwilling to add to it. "I don't remember anything about what she was wearing."

When we begin to talk about his parole situation, Sirhan becomes agitated. His anger is apparent yet he struggles to control himself. He knows that any ill-considered comment will be used against him in his next hearing and all those that follow.

Sirhan tells me the story of his first parole hearing at Corcoran in 1992. Moments before he was to be led into the hearing room he was approached by an escort officer, who told him he could only go in if he were wearing manacles and chains. Sirhan refused and he was led away, his next parole hearing to be in two years. There is no doubt in Sirhan's mind that he did the right thing. "What board," he asks, "is going to believe that I'm ready for the outside if I'm brought in tied up like an animal?"

Sirhan has come to expect disappointment at his parole hearings. "I come before the board, I have done well in school, my record is good, but they say I need more psychological tests. Two years later I have the tests, the tests say I'm fine, but then the board wants me to go through an AA program. I haven't had a drink in twenty-six years, but I go through the AA program and I come back two years later, but now they say they want to see my job offers. Job offers? Just what's supposed to be on my resume?"

Sirhan believes that he has not received impartial treatment from the parole board. "There are many people who have committed worse crimes, whom I have seen come and go," he says. "The whole thing has just become political." He pauses and then tags on a strange afterthought. "It's like we're still living under George III."

The discussion then returns to the assassination and the discovery of Sirhan's notebook, surely one of the most bizarre pieces of evidence ever introduced at a trial to prove the requisite state of mind for first-degree murder. What is Sirhan's explanation?

"I believe the notebook is mine," he says. "I just don't remember writing those things."

Does he have any memory of being angry at Robert Kennedy?

"I had a lot of affection for Bobby Kennedy," he answers, "but I felt ambivalent. I saw him as a caring, gentle person who stood up for the downtrodden, the blacks, the Latinos, but it hurt that he wouldn't stand up for everybody."

Of course, talk of motive by Sirhan must be viewed with great caution. If he is telling the truth that he has no memory of planning to shoot Robert Kennedy, then discussion of motive on his part must be after-the-fact rationalization. I point this out to him.

"I'm aware of that," Sirhan replies. "I'm just trying to explain what must have been propelling me forward. But, honestly, I don't know. Clearly I was there, but still it's a mystery, because I really don't have it in me to kill anyone—drunk or not. That's what I don't understand."

A little while later he would say, "I must have known about the jets,"*** but his words lack conviction.

In the space of twenty minutes Sirhan has just demonstrated the strange duality of mind that he has consistently maintained for twenty-six years. On the one hand, he doesn't remember planning to kill Robert Kennedy and can't imagine performing the act, on the other, he

***Sirhan here is referring to the Johnson/Eschol agreement for the United States to send fifty jet planes to Israel. [the] "jets to Israel" motive became accepted by all parties to the trial.

believes that he murdered Robert Kennedy because he was a threat to the Palestinians. Which is the real Sirhan?

For most people this has not been a difficult question. When I posed it to Manuel Pena, the former police lieutenant who helped prepare the Sirhan case for trial, he didn't hesitate. "If they ever parole Sirhan," he said, "I'll make you a bet right now that within months he's gonna jump and he'll be over there with Abu Nidal and he will be a prize, prize terrorist. He'll be doing Allah's work, which is 'Kill more whities.' "

When I reminded Pena that Sirhan is a Christian, he replied, "Yeah, but it's still the same."

Pena's view, sincerely held, is similar to that of many law enforcement officers and parole board members. It runs counter to the police investigation, which found no ties between Sirhan and any terrorist group. Sirhan barely had what could be described as a passive political life, much less an active or violent one.

In our conversations Sirhan was also remarkably nonassertive. Although he knew I was a journalist, at no time did he ever argue or hint that he might be innocent. Though he is aware that such ideas have been advanced, Sirhan never promoted the notion that perhaps he had been manipulated by others. His recounting of events, the ones he could remember, seemed straightforward.

Through the involvement of researcher Rose Lynn Mangan, Sirhan has become aware in recent years of some of the evidentiary conundrums in his case. But unlike other prisoners convicted of capital crimes, he is hardly an expert. At one point when we begin a discussion about the ballistic evidence he stops the talk with a gesture. "You must understand," he says apologetically, "you know much more about this than I do. I don't spend my time thinking about these things. If I did I would surely go crazy."

Although he seemed grateful for the company, it was becoming apparent that, for Sirhan, having visitors was stressful. He was being forced to think about things that happened many years ago, things he doesn't normally think about, things he can't change.

"I wish I had just gone up and shook his hand," he says, speaking of Robert Kennedy. "If I could bring him back to life, of course, I would do it. If I could go back and trade my life for his, I would do that too— he was the father of eleven children. But none of us have that power."

I ask Sirhan what he would like to do if he were released.

"Live a quiet life somewhere," he answers. "Help people if I could."

What kinds of things would he find enjoyable?

"I'd like to walk down a street," he says, "say hello to someone, go into a store, buy a quart of milk."

As we prepare to leave the prison, the pencils are returned, the candy wrappers are gathered. Sirhan and Adel embrace once more. There is a weary look on Adel's face not apparent before. Sirhan, in contrast, seems more lively.

"So am I the great devil you were expecting to meet?" he asks in parting.

"All that and worse," I answer to his mirth. But the jest, as intended, avoids the question. What Sirhan is really seeking is a new verdict, and, in truth, it is hard to know what to think. Evidence suggests the presence of a second gun, but there are no accomplices in Sirhan's memory. Reliable witnesses saw Sirhan with a woman, but he says he was alone the night of the murder. Sirhan claims not to have planned to shoot Robert Kennedy, yet he offers a motive for doing so. At times it's as though his mind is a hall of mirrors in which every image is a reflection of another, making him a most awkward protagonist. Nothing in Sirhan's youth appears to lead to the most pivotal moment of his life. Nothing of significance happens to him after that moment. And the moment itself is invisible to him.

Sirhan's public persona is a blank sheet upon which investigators, prosecutors, psychiatrists, con artists, parole officers, assassination buffs, and journalists get to paint a picture. Communist, terrorist, political martyr, psycho-killer, innocent dupe, robot assassin— Sirhan's tragedy is that he is exactly whomever we wish him to be: a stand-in for random societal violence, unpunished terrorism, or the dark forces suspected of murdering a generation of this nation's most charismatic leaders. He cannot be let go, because the political cost would be to appear to appease these evils or recognize their existence. Meanwhile, what's left of a human being approaches his ten thousandth day in prison, retribution for an act of violence that has never been adequately explained.

from Oswald's Tale:
An American Mystery

by Norman Mailer

Oswald's Tale, published in 1995, was Norman Mailer's 28th book. His portrait of Lee Harvey Oswald includes these glimpses of Oswald's Russian widow, Marina.

F irst, Jacqueline Kennedy was a widow, and then Marina. As the second widow, she can no longer know what it is she knows. She has passed through thirty years of interviews, more than a thousand hours of interviews, and the questions never cease. She may be the last living smoker to consume four packs a day. How can it be otherwise? The past is filled with guilt—the future is full of dread. Only the present is clear; she always suspects the motives of the new people to whom she speaks. How innocent can be their motive for approaching? These days she feels that the walls are coming closer. If she starts thinking about what has happened to her, not with pity, she will say, or sorrow for herself, but just hoping to lessen stress, she feels she is choking. She still thinks of the night Lee sat in the dark on their porch in New Orleans and he was weeping. It was such a heavy burden for him. Something, and she does not know what it was.

It is hard for her to remember details. After her Warren Commission testimony, everybody accused her of lying, but she was just a human being and if she was lying, it was honestly—because she was floating through a foggy world. Memories kept coming, going. Maybe it was some self-protective mechanism. To keep her psyche from collapsing. People were saying to her, "You're so strong"—but it was not heroic effort. "It is in every one of us—you just decide not to die, that's all. You dare not to die."

Now that she is fifty-two, Marina would agree that one doesn't need to approach her with such labels, as good woman, bad woman, villainess, heroine, someone-who's-been-treated-unfairly, someone-treated-too-well. "You can be all of that in one person," said Marina. "One can be a villain, and next time a hero.

"If we go through Lee's character, I myself would like to find out: Who is he? Was he really that mean of a person?—which I think he was—but it's a hard road for me to take because I do not want to understand him. I have to tell you in advance that, as far as Lee is concerned—I don't like him. I'm mad at him. Very mad at him, yes. When a person dies, people have such anger. They loved their husband or wife for a long time so they say, 'How dare you die on me?' Okay, but that's not my reason. For me, it's, 'How dare you abandon me? In circumstances like that? I mean, *you* die but I'm still here licking my wounds.'

"All the same, I'm definitely sure he didn't do it, even if I'm still mad at him. Because he shouldn't involve a wife and family if he was playing those kinds of games. Yes, I do believe he was on a mission, maybe even when he went to Russia, but first I have to figure out what he was doing here. It wasn't just happening here all of a sudden in America. It was a continuation. In my mind, I'm not trying to convince you or the American public—I have to resolve it for myself. But I think he was sent over to Russia, maybe. I think so. I have no proof. I have nothing. I do think he was more human than has been portrayed. I'm not trying to make an angel out of him, but I was interested in him because he was different, he would broaden my horizon, and all the other men I wanted had been taken or didn't want me."

Every time she watches a film and sees an actor playing Lee, the actor is nothing like him. He turns his head like Lee or waves his hair the same way, but, she says, your American public knows Lee only from a few photographs, and that is what this actor is copying. She sees another Lee, and she does not know the psyche of that fellow. She still has it to discover.

Her interviewers asked how she would have felt if a truck had hit Alik in Minsk—if she had been his widow then, would she have thought of him fondly? She said yes. She would have thought it was just a stormy beginning but they were breaking ground that they would later stand on in their marriage. After all, she took a chance. She had crossed the ocean for him. Of course, she was afraid of him already, even if little by little she had been learning that she did not know, never knew, where she stood. Not with him. But at least you could hope.

She will never forget that on their last night in Irving, he had kept making advances to her until he went to bed, and she had refused. She had said to herself, "No, if I don't teach him this lesson right now, this lying will continue. O. H. Lee will continue. Don't butter up to me." She tried to discipline him.

Afterward, she had to think, What if he really wanted to be close to me? What if I put him in a bad mood? It torments her. What if they had made love that last night? But she is the wrong person to talk to about this, she would say, because she is not a sexual person. Sensuous but not sensual. She didn't like sex, she would say. She was not expert, nor could she tell you how grandiose something had been, because she had never experienced that. No Beethoven or Tchaikovsky for her, not in bed, no grand finale.

Marina: In Texas, sun is very intense for me and very harsh, very bright. I love moon. It's cool and it's shiny and that's my melancholy period. And some people are shining and they are bright and they burn. You know what I mean? I'm not sun. I'm a moon . . .

I look at America, it's all wonderful. But you go to the damn grocery store and it's 200 varieties of cereal. And basically it's only oats, corn, how many things . . . Just so somebody going to make extra million off that. It's so unnecessary. If that's progress, if that's abundance, how stupid for us to want it. 300 bags of poison, maybe only two or three good [well,] that kind of progress I don't think we should strive for . . . Do I make any sense to you? Or I'm just complaining?

interviewer: No, I agree with you.

After the assassination, there were times when she was close to ending her life. She wondered when her breaking point would come. She had crossed that ocean for nothing. Still, she tried to survive. It was a lonely life. Every day. The worst of the pain was that maybe she loved him more by the end than in their beginning. Maybe grieving was just starting to happen now! Maybe! Because she had never really had such a process. Just numb, with pain always there.

She doesn't know whether they would have stayed married, but still, Lee was the person she would have liked to have been able to make it with. Through life. There was some goodness in him to hold on to, and on that last unexpected Thursday when he came to visit, he was kind of sheepish because of that big lie, O. H. Lee.

And when he came in, he said, "Hi," nice and everything, and she said, "What are you doing here?"—cold and rude.

Later, she couldn't understand. Maybe he didn't love her, maybe he cared less for her, but he loved his little girls enormously, and even thirty years later she heard a story about how in those last days, when he lived on North Beckley, he was playing with the grandchildren of the woman who ran his last rooming house. These children called him Mr. Lee. He asked one of those boys, "Are you a good boy?" and that kid shook his head in the negative, said, "Uh-unh," and Lee said, "Never be so bad that you hurt somebody." This kid was now grown-up, but he still remembered that, still told that story.

The morning when Lee left, Friday morning, November 22, 1963, she did not get up with him when he arose very early. She tried to, but he said, "Don't worry. Go back to sleep." And he left quietly.

She had gone to bed after him the night before. He was already asleep or pretended to be. Then, when she woke up in the middle of the night to check on baby Rachel, she took a look at him. The only illumination was by nightlight, very low. But Lee scared her. She touched him with her foot and he kicked it away. Then he lay so still that it was like he had died. He didn't move for the next hour. She said to herself, "Is he alive?" He looked so still. Absolutely gone. She couldn't hear his breath. She had to bend over very close to feel his breathing—she thought he had died on her. Isn't that funny? For all these years she remembered saying, "Thank goodness he's alive." And he made no sound all night and never moved again. In the morning, he made himself instant coffee, drank it in a plastic cup, and went off to work.

She sits in a chair, a tiny woman in her early fifties, her thin shoulders hunched forward in such pain of spirit under such a mass of guilt that one would comfort her as one would hug a child. What is left of what was once her beauty are her extraordinary eyes, blue as diamonds, and they blaze with light as if, in divine compensation for the dead weight of all that will not cease to haunt her, she has been granted a spark from the hour of an apocalypse others have not seen. Perhaps it is the light offered to victims who have suffered like the gods.

from Kathleen Kennedy: Her Life and Times
by Lynne McTaggart

Protestant Peter Fitzwilliam was willing to divorce his wife and marry Rose and Joseph Kennedy's eldest daughter "Kick", but she wanted the approval of her devoutly Catholic parents. The couple on May 13, 1948 set out from England to meet Joseph in France, hoping to win him over. Lynn McTaggart describes the events that followed.

P eter Fitzwilliam always traveled light. When he arrived at Smith Square on the morning of May 13 to pick up Kathleen, he was amused to find that she had packed two large suitcases containing enough resort wear for at least two weeks and for any kind of weather, although they only expected to be gone for a long weekend.

Kathleen was wearing her going-away outfit—a smart little navy suit worn with pearls. Despite Peter's influence she was still a skirt-and-sweater girl at heart. Gone altogether, however, were the flannel nightgowns of her Washington days; her suitcases contained a blue silk negligee and filmy pink peignoir as well as embroidered camisoles and knickers and black lace garter belts. She had also packed a considerable amount of jewelry—much of it loaned to her by the Devonshires after the robbery. It was understood that she would return these heirlooms if she remarried.

Peter left with her for the airport in a great hurry. They were due to fly at ten thirty and were already behind schedule. "Wish me luck," Kick said to Ilona Solymossy, waving a white-gloved hand in farewell.

"Should I cross my fingers?" Ilona said.

"Yes, both hands," Kick replied.

"I will even cross my feet," the housekeeper said with a laugh. They arrived a half hour late at Croydon, the airport outside London where Peter had chartered a DeHavilland Dove twin-engine ten-seater. Arrangements had been made for the airplane to land in Paris at noon, depart at twelve thirty, then arrive in Cannes at three thirty. After an hour stopover the pilot would head back to London.

Before takeoff the pilot, Peter Townshend, noted a squall over the Rhône Valley, an area en route to Cannes that was known for its often violent thunderstorms. Townshend planned to check conditions further during the stopover at Paris. Although bad storms all over the Continent were forecast, he had calculated that there would be enough time to get his passengers to their destination. If the weather worsened around Marseilles, in the South of France, he could always take a different route home. On a recent flight the airplane's undercarriage and two propellers had been damaged, but the repairs had been made and the plane tested to Townshend's satisfaction earlier that morning.

With the late start the Dove arrived at Le Bourget, the Paris airport, at twelve forty-five. After landing, Kathleen and Peter got out, informing Townshend that they would be gone about forty minutes. At the airport Peter decided to telephone some of his Parisian cronies. On impulse he invited them to lunch at the Café de Paris. He was known for orchestrating such impromptu get-togethers. This time he was eager for Kathleen to meet some members of the French racing set. It would be a festive start to their first weekend alone. He ushered Kick into a taxi, and they set off for Paris without informing Townshend of their change of plans.

Shortly before two Townshend walked over to the meteorological station to collect a weather update. He was handed a chart made up at nine that morning and was warned by the meteorologists that conditions were worsening over the Rhône Valley. A massive thunderstorm with abnormally heavy rainfall was expected at about 5 p.m. Townshend glanced at his watch. They had already fallen an hour and a half behind. The flight from Paris to Cannes took three hours. To avoid the storm, they would have to leave immediately, but his two passengers had not yet returned.

Townshend had trained pilots and flown RAF Liberators during the war. He was accustomed to adhering to schedules planned to the last split second and hated the thought of making alterations in his meticulously worked-out flight plan. But now he realized that he and his radio pilot, Arthur Freeman, might very well get caught in the storm or be grounded in Cannes for the night. Restively he paced back and forth from his plane to the meteorological station. "I'm going to be late," he declared in French to the official on duty. "It's annoying."

For the next hour he kept revising his flight-plan departure time. Moments after he had moved the takeoff forward for the fourth time, Kathleen and Peter, accompanied by their luncheon guests, finally appeared. They were in a gay, carefree mood. Townshend was livid. Because they had been so late getting back, he informed them tersely, they would be flying over the Rhône Valley precisely at the time that a thunderstorm had been predicted. All commercial flights were being canceled. Although private planes could fly in any weather, the meteorological station had advised him not to take off. The flight was now too risky, and he intended to cancel it.

Highly annoyed, Peter began to argue with him. He considered it ludicrous to cancel all plans because of a little rain. Kick had looked forward to the trip so much. If they didn't fly that evening, they would have to call it off entirely. With the plan to meet Mr. Kennedy on Saturday there would be no point at all in leaving for Cannes the following morning. He himself was not at all afraid of a little turbulence. He was so insistent and so charmingly apologetic for having wrecked the schedule that Townshend found himself giving in. At three twenty he started the engines.

The Dove climbed to six thousand feet after takeoff, ascending to nine thousand five hundred feet, the cruising altitude, at Fountainbleau. Despite the altered time and weather conditions Townshend continued to adhere strictly to his original plan, with only two slight corrections to avoid turbulence.

At four fifty Arthur Freeman requested a forecast for Cannes at six thirty, when they expected to be landing. Impatient to make up for all the lost time, Townshend did not have him ask for an update of the conditions over the Ardèche Mountains, where the bad weather was expected.

"Rhône ahead," Freeman announced to the station at Lyons. After receiving the forecast for Cannes, Freeman lost contact with the ground. They were in the region of Vienne, at the edges of the thunderstorm, where atmospheric discharges prevented radio communication. Freeman switched his radio to various frequencies but could pick up nothing. Up until that time Townshend had known exactly where they were, but now without radio or good visibility he could only rely on instinct. Flying blindly through a cloud formation, a pilot could easily mistake a rapid bank sideways for a sudden pull-up, since the physical sensation produced by both—a flattening against the seat— was identical. To level the plane, a pilot in that situation was apt to react by pushing the stick forward, thus forcing an already descending airplane to assume an even sharper dive.

Townshend had remained at an altitude of ten thousand feet, even though, as an experienced pilot, he knew that a tiny craft could pass safely through a thunderstorm only at either a very low or a very high altitude. He may have been waiting for Freeman to manage to make radio contact again before changing his altitude; by law a pilot had to receive permission from ground control before doing so. In dangerous weather conditions, however, a pilot was allowed to change course on his own. From the difficulty Freeman was experiencing Townshend must have known that the thunderstorm was violent; after Valence he could actually see it ahead of him. Perhaps he was waiting to drop down until he had established his exact location. He was unaware that a southeasterly wind had blown the little Dove off course. By remaining at the prearranged altitude he was heading straight into the eye of the storm.

With bad visibility, no radio directions, and all his attention focused on steadying the craft in the turbulence, Townshend passed into the storm cloud. Suddenly the Dove began thrashing wildly. Alternate air currents tossed the little craft thousands of feet in different directions. For twenty minutes Peter and Kathleen endured a terrifying ride. One minute they were thrown against their seats, the next they were forced upward, gasping from the strangulating tug of their seatbelts. They couldn't even hold on to each other because they were at opposite ends of the passenger cabin. To distribute the weight evenly, Townshend had placed Peter in the forwardmost left seat and Kathleen in the last seat to the right.

Desperately Townshend and Freeman tried to regain control. The rain had obscured all visibility. Their instruments spun uselessly. Townshend had no idea whether they were climbing or descending until the plane shot out of the bottom of the cloud and he spotted a mountain ridge a thousand feet away. With the sudden sighting of ground he realized he was in a steep dive and that the plane would crash. Immediately he shoved his stick all the way back to pull out of the dive. The elevator tab that made the plane ascend was controlled by a foot pedal. Probably because it wasn't working properly Freeman abandoned the pedal and pulled directly on the elevator cable itself. Coupled with the stress of the turbulence the sudden change of direction was too much for the little Dove. As it thrust upward the starboard wing tore off. With the sudden loss of balance one engine tore loose, then the other, followed by the tail plane. The fuselage went into a flat spin and plummeted toward a ridge on top of a mountain peak. Townshend and Freeman stuffed handkerchiefs into their mouths, a standard procedure in a crash landing to avoid biting through the tongue. For about ten seconds Peter and Kathleen in their separate seats realized they were probably going to die.

In the midst of the violent storm a farmer named Paul Petit heard a loud racing of engines overhead followed by a sharp, high-speed whistle. As he ran out to investigate the noise he watched in dazed horror as an airplane emerging from a cloud disintegrated in midair. Petit lived alone with several fierce guard dogs in a nine-hundred-year-old red stone farmhouse near the peak of Le Coran, the highest of the Cevennes Mountains in the Ardèche. His father and brother were his only neighbors.

In the fearsome weather Petit and his father scrambled up a serpentine stone trail. On a ridge near the top of the mountain they found the body of the plane, nose down. They managed to pry open one of the doors. Even in the blinding rainstorm they could tell that none of the passengers had survived.

Petit began a slow descent to St. Bauzile, the nearest village. From a coin telephone outside the town bistro he placed a call to the *mairie* and the gendarmerie, telling them of the crash. An hour later several gendarmes, the mayor of the town, and a journalist followed Petit up the mountain to the wreckage. It took them two and a half hours to make the ascent. They looked inside the cabin to check the condition of the victims. The pilot and copilot lay crumpled against the cockpit, their earphones still on. The male passenger was crushed beneath his seat. The only accessible victim was the woman, still fastened by her seatbelt, who lay in a skewed position, her legs broken. In the woman's purse the police found her passport.

In Britain the first reports at 4:30 a.m. announced only that a private British plane had gone down, claiming between four and eight victims. An American passport bearing the name "Lady Hartington" had been found on the single female passenger. Perhaps because there were two Lady Hartingtons, Kathleen and her sister-in-law, Debo, newspapers and wireless broadcasts referred cautiously to the "Lady Hartington Passport Mystery" until a body could be positively identified. In America newsmen checked the passport number and identified Kathleen as the victim.

• • •

Eunice Kennedy answered the telephone in Georgetown when a call came after midnight on May 14, from a Washington Post reporter.

"There's a story here that a Lady Hartington has been killed in an airplane crash. Is that your sister?"

"I'm not sure, I think there are two Lady Hartingtons," Eunice answered falteringly. Please let it be Debo, she thought, even if it was a terrible thing to wish.

The reporter said the victim's passport showed "Kathleen" as the Christian name.

"That does sound like my sister," Eunice replied agitatedly. She demanded to know how the reporter had learned about the name on the passport. When she hung up and told Jack of the call, she retained only the faintest hope that there had been some mistake.

Jack immediately got on the phone to Ted Reardon, his executive assistant. Reardon had been Joe's roommate at Harvard and had remained devoted to the family after Joe was killed. He promised to telephone some of his news contacts and check out the story. An hour later Ted called Jack to confirm that his sister was dead.

"Fine, Ted," Jack replied, sounding suddenly exhausted. "Will you come over in the morning and make arrangements for the family?"

Reardon's wife awoke shortly afterward and found her husband staring at an open page of As We Remember Joe. He pointed to the photograph at the bottom of Kathleen's entry. It was the single, well-publicized photograph of her wedding. A grinning Joe peered behind Billy in his Coldstream Guards uniform and Kathleen in her makeshift wartime bridal costume. "Imagine," Reardon said, "first Joe, then Billy, then Kathleen. It happened so fast to all three of them."

Joseph Kennedy was asleep at the George Cinq Hotel in Paris when a call came through from America at 6:30 a.m. Kennedy's old friend Joseph Timilty, who was traveling with him, took the call. A reporter from The Boston Globe, who had been trying to get through for two hours, notified him of the crash.

Timilty told the reporter to hold on while he woke Kennedy and broke the news. He returned to the telephone a few moments later, Kennedy had been too shocked to speak when told of his daughter's death. Timilty rushed away from the phone to be with him.

Later that morning in St. Bauzile gendarmes extracted the bodies and laid them on makeshift stretchers. The authorities removed all valuables, including Kathleen's pearls and wedding ring; when they could find only one pearl earring, they looked accusingly at M. Petit. A doctor from a nearby village arrived to perform an external examination of the victims. All four had died on impact after suffering massive cuts and bruises to the head. Fitzwilliam was terribly disfigured and one leg was crushed. Freeman's hand was burned and badly cut, with one finger nearly torn off—the result of his last-ditch attempt to pull the elevator cable. As the passenger in the rear Kathleen had suffered the fewest injuries. The right side of her face had a long gash. Along with her legs, her jaw and her pelvis had been crushed when the plane hit the ground.

Petit's hundred-year-old oxcarts lurched down the mountain, carrying the bodies to St. Bauzile. In the *mairie* the bodies were laid in makeshift coffins, then transported that evening to Privas, the largest town in the Ardèche. There they would remain until the nearest of kin could come and identify them. Harry Sporborg was the first among Peter's associates and relatives to be notified of the tragedy. After dispatching Peter's trainer to Privas, Sporborg was faced with the painful task of informing Maud Fitzwilliam that her son and sole heir was dead.

Joseph Kennedy, who told reporters he hoped there had been a mistake in his daughter's identity, spent much of that day traveling to Lyons and down the Rhône River to Privas. When he arrived, the gendarmes escorted him to the *mairie*. Flowers covered the four lead-lined coffins. An official opened one for him. Kennedy gasped and stared unbelievingly at the body inside.

When he called home that evening, he said nothing about Kick's disfiguring wounds. He told the family crowded around the telephone how "beautiful" she had looked. She had been found on her back, as though "asleep," with her shoes gone. Wasn't that just like Kick, who always went around barefoot?

"Kathleen is dead," John White wrote in mournful disbelief in his diary the day the story came over the wire at the *Times-Herald* office. "It's like a toothache. You forget it for a while." All Kick's friends, on both sides of the Atlantic, were stunned by the horror of the double tragedy. *Oh, dear God,* Patsy had thought while reading a newspaper account of the crash, *that was the trip!* In England, David Ormsby-Gore sped home after hearing a bulletin on his car radio so that he could break the news to Sissy before she heard it on her own. Janie Aiken had been readying herself to leave for Paris.

In Washington it was Reardon who arranged to get Jack and Eunice up to Hyannis Port. Overcome with grief, Jack had closeted himself in a back room, admitting only servants delivering trays of food. By evening, when Lady Astor's niece Dinah Brand Fox went over to the Georgetown house, she found Eunice and Jack waiting to fly to Boston. They kept pacing in a tense, scattered way, as though suddenly endowed with unchanneled energy.

Glowing eulogies of Kathleen appeared in British newspapers. "No American, man or woman, who has ever settled in England was so much loved as she; and no American ever loved England more," wrote one admirer. ". . . Strangely enough it was those in London who are most disenchanted with this day and age who perhaps derived the greatest comfort and delight from her enchanting personality."

In America, John White was moved to write a special tribute, using the title of Kick's old column, "Did You Happen to See . . . KATHLEEN?"

> It is a strange, hard thing to sit at this desk, to tap at this typewriter (your old desk, your old typewriter), to tap out the cold and final word—good-by.

Good-by little Kathleen.

The wires have at last stopped rattling out the details of what happened in France, Thursday, late . . . in the storm. . . .

Kathleen. Little "Kick." Where have you gone? . . .

It seems such a short time ago that you came to the *Times-Herald*. Bright, pretty, quick. Vivid. Filled with over-bubbling enthusiasm, eager, eager to learn everything. The friendliest little creature in the world, with that compelling gaiety, that merriment.

Who can weigh or measure the blessing of a high heart?

And you went away to England and married Billy, Marquess of Hartington, and four months later he was killed in France. And your brother Joe was killed and brother Jack nearly died in the Pacific.

Do you go agrieving, by the week and by the month?

Nope.

You did not.

When you came through here the other day you were merrier than even you had ever been.

"Hello-o-oo. It's Kick. What's the sto-o-ory?"

Telephones jangled and there was commotion in the city room and in the city.

So now a plane goes down.

Lady Hartington was found stretched on her back and appeared to have been asleep. . . .

Kathleen, Kathleen. . . .

The column was typeset but finally judged to be too personal and killed before the evening edition went to press.

After the initial shock wore off, Kathleen's friends were a little embarrassed for her. How awful that in dying she had been caught sneaking away for that one weekend with Fitzwilliam. It seemed so unfair that after so much suffering she could not have had even that little bit of happiness. British and American newspapers had exercised remarkable restraint in the matter-of-fact first reports of the crash. They avoided speculation as to why two unrelated titled citizens were traveling alone together, but all of London knew to read between the lines.

Her body lay in state for several days in St. Philippe du Roule, a Catholic church in Paris, after being transported from Privas. A nun of the Order of the Sisters of Hope watched over the bier, which was covered in purple brocade and banked with red, white, and pink roses. Mr. Kennedy stayed in Paris with the coffin until arrangements could be made for the funeral. Whenever questioned by the press about his daughter's burial, Mr. Kennedy replied dazedly, "I have no plans, no plans." For days Kathleen's final resting place remained undecided. The Devonshires finally pointed out that even though Kathleen had been planning to marry someone else, she had died, after all, as Billy's widow. Since she had so loved England, she herself would probably have chosen to be buried in the family plot near Chatsworth. They left the decision up to Mr. Kennedy. To their surprise the ambassador acceded without argument.

The death of the eighth Earl Fitzwilliam was a terrible blow to Rotherham, particularly since he had left no heir. On May 19 the casket was slowly driven along the straight gravel stone path from Wentworth to the twelfth-century church, built in memory of one of Peter's ancestors. Peter's body was laid beside the tomb of his father, who had died just four years earlier. It was Maud Fitzwilliam, not Obby, who made the funeral arrangements.

On May 20 Protestant nobility and important members of the British government crowded into the high Jesuit Mass sung for Kathleen at Farm Street. The only Kennedy present was her father. The rest of the family had stayed in Hyannis Port, holding a small memorial to which only a few close friends were invited. After the Mass in London some two hundred of Kathleen's friends crowded into a special train and accompanied the coffin to Derbyshire. Employees and tenants of the estate lined the streets as the procession made its way through a private entrance of Chatsworth to the quiet graveyard behind the Edensor church, where the Bishop of Nottingham conducted a short service.

Mr. Kennedy looked on as the Catholic priest prayed for his daughter in the burial grounds of a notoriously anti-Catholic family. He appeared awkward in the company of his daughter's friends—the grown children of many of those who had ostracized him ten years earlier. Among the wreaths that covered the casket was one with a hand-written note from his old enemy, Winston Churchill.

As the coffin was lowered into the ground Kennedy, standing by the foot of the grave, put his arms around Ilona Solymossy and her sister. Afterward, without so much as a nod of acknowledgment toward the Duke and Duchess of Devonshire or the priest, he turned away from the grave site, leading the two sisters toward his car. As they walked he enlisted their help in determining which of the possessions in Smith Square were to be returned to Billy's family.

Kathleen's father had left all the details of the funeral to the Duke and Duchess of Devonshire. He'd even neglected to pay the priest who served the Mass. It was the duchess who finally thought up the epitaph for Kathleen's tombstone:

JOY SHE GAVE JOY SHE HAS FOUND

Kennedy sailed home the following day, remaining in his cabin for most of the voyage. When the ship docked in New York, Joseph Dineen, one of Kennedy's cortege of friendly reporters, accompanied him for a stroll around the deck. Dineen tried to divert him from his brooding silence. "What do you think of the Marshall Plan now that you've looked over the ground? Have you changed your mind?"

Mr. Kennedy didn't even seem to hear him. "It's no use, Joe," he said finally. "Nothing means anything anymore."

But something did still matter a great deal to Joe Kennedy: the public image of the family now that Jack was moving forward with his political plans. The rude facts of the airplane crash did not square at all with the image Mr. Kennedy had been shaping over the years; a God-fearing convent-school girl did not fly off alone with a married man to the French Riviera.

Before he left Privas, he had been given Kathleen's luggage. In among her effects were a family photograph album, a set of rosary beads, and a douche.

After holding off for a few days the American press finally began asking questions about why Kathleen and Fitzwilliam had been together. Instinctively employees of the Kennedys and the Fitzwilliams had entered into a conspiracy of silence. To protect the memory of her beloved young mistress, Ilona Solymossy, whose telephone rang incessantly with calls from reporters, finally came up with the story that Kathleen had been headed on a trip to meet her father when her old "friend" Earl Fitzwilliam had offered to give her a lift. Although she did not go into the nature of the "friendship" between Lady Hartington and Lord Fitzwilliam, she told herself that she wasn't really lying because no one ever specifically asked. Members of both families adopted Ilona's initial premise and elaborated on it.

The first story broke in the New York *Daily News*, which was published by Kennedy's old crony, Joseph Patterson, who had been the one to suggest that Mrs. Kennedy be hospitalized to avoid having to answer the press's questions about Kathleen's marriage. It was headlined "Chance Invite Sends Kennedy Girl to Death." According to this account Kathleen, who had just returned from America two days before, had planned to meet her father in the south of France but had been unable to get a seat aboard a train or airline on such short notice. In the Ritz Hotel in London, the story went on, she "casually encountered" Lord and Lady Fitzwilliam. Hearing of her plans, Fitzwilliam had offered her a seat in the private plane he had chartered to visit "racehorse breeders in France." Fitzwilliam's secretary was quoted as saying that "Lady Hartington was an old friend of both Lady and Lord Fitzwilliam's. She had been delighted with the offer of a lift."

The *Daily News* story was widely reprinted. No reporter ever investigated why Kick was traveling to the south of France to meet her father, who was in Paris, or whether or not Fitzwilliam actually had stables near the Riviera (he didn't). If any reporters did make inquiries, their findings never made it into print. The "chance meeting" at the Ritz became the official explanation for Kathleen's flight to Cannes with a married man.

Subsequent features on the crash embroidered on the fiction. In describing Kathleen's place of death one story noted that she had studied at the convent school in Neuilly ("She knew and loved well the French countryside where she met death"), giving her final destination religious overtones. Several reports placed the entire family at the Derbyshire burial, while another had Mr. Kennedy implying that he had seen Kathleen in Paris before her death.

The purpose of the trip continued to puzzle many people. Those few who knew that the couple were meeting up with Mr. Kennedy wondered whether they had headed for Cannes in the storm after frantically looking for him in Paris without success. Some had heard they had been en route to Italy to request a special dispensation from the pope. That rumor probably started from a news report maintaining that Kennedy had come to Paris from Rome, where he had had a papal audience. Lady Astor was convinced that the crash had been engineered by Vatican agents, who were trying to prevent another sacrilegious union.

Catholics finally came to accept a romantic version—that Kathleen and Peter were rushing off to elope on a passionate and doomed impulse. Some even believed that that kind of unspeakable act could bring about a sudden violent death. Poetic as the image might have been, that version didn't really make sense. Lovers running off to marry might act recklessly. But even the most reckless lovers wouldn't head off in a tiny twin-engine ten-seat airplane into a raging thunderstorm, fully knowing that bad weather had swept the Continent and that all other flights had been canceled.

Some of Kick's friends who had disapproved of Peter decided that she would have come to her senses when actually confronted with the prospect of marrying him. Charlotte Harris thought it was probably better that Kick had died with Fitzwilliam rather than living the rest of her life in terrible guilt over breaking with the Church and her family. When one of Peter's friends bemoaned the gruesome senselessness of the tragedy, a companion replied, "I think that's an awful lot of nonsense. They were very much in love with each other, and they were both killed together. I think that's a very good way to die."

Evelyn Waugh blamed himself for Kathleen's death because of certain advice he had given her one evening over dinner. Years later, in delivering an unsolicited sermon to the Catholic Clarissa Churchill for marrying Anthony Eden outside the Church, he would use Kathleen's story as an object lesson:

> An American Catholic girl married outside the Church because she was in love with a man under orders for the front. It caused great scandal . . . . Then she was widowed, repented & was received back. She asked me what she should have done and I said: "If you want to commit adultery or fornication & can't resist, do it, but realize what you are doing, and don't give the final insult of apostasy." Well the girl followed my advice next time & was killed eloping. So my advice isn't, wasn't much help.

Rose Kennedy made just one connection—between the presence of the married man in the airplane and the state of Kathleen's soul. Right after the funeral Mrs. Kennedy mailed out to Kick's British and American friends a small printed Mass card with the last studio portrait of Kathleen and a prayer. The prayer was supposed to be a plenary indulgence, applicable to souls in purgatory, if said before a crucifix after Holy Communion. Many English Protestant friends of Kick's were stunned by what they viewed as the bad taste of the gesture. Even the most bigoted among them considered Kick an exemplary Irish Catholic. It was preposterous to think that someone like her would need years of prayer to escape damnation. After reading the card one old acquaintance ripped it up in a fit of rage.

The summer of the year that Kathleen died, Jack Kennedy went to England. During his stay he stopped in to see Ilona Solymossy, whom he had met in 1947. He tried to draw out of her every last recollection of his sister. At the end of the visit, as though he'd just divulged his darkest secret, he announced with finality, "We will not mention her again." Twenty-three-year-old Bobby Kennedy, who came to see Ilona a month later, similarly asked about his sister and made the same declaration before he left.

As the years went on the rest of the Kennedy family rarely spoke of Kick in public or made any gestures toward keeping alive her memory. There was no privately printed commemorative book written for her, as there would be in turn for every male in the family who died. Mr. and Mrs. Kennedy erected no buildings and set up no foundations or scholarships in her honor, as they would for their three dead sons. In 1952 the family donated three hundred thousand dollars toward the building of a gymnasium in Kathleen's name at Manhattanville College in Purchase, New York. It was the Catholic college attended by Mrs. Kennedy and her younger girls. At Manhattanville, Ethel Skakel and Joan Bennett would meet Pat and Jean Kennedy, by whom they would be introduced to their future husbands, Bobby and Teddy. Kathleen had never gone to Manhattanville, or any other Catholic college for that matter.

When Bobby Kennedy's eldest daughter was born in 1951, he decided to name her Kathleen Hartington Kennedy. The family had only one stipulation: that she never be referred to as "Kick."

The Duke of Devonshire had died two years after Kathleen's death while engaged in one of his favorite pastimes, chopping wood. A decade later, when Jack Kennedy was elected President, he invited Andrew and Debo, the new Duke and Duchess of Devonshire, to attend his inauguration. On a trip to Ireland during his presidency he took a detour to Kathleen's grave in Edensor. After leaving the cemetery Jack paid his respects to Ilona, who was employed at Chatsworth. True to his vow of a decade and a half earlier, he did not bring up his sister's name.

Once Jack had achieved the presidency, the official Kennedy literature designated Kathleen only as "the sister who died in a plane crash." Her marriage outside the Church was always played down or included with an explanation of the pressures of wartime. Occasionally the family implied that Billy and Kathleen had not settled on the religion in which they would bring up their children. Because of her involvement with the Red Cross it came to be assumed that Kathleen, like her husband, had died during the war. To one newsman, a friend of the family's, Rose Kennedy once matter-of-factly characterized Kathleen as the only one of her nine children eager to leave home.

After Jack and Bobby were assassinated, Kathleen was simply listed as one of the four children lost by the tragedy-prone family. (The tragedy of Kathleen's death seemed to pale beside the violent deaths of the two younger brothers and what turned out to be the senseless heroism of Joe Jr. when it was discovered years later that the launching site he was to blow up had been abandoned months before his fatal mission.) The "chance meeting" story remained unchallenged and made its way into biography after biography, along with information about Kathleen's "gift of faith" and the lengthy "retreat" she made after Billy's death. In her autobiography, *Times to Remember,* Rose Kennedy reversed her daughter's destination and wrote that Kick and a "few friends," returning from a holiday on the Riviera, were en route to meet Mr. Kennedy in Paris when their plane crashed.

Those few who had known about Peter Fitzwilliam wondered over the years what effect Kathleen's death had had on the relationship between her parents and whether they carried any guilt over it. But it was understood that Kathleen was to remain a closed subject in the Kennedy household. Charlotte and many of the old circle particularly knew not to talk about Kick in front of her mother.

But on one occasion a year or so after Kathleen died, Mrs. Kennedy herself brought up her daughter's name. Dinah Fox had come to visit the family in Palm Beach. All the young Kennedys were out, and Dinah had found herself alone with Mrs. Kennedy for the evening. Dinah's presence evidently stirred up memories for Mrs. Kennedy—memories of Kick and those extravagant days they had all shared long ago in

Prince's Gate before the war. Once she had begun talking about her daughter, she seemed unable to stop. "You know, I really *adored* Kathleen," she declared a number of times. "Where did her life go?" she asked in pained bewilderment at one point in the evening.

Dinah thought it was as though Mrs. Kennedy needed to know not simply why Kick's life had ended so senselessly but why she had lost her, years before she died.

At the Intersection of
Promise and Myth
by Andrew Levy

What happened to the '60s and their promise of change? The assassinations of the Kennedy brothers and Martin Luther King, Jr. seemed to rob us of possibility—but did three men represent our last hope for peace and social justice? Their lives might serve as inspiration for change, but their premature deaths can't explain our failure. Andrew Levy (born 1952) published this essay in 1994 in Harpers.

On the corner of Seventeenth and Broadway, in an African-American section of Indianapolis, there is a vacant space composed of two unused lots, sections of two parking lots, and the edge of a small park. On the evening of April 4, 1968, hours after Martin Luther King Jr. was killed in Memphis, Robert F. Kennedy Jr. climbed up on the back of a truck parked at this corner and delivered an ex tempore speech that was broadcast on local television and radio. Kennedy was just beginning his campaign in the Indiana presidential primary; he was running against a local candidate (Roger Branigin, the governor), a state Democratic machine that opposed him, and a newspaper chain that openly fought his candidacy. In Indianapolis, people either know this story by heart or do not know it at all. By local accounts, Kennedy ignored the warnings of the police chief, traveled to a neighborhood so threatening (at least on that one night) that his police escort refused to follow him, and delivered his remarks. Although there were riots in 110 cities that night,

Indianapolis remained calm. Kennedy went on to win the primary, his first victory in that presidential campaign. Two months later he was dead; a quote from the Indianapolis speech is etched on his grave-stone at Arlington National Cemetery.

Hearing the story of April 4 told today, one wishes there were a way to leaven it, to keep it from turning into an uncomfortable memorial to what we have abandoned. First, there is the matter of the speech itself, which does for us the unfortunate service of measuring the precise dis-tance between how we define an act of political courage in 1994 and how we defined it in 1968. It is impossible to picture Robert Kennedy on that truck without recalling the failure of political will that followed the Rodney King riots of 1992, when public officials on almost every level of government absented themselves from the streets of Los Angeles. It is impossible to reread the stark sentence in which Robert Kennedy reminds his audience that he knows what it feels like to have a family member murdered (the only time he would discuss his brother's death in a public venue) without thinking of Senator Albert Gore's invocation at the 1992 Democratic National Convention of his son's near death, an act somehow both moving and distasteful. It is impossible to read the passage where Kennedy quotes Aeschylus without feeling an intense sense of dislocation: what American politician today would quote a Greek poet, let alone to an inner-city crowd, let alone ex tempore?

America is as large or as small as we choose to make it. I moved to Indianapolis in the summer of 1992. There is, I believe, no city as large anywhere on this continent that has managed to remain as invisible. When I told people that I was moving from Philadelphia (not exactly a glamour capital itself) to Indianapolis, residents of both cities often asked, "Why?" The message: Don't move to Indianapolis: This senti-ment doesn't explain why people were pouring into the place (its pop-ulation expanded from 1.1 million to 1.4 million in the period from 1977 to 1990), or why anyone in the economically languishing America of 1992 would need to ask someone why he was suddenly moving to an unexpected location. I went because there was good work for me there.

People say, in dystopic visions, that the future of America will look like Los Angeles, New York, or Miami. The future will look like the movie *Bladerunner*, or like William Gibson's cyberpunk novel *Neuromancer*: high technology intermingled with widespread urban and social decay, large semi-totalitarian multinational corporations, aggressive and addicting forms of entertainment. Blacks, Hispanics, and Asians will increase in population until they outnumber (and presumably threaten) whites. This will all lead to ever larger multinational corporations, panoptic police states, innovative forms of civil unrest.

As powerful as these versions of the future (and the present) may be, they are not conclusive: they may simply be the most photogenic, the most cathartic, the most reflective of the wary paranoia that has constituted one of America's few growth industries of the last decade. It is reasonable to predict that Los Angeles or Miami will look like extrapolations of their current selves in forty years, but it is difficult to make predictions about the future of the rest of the country without reckoning with any one of the cities to which people are actually moving: cities like Orlando, Raleigh, Sacramento, Jacksonville. Conversations about information overload and the hyperreal become curiously difficult to sustain after more than a week in a city like Indianapolis, which is not really a small place, only a flat, inconspicuous one.

Here, then, is one vision of America's future. The top three employers in Indianapolis are, in order, the city government, the state government, and the federal government. The fourth-largest employer is a drug company. The best restaurants are in strip malls. There are five Gap stores and one J. Crew. There are whole neighborhoods of moderately sized, affordable homes, some aging slightly, some brand-new developments wrapped around underfilled artificial lakes. In these neighborhoods, blacks and whites live side by side.

City officials are considering a new slogan for Indianapolis: "A Model for the Twenty-First-Century City." There is logic in this. While not shedding its reputation as "The Big Nap," a nondescript, backward, corn-fed Heartland capital, Indianapolis now also appears to have been a precursor to what Joel Garreau has called "edge cities," the suburban housing developments, office parks, and shopping malls that ring increasingly barren inner cities. If the business of Washington, D.C., moves to Alexandria and the middle class of Philadelphia moves to King of Prussia, then the people of Indianapolis might say, with justification, we've been living like this all along. We have a proper downtown to show to visitors, but only 12,000 people live there. We have bad neighborhoods, but they are not as bad as yours. And everyone has convenient shopping.

In many ways, Robert Kennedy's remarks on the night of Martin Luther King's assassination did not make a great speech. "What do you think I should say?" he asked Fred Dutton, his aide, minutes prior to its delivery. Kennedy begins by announcing to his listeners the news that King has been murdered; many in the crowd of a thousand do not hear him properly, however, which leaves him with the disconcerting task of addressing a crowd half of which is stunned into silence and half of which is innocently cheering his reverent descriptions of King. Since the details of the murder are still hazy, Kennedy is forced to build his rhetoric around conditional clauses—"considering the evidence there evidently . . . were white people who were responsible"—that disrupt his cadence. He seems struck by the word "difficult" and repeats it, mantralike, amid pleas for understanding and compassion: "We can do well in this country. We will have difficult times. We've had difficult times in the past. We will have difficult times in the future." He repeats phrases, searching for the right combination of words. He reminds his audience that King was murdered, until he is sure everyone has gotten the message.

It is, in many ways, not a political speech at all; it is a response to trauma, a sudden synapse failure in the body politic. An open space. One wonders what Kennedy must have thought as he said that sentence, "I had a member of my family killed, but he was killed by a white man." One wonders what his audience thought of that confessional moment submerged in tortured syntax, John Fitzgerald Kennedy's assassination suddenly becoming a footnote in history, not a primal scene. Was it enough? In retrospect, it seems like a verbal turn tested, then abandoned: my sorrow, he seems to be saying, may feel like yours, but maybe not. The language, he seems to say, isn't ready yet.

As a referendum on the progress of race in America since the 1960s, Indianapolis offers drastically divergent evidence. There are the calm, interracial neighborhoods, whose existence can be taken as evidence of Great Society reforms, but whose muted and suburban character also reflects a distinctly Republican social consensus that must be considered Ronald Reagan's (or, more likely, Indiana's own) success story as much as Lyndon Johnson's. But within walking distance of these neighborhoods are the neighborhoods where white families drive out black families (and vice versa) and the neighborhoods that seem more despondent than ever (the poverty rate in Indiana rose from 9 percent to 15.7 percent between 1980 and 1992).

Ultimately, Indianapolis is a story about how slowly change comes, not how it sometimes comes too strong. Observing the persistence of organizations like the Ku Klux Klan and the Black Panthers (who clashed twice on the statehouse steps last winter), one finds graphic evidence that even government intervention on the scale projected by 1960s liberalism has been inadequate to the heavy task of eliminating poverty and racism in a nation as enormous and inchoate as ours. Indianapolis served itself well in the 1970s by absorbing its adjacent suburbs and improving its tax base, but now its new suburbs are flooding with wealthy emigres from the city, concerned about their taxes and their safety, or perhaps caught in the ideological centrifuge that draws Americans further away from one another in permanent pursuit of a larger yard and a neighborless horizon.

For these reasons, it is appealing to believe that Robert Kennedy's brief presence here somehow made coherence out of these mixed feelings and divergent evidence, that his victory in the Indiana primary constituted a rare and exemplary moment of consensus across the political spectrum. As exhilarating as some aspects of his campaign may have been, however, what appears to have actually occurred was a dubious electoral victory that tempers any mythologization of that month in Indiana. Kennedy's Indiana campaign was, in fact, a haphazard affair. He often told conservative white audiences what they wanted to hear and then adjusted his speeches for minority audiences. If Kennedy adopted the Indiana primary as a test of his own synchronicity with the American spirit, he seemed to spend the month testing the extent to which he needed to compromise and the extent to which the American spirit, as he perceived it, needed to compromise. This is, one supposes, exactly what a young politician in the early stages of his first national campaign must do. And it can be said with certainty that Kennedy lost nothing by standing his ground, which is no small victory. For those of us seeking historical lessons from his visit to Indiana, however, it scarcely constitutes a program.

The corner of Seventeenth and Broadway is a T-shaped intersection. It is a quilt of empty spaces. There is a vacant lot on one side, small, littered, and unmaintained; it is bordered by a chain-link fence. Opposite this lot sits another vacant lot, grassy and freshly mown, but suggesting no civic purpose. On the north side of this space there is a parking lot for a senior citizens' home; on the west side, a full-length, well-kept basketball court and a children's playground. A sign on that side of the street reads "Martin Luther King, Jr. Park." There is no one in the park. There is a public building on each side of the corner: the Citizens' Health Center on the east and Citizens' Multi-Service Center on the west. Both buildings look new, and their parking lots are full.

There are few people around. They move slowly across the landscape or sit waiting in cars. It is unbelievably quiet.

In May, President Bill Clinton, Indiana governor Evan Bayh, Indianapolis mayor Stephen Goldsmith, Senator Edward Kennedy, and a list of guests including Dexter Scott King and Martin Luther King III attended a ground-breaking ceremony at the corner of Seventeenth and Broadway for a joint memorial to Martin Luther King Jr. and Robert Kennedy.

The memorial, "The Landmark for Peace," is to be constructed from melted-down weaponry gathered from community gun-buyback programs. Although funding and design plans are incomplete—it is believed that Clinton's plan to visit Indianapolis for a fund-raising luncheon and a round of golf with the governor rushed and even inspired the announcement of the memorial—sponsors envision a dedication date within two years. But at the moment, the monument is no more than a trampled patch of grass at the corner of Seventeenth and Broadway.

And perhaps this is fitting. Perhaps ambiguous and ambivalent political moments deserve ambiguous and ambivalent monuments. The Vietnam War Memorial forces its visitors underground in an unambivalent mourning ritual but cannot control the strange communion they often experience there; Mount Rushmore challenges its visitors to contrast the grandeur of our most regal presidents carved into the side of a mountain in the middle of the most holy land of the devastated Sioux. If the corner of Seventeenth and Broadway was a premeditated monument, we might say that its designers chose its array of empty spaces, its solitary yet central location, and its lack of a formal marker as a symbolic commemoration of the people and events we can't see, placed in the middle of a city we don't see—a memorial to turning away, an unmemorial.

Still, immediately surrounding that vacancy is a series of public structures that seem to be a tribute to Kennedy's vision of an activist government providing support to inner-city communities. Stand at the spot where Kennedy stood and turn in every direction. You will see clean, formidable buildings devoted to health care and education, a senior citizens' home, and a well-nurtured park named for the man Kennedy memorialized, a man whose mission was ultimately more essential to the lives of the people who reside in the neighborhood. It is hard to imagine that Kennedy would not be pleased.

At least briefly. Perhaps it is churlish to add that if you lift your eyes further you find that surrounding that circle of public buildings lies a census tract where the promise that activist government extends to blasted neighborhoods has taken, at best, a tentative foothold and where those impressive public buildings are as anomalous as they seem necessary. One goes to the corner of Seventeenth and Broadway for communion with an uncommemorated moment in American history and finds instead a communion with the unanswered questions of the civil-rights movement and the welfare state in America. Stand at the spot where Kennedy stood and ask: Did activist government try and fail? Was it attempted without the necessary vigor, or the necessary spirit, or the necessary patience? Or was activist government a success but still inadequate against the entropic forces that have afflicted neighborhoods across the country in the last twenty years; inadequate against the endemic mistrust that stands between separate races and separate classes? Stand at the spot where Kennedy stood, in the middle of a city that prides itself on being a model for the twenty-first century, and it will feel like no time at all has passed since Kennedy stood there and tried to find the words that would make the sorrow of one race comprehensible to another. History revolves all around you. The language is still not ready; the twenty-first century, one thinks, is going to feel like starting over.

acknowledgments

Many people made this anthology.

At Thunder's Mouth Press and Avalon Publishing Group:
Neil Ortenberg and Susan Reich offered vital guidance and support. Dan O'Connor and Ghadah Alrawi also helped. Maria Fernandez oversaw production with scrupulous care and attention, with help from Paul Paddock and Simon Sullivan. David Reidy designed the book's cover.

At the Portland Public Library in Portland, Maine:
The librarians cheerfully worked to locate and borrow books from across the country.

At Shawneric.com:
Shawneric Hachey deftly handled permissions and found just the right photographs.

At The Writing Company:
Nate Hardcastle helped find the selections for this book and kept things moving. Deborah Satter helped with preliminary research. Taylor Smith, Mark Klimek, March Truedsson and John Bishop took up slack on other projects.

Among friends and family:
Will Balliett made it fun. Jennifer Willis gave me good advice. Harper Willis and Abner Willis made me smile.

Finally, I am grateful to the writers whose work appears in this book.

We gratefully acknowledge all those who gave permission for material to appear in this book. We have made every effort to trace and contact copyright holders, but if errors or omissions are brought to our attention we will be pleased to publish corrections in future editions of this book. For further information, please contact the publisher.

"Superman Comes to the Supermarket" from *The Presidential Papers* by Norman Mailer. Copyright © 1963 by Norman Mailer and reprinted with the permission of The Wylie Agency, Inc. ✤ "Calling Mrs. Martin Luther King" from "The Making of a President: Another View" from *Of Kennedys and Kings: Making Sense of the Sixties* by Harris Wofford. Copyright © 1980 by Harris Wofford. Reprinted by permission of Farrar, Straus & Giroux, LLC. ✤ "First Lady in Waiting" from *The Time of Our Time* by Norman Mailer. Copyright © 1963 by Norman Mailer and reprinted with the permission of The Wylie Agency, Inc. ✤ Excerpt from *Conversations With Kennedy* by Ben Bradlee. Copyright © 1975 by Benjamin C. Bradlee. Used by permission of W.W. Norton & Company, Inc. ✤ Excerpt from *President Kennedy: Profile of Power* by Richard Reeves. Copyright © 1993 by Reeves-O'Neil, Inc. Reprinted with the permission of Simon & Schuster. ✤ Excerpt from *The Dark Side of Camelot* by Seymour M. Hersh. Copyright © 1997 by Seymour M. Hersh. Used by permission of Little, Brown and Company, Inc. ✤ "The Exner File" by Michael O'Brien. Reprinted with the permission from *The Washington Monthly*. Copyright by The Washington Monthly Company, 733 15th St. NW, Suite 1000, Washington, DC 20005. (202) 393-5155. Web site: www.washingtonmonthly.com. ✤ "The Conspiracy Theories" by Pamela Colloff and Michael Hall. Reprinted by permission from the November 1998 issue of *Texas Monthly*. ✤ Excerpts from *Last Brother: The Rise and Fall of Teddy Kennedy* by Joe McGinniss. Copyright © 1993 by Joe McGinniss. Reprinted by permission of Simon &

bibliography

The selections used in this anthology were taken from the editions listed below. In some cases, other editions may be easier to find. Hard-to-find or out-of-print titles often are available through inter-library loan services or through Internet booksellers.

Bradlee, Benjamin. *Conversations With Kennedy*. New York: W.W. Norton & Company, 1984.

Collier, Peter and David Horowitz. *The Kennedys: An American Drama*. New York: Summit Books, 1984.

Colloff, Pamela and Michael Hall. "The Conspiracy Theories". Originally appeared in *Texas Monthly*, November 1998.

Henggeler, Paul R. *In His Steps: Lyndon Johnson and the Kennedy Mystique*. Chicago: Ivan R. Dee, 1991.

Hersh, Burton. "The Thousand Days of Edward M. Kennedy". Originally appeared in *Esquire*, February 1972.

Hersh, Seymour M. *The Dark Side of Camelot*. New York: Little, Brown & Company, 1997.

Klaber, William. *Shadow Play: The Murder of Robert F. Kennedy - The Trial of Sirhan Sirhan, and the Future of American Justice*. New York: St. Martin's Press, 1989.

Levy, Andrew. "At the Intersection of Promise and Myth". Originally appeared in *Dissent*, December 1994.

Mailer, Norman. *The Time of Our Time*. New York: GP Putnam's Sons, 1963. (for "First Lady in Waiting.")

Mailer, Norman. *Oswald's Tale*. New York: Random House, 1995.

Mailer, Norman. *The Presidential Papers*. New York: G.P. Putnam's Sons, 1963. (for "Superman Comes to the Supermarket.")

McGinniss, Joe. *Last Brother: The Rise and Fall of Teddy Kennedy*. New York: Simon & Schuster, 1994.

McTaggart, Lynne. *Kathleen Kennedy*. New York: Doubleday Dell, 1983.

Newfield, Jack. *Robert F. Kennedy: A Memoir*. New York: EP Dutton, 1969.

O'Brien, Michael. "The Exner File". Originally appeared in *The Washington Monthly*, December 1999.

Reeves, Richard. *President Kennedy: Profile of Power*. New York: Simon & Schuster, 1983.

Steel, Ronald. *In Love With Night: The American Romance with Robert Kennedy*. New York: Touchstone, 2000.

Stein, Jean, edited by George Plimpton. *American Journey*. Orlando, FL: Harcourt Brace, 1970.

Vidal, Gore. *Reflections Upon a Sinking Ship*. New York: Little, Brown, 1963. (for "The Holy Family.")

Wofford, Harris. *Of Kennedys and Kings: Making Sense of the Sixties*. New York: Farrar, Straus & Giroux, 1980.

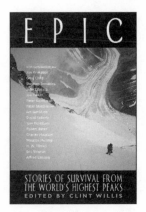

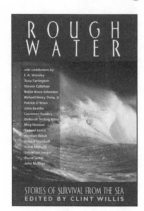

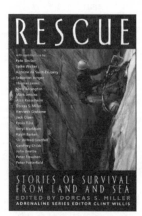

adrenaline®

Exciting titles from Adrenaline Books

WILD BLUE: Stories of Survival from Air and Space

Edited by David Fisher and William Garvey
Series Editor, Clint Willis

Wild Blue collects the most gripping accounts of what may be the greatest achievement of the century: manned flight. From flying a Piper Cub over the Rockies at the age of 16 to a nigh-time carrier approach, *Wild Blue* puts you right in the cockpit.
$16.95 ($26 Canada), 352 pages

BLOOD: Stories of Life and Death from the Civil War

Edited by Peter Kadzis; Series Editor, Clint Willis

The most dramatic moment in this nation's history, also produced some of our greatest literature. From tragic charges to prison escapes to the desolation wrought on those who stayed behind, *Blood* is composed mainly of the vivid stories of those who were there. Includes accounts by General George Pickett, Walt Whitman, Ulysses S. Grant, Michael Shaara and Shelby Foote among others.
$16.95 ($26 Canada); 320 pages

THE WAR: Stories of Life and Death from World War II

Edited by Clint Willis

The greatest writing about the War, from Okinawa to Normandy. This entry in the Adrenaline Books series is about courage, conscience, and loss. It features work by Stephen E. Ambrose, A. J. Liebling, William Manchester, Paul Fussell, and 13 others.
$16.95 ($26 Canada), 384 pages

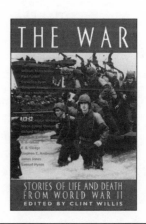

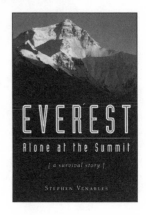
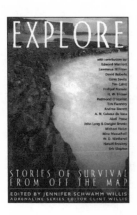

adrenaline®

Exciting titles from Adrenaline Books

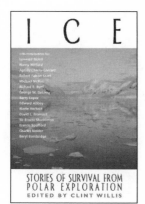

ICE: Stories of Survival from Polar Exploration

Edited by Clint Willis

The Arctic and Antarctica were the sites of many of the twentieth century's most gripping adventure stories. *Ice* features 15 of the best and most exciting accounts by the greatest explorers and observers of the polar regions—from Robert Scott, Ernest Shackleton and Richard E. Byrd to Barry Lopez, Nancy Mitford, and Beryl Bainbridge. $16.95 ($26 Canada), 384 pages

SHACKLETON'S FORGOTTEN MEN: The Untold Tragedy of the Endurance Epic

By Lennard Bickel; foreword by Rt. Hon. Lord Shackleton, K. C., P. C., O. D. E.

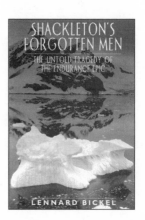

The drama of Shackleton's Antarctic survival story overshadowed a near-simultaneous expedition that the explorer launched—but did not lead—to lay support depots across the Great Ross Ice Shelf in preparation for the Shackleton party. Now Lennard Bickel tells the tragic story of these forgotten heroes in a thrilling account, about which *The New York Times* wrote, "This is more than a tale of survival against the odds. Like all the best stories, it is about the triumph of the human spirit." $21 ($32.50 Canada), 256 pages

All **Adrenaline Books®** are available at your neighborhood bookstore, or via the Internet. To order directly from the publisher, please call Publishers Group West at (800) 788-3123

For more information about Adrenaline titles, visit www.adrenalinebooks.com